The Other Side of the Dream

CLEM BURKE

The Other
Side of
the Dream

My life
in and out
of Blondie

HarperCollins*Publishers*

HarperCollins*Publishers*
1 London Bridge Street
London SE1 9GF

www.harpercollins.co.uk

HarperCollins*Publishers*
Macken House, 39/40 Mayor Street Upper
Dublin 1, D01 C9W8, Ireland

First published by HarperCollins*Publishers* 2026

1 3 5 7 9 10 8 6 4 2

Editorial Direction: Kathy Valentine
Development Editor: Peter Stoneman

HB ISBN 978-0-00-869551-4
PB ISBN 978-0-00-869552-1

Printed and bound in the UK using 100%
renewable electricity at CPI Group (UK) Ltd

CONTENTS

YOU ARE ALREADY HERE

By Fred Armisen

Clem Burke is my favorite drummer ever. I don't mean that with any sub-categorizations of genres or eras. Ever in my whole life. We all already know that the drums are the best instrument. That's just a technical fact. Watching and hearing Clem play the drums makes me feel like there's a higher purpose to life, and I am not exaggerating. His music makes me happy that music exists at all. The ultimate celebration of everything great.

The way he incorporates the toms into the pattern of a beat is what gets me, as opposed to the toms only being used for fills. He uses the whole kit all the way through a song. I don't want to write anything more about what his drumming sounds like, because every time I read a description of how a musician plays an instrument, it's never quite right. They're just words that sit there and evoke nothing, as far as sound. So I'll just leave it at those two sentences up there at the start of this paragraph. You are already here, so you most likely already know what he sounds like. Even giving you a list of songs that you should listen to will feel like homework. Every song he's played on is a perfect example of his drumming. We are already in agreement.

To me it's an aesthetic thing, too. The way he sets up his kit. The color choices of his shells, the angles of the drums, the configuration of the cymbals. That matters to me. That's part of the show, what the drums look like. There is also the element of what *he* looks like. How nicely he dresses. Endlessly cool. What his hair is like. His posture. I like that somehow he's also not trying to show off or steal the show. He is in perfect harmony with the band. Supporting them while at the same time making his part of the stage a beautiful spectacle.

I noticed throughout the years he has a kind of humility when it comes to interviews. I don't think I've ever heard him give advice. He embraces his role as a drummer and lets his drumming style speak for itself. A pure musician. I've been very lucky to get to know him over the years. He is the best! I'm telling you. What's fun about talking to him is that he is a huge music fan. He loves talking about records and bands. He's one of those guys who know facts and trivia, but also actually interesting information that I hadn't heard before. Original names and lineups of bands, notable TV show appearances, that kind of thing. It makes sense when you watch him play. That's someone who loves the lineage and explosiveness of great music.

I once visited Clem before a Blondie show at the Greek Theatre in Los Angeles. I saw something displayed in his dressing room that melted my heart. I don't think he even pointed it out. He set up a couple of framed pictures of Keith

Moon. Can you believe it? It says so much about Clem Burke.
I had to take a picture. Here it is:

Thank you, and Clem: THANK YOU.

ROCK AND ROLL SURVIVALIST

In the mid-1980s, I read Pete Townshend's book *Horse's Neck*. He wrote about Keith Moon's death, reflecting that while Keith hadn't made it, he himself was still here, alive and kicking. It wasn't exactly callous, but it stuck with me. Survival is a primal instinct, even more so than rock and roll—and while I've been inspired and driven by the latter, it's the former that I've always carried in the back of my mind.

In my book, I write about the highs, lows, ups, downs, and everything in between, all from the perspective of a rock and roll survivor. Blondie made it as far as any of us might have dreamed, but there were so many other bands, so many chances at greatness. On each and every level, I found the same whiplashes of anticipation to disappointment, from hopefulness to disbelief that everything was gone. I recount opportunities that were fleeting, lost, or fucked up, and successes that were beyond what any kid with a drum kit could envision.

Rejection and betrayal and being ripped off and let down are as much a part of the story as record deals, hit songs, and sold-out tours. Many of us aren't mentally or emotionally prepared to deal with either side of things. It takes fortitude and a strong constitution to handle the psychological pain and hurt. It takes being grounded and having a work ethic to manage the exhilaration of achieving your dreams. Doing my job and being the best I could be was the easy part. If I couldn't duck and dive and roll with the punches, I wouldn't have survived either.

Chapter I

THE SIXTH BOROUGH

I was born in Bayonne, New Jersey, a working-class town across the Hudson River from Lower Manhattan. It's an anomaly of a place, tucked away on a peninsula. To the north of us sat Jersey City and Hoboken, the birthplace of Frank Sinatra, but to the south, a mile across the Bayonne Bridge, was Staten Island, one of the five boroughs that make up New York City. My friends and I always thought of our town as the sixth borough—the city felt so close; it was almost as if I could touch it.

There were folks who lived their entire lives in Bayonne without ever setting foot across the Hudson River. It seemed like some locals were afraid of the mean streets of the big city. But if you wanted to get out of Bayonne, there were three escape routes: the Holland Tunnel, the Lincoln Tunnel, and the George Washington Bridge. That's why you get people in Manhattan saying "Bridge and Tunnel crowd." It's a flip phrase coined to describe people who come to the city but don't live there. That's how the crowd at CBGB was marked out. There were true New Yorkers, and then there were the Bridge and Tunnel crowd. Still, wherever you arrived from, the point was, you could get there if you wanted to. I really wanted to get there.

Our home was at the southernmost point before the land touched the water. If I wanted to reach Lower Manhattan, I hiked across town from my house to Hudson (now John F. Kennedy) Boulevard and caught a bus to Journal Square in Jersey City. From there, I'd take the PATH (Port Authority Trans-Hudson) train into Lower Manhattan. Trains ran through the night, but the service was patchy. If I played a show at Max's Kansas City or CBGB and got out of there at four in the morning, it was back on the train to Jersey City, where I'd face an hour's wait in the darkness for a bus to take me home. It seemed odd to be so close and for the journey to be so arduous, but that was the lay of the land. Bayonne was a blue-collar, working-class town. Everyone worked for Standard Oil or one of the nearby refineries. My grandfather worked there, as did half the people in our neighborhood. My dad worked as a truck driver, then as a foreman in a factory across the bay in Newark. He was there in the summer of 1967 as the race riots were raging, a stone's throw from where he was working. Storefronts were shattered, businesses were razed to the ground, and twenty-six people died. The National Guard was called in when the police lost control. Also, in the '60s, Bayonne's blue-collar kids came of age and were declared 1-A and drafted to fight a war on the other side of the world. The Vietnam War wasn't just background noise, it was on the nightly news, and everyone had a nephew or a son or brother out there, just hoping for their safe return. One of my cousins was drafted, and I remember it seemed hard for anyone to express their feelings about it.

My dad's generation fought in World War II, so they had stoicism baked in. No one wore their heart on their sleeve back then. Emotions were locked up tight and you swallowed the key. As an outlet, I guess, my dad and his brothers raised homing pigeons, like characters from *On the Waterfront*. They had their pigeon coops on the roof of their houses or in sheds out back. It was a manly pursuit, something of a lost art. These big blue-collar guys, talking tough, but tending their birds with real gentleness. They'd release the pigeons and anxiously wait for them to return, cracking big smiles when the birds found their way back home.

My family roots are Polish American on my father's side and Italian on my mother's. My name at birth was Clement Anthony Bozewski. I grew up surrounded by aunts, uncles, and cousins from both sides. When I first saw *The Sopranos* on TV, and they flashed back to Tony's childhood in the 1960s, it felt like an unearthed time capsule of my own life. David Chase, *The Sopranos*' creator, is from the same part of North Jersey as me—I recognized all the references immediately. The way people looked at things, the vernacular, the mindset, all of it reminded me of my upbringing in Bayonne. When I see a film like *Goodfellas*, I always get reflective and nostalgic. That was the way people were where I grew up, how they spoke, how they dressed. I'm sure there were some low-level underworld people and borderline gangsters living around our neighborhood, but it wasn't a big deal. Everyone owned something that had fallen off the back of a truck. That was standard. New washer-dryer? Back of a truck. New bicycle? Back of another truck. Everyone knew someone to ask if you needed something. Being connected just seemed like another blue-collar occupation. On my paper route, I delivered *The Jersey Journal* to our district congressman. His place was the grandest on that block. No one batted an eye when it came out that the guy was in the pocket of the Bonanno crime family and that he ran interference on their behalf. If someone wanted to gamble, that was no problem; the candy stores all ran a numbers hustle if you wanted a piece of the action. It was illegal in New Jersey to buy or sell fireworks, but there was always a local wise guy who could get them if you had the money. Come the Fourth of July, my friends and I killed time setting off fireworks until the neighborhood dogs were barking in a frenzy.

The daily number was a mob-run racket, and everybody played. Everyone had an aunt or a priest or a kid's schoolteacher, hoping against hope their number would come up. If it was illegal, I didn't pick up on it. I was a kid and had my own thing going. I know it worked like a lottery: pick an arbitrary set of numbers, place your bet with the local bookie, and if your numbers came up in the *Daily News*, you'd win a bunch of money. Every week, regular as clockwork, my dad used to drive us out in his Chevy Impala to this candy store across town. He'd pick up a newspaper and he'd place his bet. Meanwhile, I'd wait in the car, tapping out a beat on the back of the seat, with the radio tuned to one of the Top 40 stations.

What else can I tell you about my childhood? I started out okay. In grammar school, probably without trying too hard, I was always an honor student. I was in the drum and bugle corps with a friend of mine, Joe Munn. Joe lived on my block, and if it rained hard enough, we'd take our fishing poles and go puddle fishing around the neighborhood. My mom's sister lived with us, so growing up, it was like having two mothers, and probably I was a spoiled brat because of it. I played some sports. I was a pitcher in a Little League baseball team. All that American Dream type of stuff. Briefly, I played the saxophone and then started playing the drums in the school orchestra. Eventually, I was kicked out for playing too loudly, but I should give the drum and bugle corps a lot of credit for getting me off on the right foot. Like many of my favorite players—guys like Billy Cobham and the session player Steve Gadd—I learned a lot of my craft in the corps. For starters, you soon understood the importance of stamina. When you're marching in the summer heat in a heavy drum corps uniform, not passing out from exhaustion is important.

Before the Beatles and the British Invasion, my first love was Top 40 radio and—particularly—Frankie Valli and the Four Seasons. The Four Seasons were the New Jersey equivalent of the Beatles, and everyone in my town identified with them. They scored lots of hits in the early 1960s, and when I started out drumming, I played along with the *Four Seasons Greatest Hits* LP all the time. It's still one of my ten favorite albums. Then, when I was ten years old, the Beatles appeared on the Ed Sullivan Show, and the world shifted on its axis. The next day I had my regular after-school music lesson at Sickles Music, on Newark Avenue, in Jersey City over on Five Corners. We had to take two buses, changing halfway, to get there. After the lesson, my mom bought me my first 45, "I Want to Hold Your Hand." I think in that moment, it was like a switch had been thrown because after that I got myself a paper route so I could buy the latest 45s for myself. In no time at all, my bedroom wall was completely covered in Beatles cuttings and posters and pictures of the other British bands. There was always music in the house. The radio was never off, and it was always tuned to a Top 40 station. The New York/New Jersey metro area had two big stations: WMCA and WABC. The disc jockeys on WMCA were called the Good Guys. When I came downstairs for breakfast, my mom would have WMCA on and she'd be singing along to the hits of the day. In 1964, one of those was Louis Armstrong's version of "Hello, Dolly!," from the Broadway musical. I especially liked that song because my mom—whose given name was Antoinette—was known to friends and family as Dolly. And who doesn't like Louis Armstrong? Even Joey Ramone covered Satchmo's "What a Wonderful World" on his solo album.

All in all, we were a musical household. We had a piano in the house, which my mom played. Before the war, my dad had been a drummer with his family band, alongside his two brothers and his father. They were what we used to call a society band, playing weddings and bar mitzvahs around the state. When my dad returned from serving in World War II, he put the drums in the attic, and they were left to gather dust for twenty years or so. I can remember the day I got them down and my dad helped me set them up. It was a set of those grand Slingerland Radio King–type kits, a real throwback to the big band age, with calfskin heads and a 26-inch bass drum and completely beautiful. As a kid with aspirations to be Ringo Starr or Dave Clark, they seemed old-fashioned, but in years to come, guys like John Bonham returned to using those type of kits. I traded mine in because I wanted something more modern. I regret parting with them now, but the die was already cast for me. I'd joined a band with a few other teenagers, and I desperately wanted a set like Dave Clark's, on the cover of the Dave Clark Five *Coast to Coast* album: a white Rogers Marine Pearl with a smaller 20-inch bass drum. Once I had the drums, I had to make a choice between the St. Andrew's drum and bugle corps and the rock and roll band I formed with my friends. Clearly, I chose the latter.

MY FIRST BIG BREAK

My first band did covers of the Top 40 hits of the day. We were called the Environment, later changed to Total Environment. I was only thirteen, but I was dead serious about it. We rehearsed in my living room, and once my parents realized I had this passion for being in a band, they got right behind me. I may have been young, but instinctively I knew I was on the path to doing the thing I was going to do for the rest of my life.

At the time, I was at Bayonne High School. My band-mate—Tom Kochanski on lead vocals—attended the all-boys, Catholic Marist High School in Bayonne. Guitarist Mike Topolski and Russ Pepe, our bass player, went to another Catholic boys' school one town over in Jersey City. One of the brothers at Marist took us under his wing and arranged for us to rehearse in the school cafeteria. For a Catholic brother, he was a cool guy and was a real patron of the band in that first year. Having him on our side wasn't without its drawbacks though. One afternoon we were rehearsing a run-through of the Zombies number "Time of the Season." If you've ever studied the lyrics to that song, they're quite deceptive. At first listen, the song sounds sweet, but on closer inspection, you realize it's sort of sexually charged. I think the line "And let me try with pleasured hands" set an alarm bell ringing in the Catholic brother's brain. As Tom sang, our patron brother stopped in his tracks, suddenly paying close attention. When the song ended, he offered to transcribe the lyrics for us while we were working on the arrangement. Upon return, he was visibly shaken. "Boys, boys! You can't sing this." You could see he was caught up in a real ethical dilemma. "You need to change the words," he said, and promptly went away and rewrote the lyrics to something more appropriate for a Catholic high school crowd. I was too naive to notice the subtext, but after that, I realized there's a sexual undercurrent present in all rock and roll. I mean, rock and roll *is* basically a euphemism for fucking, right?

To allay the brother's fears, we ran through the censored version once, but in the spirit of rock and roll—and I guess, the spirit of fourteen-year-old kids—we consigned the rewritten lyrics to the trash. His patronage was appreciated, but after that rehearsal, we only played the song as originally written. A few decades down the road, I was on a panel at South by Southwest with Colin Blunstone and Rod Argent from the Zombies and got to tell them that story. I think they enjoyed hearing about their role in the stand a bunch of high school guys made against censorship.

The first well-known bands I saw live were at Marist High School, in the school gymnasium. Tom, the self-designated leader of Total Environment, was also the social secretary on the student council and booked all the shows. I saw Vanilla Fudge—the concert had a powerful impact on me. Vanilla

Fudge was a hard rock band known for their hit cover of the Supremes' "You Keep Me Hangin' On." They had a great drummer, Carmine Appice. Carmine was a huge influence on my drumming style and loads of other drummers, too—not the least of which was Led Zeppelin's John Bonham. Carmine has played on some great records over the years, and he's a friend of mine to this day. After the show, I found my way backstage and managed to take some Polaroids of the guys. Come to think of it, this was my first backstage hang—the first of many.

Total Environment played our first show at Our Lady of Mount Carmel Grammar School in Bayonne, supporting a local band, the Uncharted Bus. The Uncharted Bus had a few years on us and were popular around the area. We had to audition for them to get the slot and were thrilled to get the gig because we were all fans. Looking out that night on the crowd of teenage kids from the back of the stage behind my Japanese red sparkle drum kit, I was hit with a wave of excitement. I thought, this is it—I was completely convinced this was how my life was going to be from then on. We played a tight forty-five minutes, including the Doors' "Light My Fire" and "In-A-Gadda-Da-Vida," the Iron Butterfly opus, with the extended drum solo. For a bunch of kids, we were pretty good. Good enough to take us all the way from Jersey to Carnegie Hall at the very least.

We got the name Total Environment because we used to have a Fillmore East–style Joshua light setup when we played a big gig. It was the heyday of psychedelia, and we wanted to emulate the stage presentation of the bands playing at places like the Fillmore, with the swirling liquid light shows and strobe light effects. Once we had the lights and the band playing at full tilt, it was like we created a *total environment*. The guy who ran the lights was called Ray Goodman, and Ray went on to make a career for himself in New York fashion that ran parallel with the rise of the CBGB scene. He was a real NYC entrepreneur. Over the next decade, Ray went on to create a fashion empire that was unique to Manhattan. He had fingers in pies all over town. He had the clothing line Tripp NYC. He bought the East Village boutique Limbo, an old hippie emporium and one-stop shop for fringe suede jackets, Afghan coats, and bell-bottoms on Saint Mark's Place and opened his own store, Trash and Vaudeville, in its place. He and his wife, Daang Goodman, started designing their own clothes and importing cool 1960s mod suits from the King's Road in London, but as the 1970s wore on, Trash and Vaudeville evolved into *the* place to get all your punk apparel—everything from skinny jeans right down to the ubiquitous Schott motorcycle jackets we all wore—the Ramones trademark look.

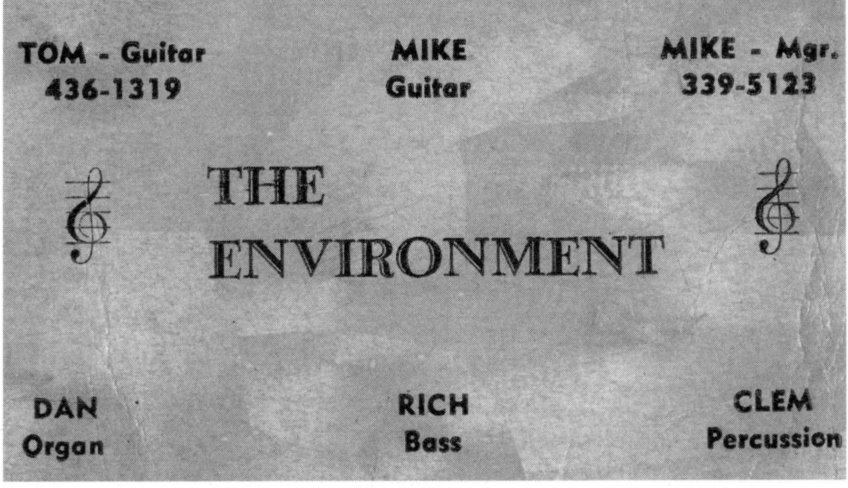

Business card for the Environment

Total Environment had gigs pretty much every weekend. It was a routine, but not a bad routine like getting up for school or going to work. One of my bandmate's folks owned a restaurant, and they let us use their catering van if we had a show out of town. In our time, we probably hit every local youth club, church hall dance, and Jewish community center. One time, we even played at a school for the deaf and went over great. The number of shows we were playing caused our PA rentals to escalate, so we decided to go more professional by buying our own. We had our eye on a Shure PA and mixer—out of our price range at $500. Tom's father worked at this place called the Hess Corporation—one of the big oil companies. Somehow, he persuaded his boss, Mr. Hess, to front the $500 for the PA, with the understanding we could pay him back in installments from the money we made playing weekend gigs. At the time, Leon Hess, as well as being an oil magnate, owned the New York Jets. I don't know if we ever paid him back, but I'm sure he didn't miss the money if we didn't.

The nighttime DJ on WABC-AM at the time was "Cousin Brucie" Morrow, who addressed his listening audience as his "cousins." He hosted an annual local battle of the bands called Cousin Brucie's Big Break. In 1969, we sent in a tape of Total Environment performing "Somethin' Goin' On" by Blood, Sweat & Tears. It's a great number, with some neat guitar and keyboard solos and even a cool drum break. A week later, we got a call saying we'd been accepted for the competition and were invited to ABC Studio on West Fifty-Sixth Street to record the song. Our song was later played on Cousin Brucie's show, and so many listeners called in with votes, it led to Total Environment being asked to play live at the Big Break Battle of the Bands. Usually, the show was held in a hotel ballroom like the Hilton, but this one was set to be staged at Carnegie Hall. I was fourteen, recording in a professional studio and playing at the most prestigious concert hall in the United States.

My band didn't win, but I'll never forget looking out, seeing this grand theater filled with people, knowing my parents were among them, and being overwhelmed with the idea that I'd be playing drums with my band on that stage. A few years later, around *Parallel Lines*, I was back at ABC to record an interview. Toward the end of the session, I mentioned I'd been in the same studio with my teenage band. It turned out the engineer recording the interview had been our engineer that day. To complete the crazy circle of coincidence, he handed me a quarter-inch tape box containing our original recording.

Prior to the Brucie's Big Break success, Tom had been the focal point and lead vocalist of the band, giving him a measure of control over what we did. But "Somethin' Goin' On" was sung by Mike, a decision Tom wasn't happy about. It was the right call given how things turned out. The song was an ambitious arrangement for a bunch of kids to take on. The choice of song and singer was Dan's, and as I think about it, this might've been the first of a lifetime of band dynamics and politics playing out. Dan and I are still friends. I think of him as the mastermind behind Total Environment. He was far and away the most gifted musician. We were all listening to Top 40 radio, but Dan was older and had developed a more refined musical palette—he was already a jazz freak. We were just kids, but he was digging Miles Davis, and he'd been following these cool jazz cats like Jimmy Smith since he was a kid.

I assumed our career was on the up, but the inevitable so-called musical differences of band life started to take a toll. We were still booking a lot of school dances on the local circuit, but I think the earlier discord with Tom being side-lined was smoldering. Despite all this, we still had momentum. Recently, someone sent me a press cutting from the local newspaper, *The Bayonne Times*, and a one-page feature on Total Environment, dated April 1969. There're some grainy photographs of us rehearsing for a show at Marist and a mention of our recent television debut on Channel 47 a couple of weeks earlier. We'd been booked to perform on a show called *Up and Coming*, over in Newark. The show was way, way down the dial, among the UHF band TV channels, so it wasn't exactly the Beatles appearing on Ed Sullivan, but it was a start—appearing on any TV felt like a very big deal indeed.

ROCK COMBO — Members of Total Environment take time out from a rehearsal. Seated is Mike Topolski; standing, (l. to r.), Russ Pepe, Clem Bozewski, Dan DeSenta and Tom Kochanski.

Bayonne Rock Group Hopes For Its 'Big Break' Today

My first press

Our host was this guy John Zacherle, who presented the monster-of-the-week horror movie on late-night TV. Whenever you watched *The Wolf Man* or a Friday night *Frankenstein* double feature, you'd see Zacherle beforehand. Playing with us on *Up and Coming* were Billy Joe Royal, riding high on his hit "Down in the Boondocks," the Hassles, a psychedelic blue-eyed soul band out of Long Island, and an English band, the Nice (Keith Emerson's band prior to Emerson, Lake & Palmer). Keith was thought of as the Jimi Hendrix of keyboard players, so he played up to that wild image. He wore a motorcycle jacket, and as part of his performance he dry-humped his Hammond organ and attacked the keys with a Bowie knife he carried on stage. Backstage, some guy from the Hassles tinkered around on the grand piano they had back there. We all looked on as he started playing "Martha My Dear," Paul's tune from *The White Album*, which had recently been released. Down the road, the Hassles guy released a record, *Piano Man*, and I suddenly realized I'd shared a stage with Billy Joel. Years later, when Blondie had the same agent as Billy, a great guy called Dennis Arfa, we wound up on a bill together at a festival in Ottawa. At the show, I cornered Dennis backstage, telling him I had to see Billy and ask if he remembered that night. I figured he would remember that show because the sight of Keith Emerson humping his organ is something you don't easily forget. Dennis took me over to meet Billy.

"You don't remember? Newark, New Jersey?" I asked. "Keith Emerson? John Zacherle? 'Down in the Boondocks'?"

"I got no idea what you're talking about," he said, laughing. "How do we get hold of a copy?"

Probably that tape was recorded over a long time ago, commonplace back then, and the moment was lost to history. Billy Joel has probably appeared on countless TV shows, so it's a matter of perspective. For us, being on *Up and Coming* was a big deal, but for Billy, it was just another day on the job. When I think back to that night, I can't remember what song we played, so my memory isn't what it used to be either.

Chapter 3

GETTING HIGH SCHOOL

By the time I was in high school, I had no interest in being there. I was just mad for rock and roll and being in a band. Then my mother got sick with cancer. After that, I checked out of school completely. I'd arrive late or not at all, because I was taking care of her. When she died, my world was turned upside down. I was seventeen. My dad slipped into his own world, and his life went sideways.

She'd been his anchor. We were a small family but large in terms of having two sets of relatives living within a couple of square blocks. My mother was the glue that held us all together. She was social, the first to invite people over for dinner or to throw a birthday party—the classic New Jersey matriarch. When dinner was ready, she'd send me down to the corner tavern where my dad was shooting pool and hanging out with his buddies to tell him to come home. With my mom gone, and my dad withdrawn into solitude, music became my escape. When I turned up for school, I only did the bare minimum to get by. Unlike a lot of kids, I didn't take to drinking, but I did start smoking pot. When we graduated from Junior High. I remember seeing my classmates getting drunk and puking everywhere. After seeing that, I was never really into drinking much; I didn't like that feeling of not being in control. Smoking weed was a different story. During high school lunches, I'd gather with my buddies, and we'd pass the hour smoking pot and talking about music. Compared with the space cadet kids who dropped a tab of acid before a science lesson, smoking your way through a nickel bag of weed seemed like tame behavior, but we weren't exactly seen as good students. Sometimes, I'd get kicked out of class for wearing a motorcycle jacket instead of a tie, but none of us were bad kids. As I grew a little older, I got harassed from time to time because my hair was long, but already I was biding my time. Waiting for school to be over so I could get on with living my life. I have no idea how I graduated or even got to college.

By 1971, Total Environment had run its course, and we went our separate ways. I've come to realize bands aren't meant to stay together permanently. That whole "together forever" notion is like something out of a corny movie about a rock band, probably instilled by the Beatles in *A Hard Day's Night* and *Help!*—like they're all best friends. Obviously, there are exceptions. I've been on both sides of that fence. Somehow, Chris, Debbie, and I have managed to buck that trend and stay the course, but for the most part, the idea that bands are not a forever thing holds true. I loved the sense of brotherhood and the camaraderie, but when Total Environment called it a day, I set my sights on what was next. I was hooked on the idea of being in a band, so we started a new group. Our new venture, the Sweet Willie Jam Band, was less Top 40 focused and more like the FM radio album rock sound of the '70s. We played Santana, the Allman Brothers, the Band, Joe Cocker. We were in our last couple of years of high school and smoking a lot of pot. We had two drummers, which is exactly the kind of idea you come up with when pot is involved. We recruited Joe Munn, my drum and bugle corps buddy, to fill the other drumming seat, and we were good to go. When we weren't rehearsing or strategizing, we went to the Schaefer Beer–sponsored Music Festival shows in Central Park at the Wollman Skating Rink; concerts for a dollar or maybe a dollar fifty. That's where I saw the original lineup of the Allman Brothers, Led Zeppelin, Procol Harum, the Band, and even Miles Davis. Not bad for a buck. A few years later, I found myself headlining on that same stage with Blondie on the *Parallel Lines* Tour.

In Sweet Willie we were too young to play pubs and bars, but we picked up where Total Environment left off and became a real draw on the Jersey high school circuit. I was making a little money, maybe fifty to a hundred bucks if it was a good weekend. Enough to buy a couple of records, a pack of cigarettes, and maybe a nickel bag of pot. My whole social life revolved around music and being in a band—but as high schoolers, we had other things on our mind too. Meeting girls was definitely a perk of being in a popular band. In my senior year, I met my first serious girlfriend and endured my first big heartbreak when she went off to college. She was very cool. I guess you'd call her a hippie girl. We'd all hang out at my friend's place—which was the band's HQ—and when his mom left for work or went out to play bingo, all the band members' girlfriends would come over, and we'd splinter off into separate bedrooms and make out. Once or twice, his mom came home early and the make-out sessions would end with panicked scenes as everyone hunted for their sweaters and scrambled to make a quick getaway.

During the days of the Sweet Willie Jam Band, I graduated high school and started at Jersey City State College (now New Jersey University) before transferring to New York University. Jersey City State was a liberal arts college, so I studied English, drama, and electronic music. There were various other subjects, but like in high school, I was completely focused on music. I didn't pay too much attention to academics but hung in there until my rock and roll life completely took over.

Chapter 4

CLUB 82

In 1973, the draft for the Vietnam War was over, bringing a collective sense of relief to guys my age. I was fresh out of not caring about high school and had moved on to not caring about college either. My music career was on track, working the bars of Jersey and Lower Manhattan with a glitter rock four-piece band, Sweet Revenge. This group followed a short-lived progressive band I had with some college classmates called Rondo Hatton—named after the obscure B movie actor. But after getting caught up in the Bowie glitter rock thing, I realized Sweet Revenge was better suited to my rock and roll aesthetic, which was still forming at the time. I didn't hang out with jocks or intellectuals, just the rock and rollers.

When I joined Sweet Revenge, I didn't answer an ad. I didn't audition. As I do to this day, I just gravitated to other musicians, and things happened organically from there. Either I was friends with, or I had a rivalry with, some other guy in some other band. I don't think of myself as being adversarial because I always loved the camaraderie of rock and roll, but I admit that part of me wanted to be better than my peers. There was always this idea at the back of everyone's mind about who was the best drummer, who was the best singer, the best guitarist, or whatever. I'd been playing in bands long enough that I had a reputation around the metro area as one of the best drummers, so, via word of mouth, the members of Sweet Revenge just drifted into my orbit. What else was I going to do but be in a band? I had a half-formed idea that if music didn't work out, I'd become a cop or enlist in the army, but we're talking plans Y and Z here. It was really plan A or nothing. I wanted to be a rock and roll star. Sign a deal. Make a record.

Sweet Revenge was me, a great friend of mine, Lee Boyce on guitar, who modeled himself after Jeff Beck; our androgynous singer, Charlie Pip; and this flamboyant redhead, Bobby Armstrong, filling out the lineup on bass guitar. We used to rehearse above an abattoir on Route 22 in Jersey City. Essentially, our setlist was a bunch of David Bowie and Mott the Hoople covers, but we had a few originals. One was "Fuck the World," an anti-establishment anthem with a punk attitude. I was juggling various elements of my life, still attending some classes, but for the most part daylight was for sleeping, not studying. I was living my life at night. I was also becoming tired of New Jersey; I just hadn't quite figured out that it was time to leave.

Ronnie Kankas, aka Ronnie Toast, was a friend of mine from high school and one of the few who was also into Bowie, the New York Dolls, and the Stooges. Sometimes, he'd get his dad's car and swing by my house, and we'd hit the road to nowhere and drive into the night, just killing time. We'd drive out on these mad, vague quests to find the Jersey Devil. Half-serious, half-joking, we wanted to see if the legend was true. According to local folklore, the Jersey Devil was a winged, cloven-hooved creature with a goat's head and a forked tail, said to live in the Pine Barrens in South Jersey. We'd scour the back roads, probably a little wasted, trying to catch a glimpse and listening out for its high-pitched screams over the sound of the car radio.

One time we just took off and drove around for hours before we started running out of gas. We pulled into a gas station, and Ronnie rolled down his window and asked the guy for $5 worth of gas. In New Jersey, it was illegal to pump your own gas, so when you pulled up to the pump, you needed to wait for an attendant to put the gas in the tank for you. So, we're sitting in the car, and the guy puts the nozzle into the tank and starts pumping, and the pump is ticking over, $1, $2, $3, and we're not paying any attention. Then I look over at Ronnie, about to say something, and he's got this wild look in his eyes. Maybe I didn't need to look so far to find the Jersey Devil, I figured, because without warning, Ronnie slammed his foot on the gas pedal and pulled out of the gas station. When I looked back, the hose was snaking around and spilling gas all over the ground while the gas station guy frantically tried to bring it back under control. We were whooping and hollering and killing ourselves laughing as we drove off.

We got lost in the night, heading up and down country backroads with the radio cranked up loud until we found ourselves on a narrow dirt road. It was autumn, so it was colder, and the ground was covered in dead leaves and mud. Without even realizing how it happened, we were hemmed in on three sides by dense forest. Ronnie passed a joint, I took a drag, then passed it back while we wondered what to do. We're in the dark forest, in the dead of night, wasted, and "Life on Mars" starts playing on the tape deck. We must have been too stoned or too stupid to panic because we just fell asleep in the car. I woke up the next morning with the sun breaking through the branches, and I could see a way out. I woke Ronnie. He yawned and stretched, put the car in reverse, and it seemed like we were going to make a smooth exit, until the car got stuck. He kept pumping the pedal, but the wheels wouldn't turn. We were inches deep in autumn leaves. The motor was running hot and a spark from the engine must have ignited the dry leaves, because within a few seconds, flames were lapping at the windows. We jumped out okay, we were panicking now—and stood back watching as the car was engulfed. Once the fire burned itself out, we shrugged and made our way down the road. It was a depressing hike back to civilization, but eventually we got out of the woods and to the main highway where we were picked up by some passing cops who took us back to the station. They got in touch with Ronnie's parents, and Ronnie's dad, who was understandably pissed, eventually came and got us.

Along with Ronnie, my most like-minded friends were Gary Lachman, my buddy from high school, and another guy, James Prasch. We came together because we were the only people in Bayonne turned on to Bowie and the Stooges. That was the commonality that helped to bind us, but I was the one pushing for us to get into the city and to see bands and start living the rock and roll life. The other guys were deep into William S. Burroughs and black magic and Aleister Crowley, but these were formative friendships, and we lived in each other's pockets and shared the same outlook.

I saw Bowie that September at Carnegie Hall on the *Ziggy Stardust Tour*. Despite his UK notoriety, he was still somewhat unknown in the US, except to us in the know. I was already well on my way to a lifelong Anglophile disposition, maybe at that point second only to my appreciation of NYC's rock and roll underbelly. The Carnegie Hall show was Bowie's big debut gig. I went by myself and found my seat in the balcony, noticing Andy Warhol—always easy to spot— making his way to the front. As the hall filled, the atmosphere got more electric, until finally the theme from *A Clockwork Orange* boomed out of the speakers and the band came out and launched into "Hang On to Yourself." I'd never seen a standing ovation at the start of show, but that was just the baseline of the night. People were in the aisles, on their seats dancing and screaming, everyone mesmerized and completely under the spell of Ziggy and the Spiders from Mars.

I was already committed to the rock ethos, but that concert significantly amped up my motivation to fully immerse myself in glam culture. I'd sleep all day, drag myself out of bed, and convene at someone's apartment on Journal Square, off Route 1/9, the direct route to the Holland Tunnel. It was right at the edge of Jersey City, so you could see Lower Manhattan out of the apartment's dirty windows. We'd smoke a little pot, shoot the shit, drink a couple glasses of blackberry brandy or whatever cheap wine we got from the grocery store, and take a late PATH train into Manhattan. First stop, Christopher Street, then on to Ninth Street station, where we'd disembark. We were decked out in our velvet pants, 1950s-style black-and-white jackets, teetering platform shoes, and shag haircuts, hitting the city like associate Spiders from Mars. Strolling to the corner of Sixth Avenue and Ninth Street, the intersection that marks the boundary between the East and West Village, we'd grab a bodega beer, smoke a joint, and travel farther east down Eighth Street, maybe grabbing a hot dog from Nathan's all-night hot dogs on the corner of Eighth and Sixth on our way into the East Village. We'd pass by 1 Fifth Avenue, later the site of Robert Mapplethorpe's photo session with Patti Smith for her first album cover. The journey continued down Eighth Street, until we hit Saint Mark's Place, home of the Electric Circus and the Dom, where, in the late '60s, the Velvet Underground performed as part of Andy Warhol's Exploding Plastic Inevitable.

At the intersection between Saint Mark's and Second Avenue, we'd give a nod to the Gem Spa, the famous newsstand and candy store featured on the back cover of the first New York Dolls album and home of the best egg cream in the city—a traditional New York fountain soda consisting of Fox's U-Bet chocolate syrup, seltzer, and milk. Finally, we'd take the turn onto Second Avenue and keep walking until we hit East Fourth Street and a whole new world. A scene of our own.

I had my antenna up for a break on the Manhattan scene. Ronnie was writing a lot of poetry and working with James, who had this type A personality, a real frontman swagger. James was the first of my peers to move out of his parents' and live on his own. His apartment overflowed with people crashing out or in various states of inebriation. James was the de facto leader of our little pack. He held down a straight job with the New York City Transit Authority, but he always wore a dab of eye makeup and flowing scarves, in deference to the glam era that was bubbling up around us. Later in life, he found God, or maybe God found him. I don't know, but even at that tender age, he was wrapped up in that nihilistic, end-of-the-world-is-nigh mindset. Maybe he had a point, because it felt like we were living through apocalyptic times. I'd spent my childhood looking across the bay at New York as this shining beacon, but we arrived to find a city on life support. New York was literally crumbling around us. Businesses were abandoned. The people with the means had escaped to the suburbs, leaving the streets piled high with garbage—still it was incredibly exciting to me and my friends.

Over the course of this period, Gary became estranged from his parents and moved away from New Jersey. Downtown rents were practically zero, so he started living in this Lower East Side storefront on East Tenth Street that Jimmy Prasch was renting. Because we were members of the Bridge and Tunnel crowd, that storefront became our crash pad and unofficial HQ. The battered storefront had a padlocked security fence you needed to screech to one side to get into a four-foot-square vestibule in front of the entrance. Across the threshold there was one large spartan room with a couple of couches and the bare necessities, like a toilet and a stove. We blocked out the store windows on either side of the doorway, so you could wake up inside and have no idea whether it was day or night. Usually though, you could hazard a guess. We generally woke up around 6 or 7 p.m., and if we had a buck left from the previous night, we'd head out for a bowl of borscht or something before starting the whole cycle again.

East Tenth Street was at the heart of New York's Ukrainian neighborhood, just a block away from the restaurant Veselka, which is still there today. A few doors down from Veselka, in the basement of one of the buildings, was another Ukrainian place I used to take my dad when he was in the city. You walked down from street level into the bowels of this building, and suddenly it was like you were back in Eastern Europe, twenty, thirty years before. For my dad, it must've been like a taste of his childhood. You're fifty feet down from the street, but everyone's eating cabbage and pierogi and speaking Polish and Ukrainian. Most crucially for me, geographically speaking, sleeping on the couch at Jimmy's storefront meant we were only a few short blocks away from Club 82.

Club 82 was our regular haunt in the heart of the East Village. It was run by a crew of tough lesbians, decked out like the supporting cast of *Rebel Without a Cause*: DA haircuts, white T-shirts, packs of Camels rolled up in the sleeve, cuffed Levis, and biker jackets. The club mainly presented drag shows, followed by a gay disco that lasted well into the morning. Wednesday nights were reserved for something different. Someone convinced Tommy, the James Dean lookalike who ran the place, that she should have rock and roll bands play once a week. The New York Dolls played one night, one of many nights, and after that experience, we were hooked. Club 82 became our home away from home.

The 82 was set in the basement of a majestic apartment building at 82 East Fourth Street. The place itself is steeped in the dark side of New York legend. Anna Genovese—the wife of the mobster Vito Genovese—ran the club when it first opened in the 1950s. Vito was an associate of Lucky Luciano and later headed up the Genovese crime family. The New York of the early 1970s still had those ties to that era, and you were always aware of that undercurrent, especially if you were moving around the city after dark. There were a lot of illicit after-hours clubs springing up. Here-today, gone-next-week drinking dens and gambling clubs, open from the early hours of the morning until the following afternoon, creating a mob service industry around all of it. There were enforcers, guys in sharkskin suits hassling club owners for their weekly protection money, and guys wheeling trollies of hijacked booze from the street down to the bar, like something out of a Scorsese film. Add the drug trade into the mix and a bunch of glam rock kids hankering for a baggie of pills to see them through till dawn, and it was obvious our world and theirs were sometimes closer than we imagined. I didn't know anyone who was involved in organized crime, but I wasn't naive. Hudson County, where I grew up in Jersey, was known as the most corrupt county in the state. We knew we were rubbing shoulders with some serious people sometimes, but also, those connected guys were our classmates' uncles or cousins, and we knew them from around town, or standing out front of their houses, cracking open a cold brew or fixing the transmission on their car. In the city, the mob had ties to every after-hours drinking den, and we went to them all. You didn't have to look too hard to find somewhere to get a drink and have a good time, and we found some new dive practically every week. Club 82, though, that was the one that stuck.

The streets outside were dirty and dangerous, but inside, we were one or two degrees of separation from the real-life New York underground. Club 82 was a schizophrenic place. Kind of a drag club, kind of a night club, with dark corners, hidden tables, and discreet booths to get up to whatever you might be into. There was a sinister edge, but we sure didn't mind. We were just drinking in the atmosphere, which still hung heavy with the influence of the Velvets and the Beat poets who used to live around the Village. Whenever anyone asks me what that moment in time felt like, I always tell them, it felt like we were in a holding pattern, waiting for the next thing to happen. Then we realized, it was happening all around us.

Band night at Club 82 brought in too many bands to mention, but to name a few, I saw Teenage Lust, the Harlots of 42nd Street, Another Pretty Face, Wayne County, and Queen Elizabeth. Eventually, I got a booking for Sweet Revenge. At first it was the best place to hang; then it became the only place. We started out as observers of the scene, but before we knew it, it became our lifestyle. Sleeping all day in the storefront, buying a cheese sandwich and a pack of potato chips and a coffee for sustenance, and then walking down to Club 82—this became our entire existence. It didn't take long to get a foothold in the scene that formed around bands like the New York Dolls. David Bowie was huge in England, but stateside, glam, or glitter rock, or whatever you want to call it, was an underground pursuit, and we were right in the heart of it. I know if it hadn't been for Bowie and the Dolls, my life would've been entirely different. Probably, I would've been at a Grateful Dead concert with 99 percent of the people I'd left behind. None of what followed would have happened. No Blondie. Nothing. Just a completely different musical path.

The cast of characters was vast and constantly evolving. Some nights you'd run into Jeff Starship from the band Sniper (Jeff, of course, was later known as Joey Ramone), Lenny Kaye, Thomas Erdelyi (soon to become Tommy Ramone), the Neon Boys' Richard Hell and Tom Verlaine, Elda Stiletto, some guy called Chris Stein, a girl called Debbie Harry, and a hundred others who'd go on to find some level of infamy. If you had a sharp eye, you might catch sight of Lou Reed, Bryan Ferry, or even Bowie. People who were gods in our eyes, but who'd yet to make it in the straight world.

We had an inside track on knowing when Bowie was in town via a friend of ours, Sue, who became part of our extended entourage. Sue was friendly with Bowie's chauffeur, Tony Mascia—the same guy seen driving Bowie's Lincoln Continental in *The Man Who Fell to Earth*. We spent a lot of time getting intel from Sue, trying to figure out Bowie's movements whenever he was in the city. Bowie was the prince from across the water, but the Dolls ruled the roost. Even if they weren't playing, one Doll, if not all of them, could usually be found in some dark corner of the 82 or another club. The first time I saw Johnny Thunders offstage was at Club 82. As I descended into the club, he was reclining across the bottom of the stairs, nodding out in his own private world. I thought for a minute what to do. He's a New York Doll. Do I just step over him? Well, I did just that and he didn't stir.

Over time we got friendly with the people who ran Club 82, and once our faces were known, we'd get half drunk outside, and Tommy would comp us and nod us through. Once inside, there were a hundred faces, all seeking refuge from the dirty streets. It was the early days of the still-deep underground disco scene, and everyone danced all night under a vast mirror ball, sniffing amyl nitrate and taking amphetamines and quaaludes to keep themselves on their feet until the sun came up. Away from the prying eyes of society, we were experimenting with drugs, sexual ambiguity, and androgyny.

I didn't know it at the time, but my future was about to begin. I went along one night to a Dolls' show and caught the support band, the Stilettos, a New York group that included Debbie Harry and Chris Stein. They were faces on the scene I'd seen around a few times; we'd even sized each other up a couple of times. But we moved in our own circles and lived in our own self-curated bubbles. All of us had become associated with another venue, a block or so away on the Bowery, after the Dolls imploded and the 82 just vanished from the cultural landscape. It was like the world shrugged, and we all moved our lives around the block to another place. Looking back, it's curious how the glamour of that scene evaporated in the fashion austerity that ruled the Bowery a year or so later. The new ground zero was a couple of blocks away, and it's almost as though all the glam rockers on East Fourth Street stepped out of their platform shoes, cut their hair, walked around the corner to 315 Bowery, and transported the scene from one site to the other. Like everyone, I didn't know what was coming next; I just knew I wanted to be a part of it.

Chapter 5

NEW YORK DOLLS

The New York Dolls were the perfect rock and roll band. If you saw them in their prime, you can consider yourself very fortunate. Gigs at Club 82 and the legendary Halloween show at the Waldorf Astoria in 1973 are forever etched in my mind. They were like superheroes, larger than life. Experiencing the Dolls live was a spectacle of unchained raw charisma and attitude—they were the incarnation of cool. At eighteen, I was already a regular on the PATH train, traveling from Jersey to the Village to hang out at Ashley's or shop for clothes at Ian's on Grove Street, where the Dolls bought their outfits. The idea they might be hanging out in the same zip code as me and my friends and that we might one day run into one of the Dolls blew our minds.

After Bowie, it was the Dolls whose trajectory I followed most closely. I knew their every move, looking on while they were scouted by every label in New York before finally signing to Mercury Records in early 1973. Their first album, produced by Todd Rundgren, was released on July 27. I had the date marked on my calendar. On the cover they're wearing heavy makeup: eye shadow, lipstick, and rouge. Their image was like a hybrid of Little Richard and the Rolling Stones. I never thought of them in terms of gay or transvestite—that stuff didn't matter. They were enlightened in the way they challenged binary norms—encompassing androgyny, machismo, and everything between. Johnny Thunders was a fan of 1960s girl groups like the Shangri-Las and the Ronettes and evoked Ronnie Spector in his look. Occasionally, they performed the Shangri-Las' "Give Him a Great Big Kiss," even taking a line for the introduction to their own song, "Looking for a Kiss."

A week after the album's release, the Dolls played their biggest hometown show to date, opening for Mott the Hoople at Madison Square Garden's Felt Forum. My dad used to take me to the Felt Forum to see the fights, but now it felt like a perfect setting for a rock and roll show.

Maybe foretelling the chaos that would surround this show, a few hours earlier and across town, the dilapidated building that housed the Mercer collapsed into a heap of rubble, killing four people. With the history the Mercer and the Dolls had—they largely built their rep there—the tragedy provided a curious footnote to their story. The Dolls had a lot on the line that night: a brand-new record in the stores and facing a crowd that mostly had never seen them before. I'd love to tell you they hit it out of the park, but it wasn't one of their best shows. While they waited in the wings, Murray the K, the New York radio DJ and self-proclaimed fifth Beatle, did the first of a series of buzz-killing introductions. Wolfman Jack appeared, followed by Todd Rundgren, who brought the Dolls on to tape of traffic noise. They came out fully loaded with swagger, but Mott's audience wasn't sold; in fact, they seemed indifferent. It didn't help matters that the sound was muddled and plagued with problems. The crowd's lackluster vibe seemed to rattle the Dolls; they were used to being the star attraction and not the support act. Their short set went down in flames, ending with "Frankenstein" and "Jet Boy." There was no encore.

That December, I was visiting a friend at George Washington University when the Dolls had a show at the school's Lisner Auditorium. I arrived at the venue early to get a spot in front, but I needn't have worried: the show was general admission and sparsely attended. They might've been kings of New York, but once you left the city, the hype and controversy around them drew more curiosity seekers and hecklers than fans. Still, there was at least one die-hard Dolls fan in the auditorium that night. I endured Babe, a horrible prog-rock cover band as the opening act, and then, with minimal fanfare, the Dolls appeared and launched into "Personality Crisis." With most of the audience standing a good distance back, I easily made my way up and stood front and center, transfixed the entire set.

The Dolls were dressed down. Johnny wore denim with a wide red leather belt wrapped around his waist. David was wearing jeans and a beat-up black leather motorcycle jacket. Bassist Arthur Kane was out of it, but his playing was still incredible. They were all great rock and roll musicians; claims to the contrary were usually the result of their level of sobriety on any given night. This night they seemed more focused on the music than putting on a show; David even toned down his onstage patter. In the middle of the set, two chairs were brought out to the front of the stage—directly in front me—and David and Johnny played an acoustic "Lonely

Planet Boy." Johnny was playing a beautiful Gibson Hummingbird. I feel privileged to have seen any Dolls shows, but witnessing that performance in Washington, DC, was magical—a sort of heart-wrenching glimpse of everything they could or might be.

The Dolls released their second album in 1974, but the band fell apart the following spring. It was a sad end to that chapter of rock and roll history. Over the years, I came to know each of them as friends. Occasionally, I'd find myself in the depths of some dark after-hours club or in Ashley's in the East Village, snorting a line of coke with Johnny or sharing a joint with Sylvain Sylvain. When Jerry and Johnny started a new band, the Heartbreakers, I saw them every chance I got. Johnny would spot me in the crowd and break into the Surfaris' "Wipe Out"—the classic surf instrumental with the ferocious drum break. No matter what shape I was in, he'd coerce me to join him onstage. One night at the Limelight on Sixth Avenue, I didn't even wait to be invited, I just got up onstage. That was probably the only time I was more fucked up than Johnny Thunders was. I never stopped holding every one of the Dolls in the highest regard—especially Johnny. His presence and charisma always shined through, whatever state he was in. In August 1976, Blondie and Talking Heads supported the Heartbreakers at CBGB for three nights, two shows a night. Fortunately, I have the poster to prove it happened, because I remember very little, if anything.

Ultimately, the Heartbreakers disbanded, only to get back together sporadically for "rent" parties. Johnny eventually went out on his own and released a solo album, *So Alone*, in 1978, which featured "You Can't Put Your Arms Around a Memory." According to Sylvain, Bob Dylan once told him he wished he could write a song as good as that. Johnny took the title from a line on the Jackie Gleason sitcom *The Honeymooners*. In the episode "Better Living Through TV," Gleason's character, bus driver Ralph Kramden, threatens to leave his wife, Alice, and warns her, "You can't put your arms around a memory." She responds, "I can't even put my arms around you."

In early 1989, I was visiting my dad in Jersey with my girlfriend, Kathy Valentine, when I got a message from Johnny asking if I'd join him for an upcoming gig at the Ritz. At the time, Johnny had a band called the Oddballs, all of whom were in New York except for their drummer. Of course, I agreed to the gig. We scheduled three days of rehearsals in the same building on West Thirtieth Street where I first played with Chris, Debbie, and Fred Smith in Blondie. Being back in the "Music Building" brought back waves of memories—both positive and negative. The first day went fine. John was a great bandleader, and the other musicians knew the material, making it easy for me. Afterward, Johnny pulled me aside to "talk business." I'd have played for free, but we agreed he'd pay me $500. With another rehearsal set for the next day, we said our goodbyes. As I was leaving, Johnny pointed to a sticker he had placed on his guitar—"Cottage cheese for brains"—and we shared a laugh.

True to form, Johnny skipped the next two days of rehearsals, and we didn't see him until midnight on the night of the show. Regardless, the band had rehearsed hard without him, and we were ready. The Ritz, one of the premier NYC venues at the time, was sold out, and we went down well. Kathy went down not so well, getting so drunk, I had to look for her and carry her out of the club. It was a last hurrah for her, bookended by her boyfriend spending a week playing with Johnny Thunders. She went back to Los Angeles, got sober, and has stayed that way ever since. Johnny wasn't so lucky. He died in New Orleans on April 23, 1991.

After his death, I flew to Toronto to collaborate with Sylvain on an album of Johnny's songs. The sessions went great, and it was fun to play those numbers. Sadly, the record never came out, and Sylvain died in 2021. As for Arthur Kane, Frank Infante and I worked with him backing Sonny Vincent of Testors on a Little Richard tribute record. Arthur was such a gentle, kind human being and a wonderful player. We had a great time that day jamming on songs by the Yardbirds, the Kinks, and the Who—Arthur knew all the licks perfectly. His drinking led people to think he couldn't play, which couldn't be further from the truth. Arthur was in the same league as John Entwistle. With him dying in 2004, and the last Doll standing, David Johansen, dying in 2024, their legacy lives on. I vote for them to be elected to the Rock & Roll Hall of Fame every year, where they absolutely belong.

It's hard to overstate the sense of disappointment I felt that the Dolls didn't last as a band, and that the New York glam thing was over. Following the Dolls' demise, I think all the bands in the city took a collective breath and realized we were going to have to capture our own moment, whatever that was.

Chapter 6

DEBBIE AND CHRIS

On March 10, 1975, a small advertisement in the Musicians Wanted section of the *Village Voice* caught my eye. It read:

Freak energy Musical Experienced drummer needed female fronted estab. working NYC rock band. Excell oppty. money. Fun. Call NOW 925-0531

Before social media, the want ads were where you looked to find anything from an apartment to a job, or in this case, a drummer.

I presumed the abbreviations were to keep the cost of the ad down. So much for money, I thought, but I figured it was worth a call. A bored, stoned-sounding voice told me the

Freak energy Musical Experienced
drummer needed female fronted estab.
working NYC rock band. Excell oppty.
money. Fun. Call NOW 925-0531

The advert that started it all

name of the band was Blondie and gave me the address of their rehearsal studio, and we agreed to meet the next day.

For that meetup, I picked out some suitably freak-energy clothes and threw them on the bed. I was dressing in the glam rock style of the day, a hybrid of Trevor Bolder from the Spiders from Mars and Russell Mael, the singer of Sparks. I had the same shag haircut and chose a blue sailor's uniform top, inspired by a picture I'd seen of Keith Moon wearing one. I paired this with some red platforms from Arrowsmith Shoes on West Eighth Street. After checking my reflection, satisfied, I called my girlfriend, Diane, to come along.

Arriving at the building on West Thirtieth Street, we went up the elevator, and I was surprised to find that the band in need of a drummer was, in fact, two familiar faces from Club 82. It was Chris and Debbie from the Stilletos, the band I'd seen opening for the Dolls a few months earlier. The rehearsal space was in a dormant office building in the garment district they were renting on the cheap, with another band, The Marbles.

The next surprise was that they didn't want to jump into playing. It was more like an informal interview, with Chris doing most of the talking. Everything he said sounded kind of laconic, like his mind was on something else entirely. I told them a little about myself and the bands I'd been playing with, and we talked about music and life, generally sizing each other up. We seemed to get along okay. They were a few years older than me, and in time, they became like the older brother and sister I'd never had—in a very dysfunctional family, aka Blondie.

It was clear we had a mutual love of a lot of the same music: the Velvet Underground, the Stooges, the New York

Dolls. We were all fans of the 1960s girl groups like the Ronettes and the Shangri-Las and, of course, of Phil Spector's Wall of Sound. That music's surface sweetness mixed with a streetwise toughness was going to be a pivotal element of our early sound.

They were writing their own songs too. Good songs. Debbie, the singer, was a Jersey girl who'd transplanted to NYC in the 1960s. As I pulled up a chair, she remarked on my red shoes, so I give my choice of footwear a lot of credit for me getting in the band. The guitarist, Chris, was Brooklyn born and bred. His claim to fame was that one of his old bands opened for the Velvets one night. He rarely rose from his seat the whole time I was there. He was in a state of constant repose, idly strumming his guitar as we spoke. Chris cut a curious figure in his glam rock regalia: long rooster hair and heavy black eye makeup, like a doppelgänger of Alice Cooper. I really didn't know what to make of this first encounter, but the conversation was enough to decide we wanted to get together again and actually play music.

Over the coming days, I transported my drums piecemeal on the train over to the studio, back and forth between home and the city until I had the full kit in Chris and Debbie's studio. For a while, we rehearsed with Chris reclining in his chair at a permanent forty-five-degree angle, with this guy Fred Smith on bass. When we started to make a little noise, it was distinctly unpolished. Still, even at first glance, Debbie had all these facets to her, all vying for your attention. There was a touch of Warhol cool, a sprinkling of Marilyn Monroe's vulnerability, a bit of Jean Harlow platinum blonde Hollywood chic all in the mix, combined with her easy beatnik charm and intelligence. I knew right away she was destined to be a star. She was basically a star already. It would just take the world a couple of years to catch on. In a small way, I feel like I discovered Debbie Harry. I'd been honing my talent, hoping to find the perfect frontperson, someone with the creativity, the star power, the energy of a David Bowie, a Marc Bolan, or a Jim Morrison—I never imagined that my frontperson would be a girl.

Blondie was a long way from the finished product. Things were rough around the edges, but Fred Smith was a good player. He'd played with Debbie and Chris awhile and was with the band when they were still going under the name Angel and the Snake. Angel and the Snake morphed over time to become Blondie and the Banzai Babies, and then, finally, a few months before my arrival, just Blondie. Supposedly, I was the fiftieth drummer who replied to that ad. I don't know, I just know I got the gig. It wasn't like I signed a contract or anything. It was all very loose and informal, but nothing was ever official in those days. I know it's the music *business*, but the business side of things hadn't entered our lives. There were no plans for world domination, and making money seemed like it was still an afterthought. It was more a case of, we have these songs, do you want to play music together?

Debbie and Chris were managing the band, and neither of them were what you might call businesspeople. Home base for them was a walk-up apartment on Thompson Street in New York's SoHo district, with a bathtub in the kitchen, old-school tenement style, that also served as a counter when it was covered. Sometimes, when I came over, Chris would be sitting in the bathtub holding court. A year later, I'd have the same bathtub accommodation in my apartment in the West Village on Christopher Street.

One thing they had going for them was they had a few connections around town, particularly in terms of the underground club scene in Lower Manhattan. Crucially, they knew Hilly Kristal, the man behind CBGB. Hilly, in my opinion, needs to be in the Rock and & Roll Hall of Fame, for obvious reasons. Through Hilly, Chris and Debbie had lined up a couple of CBGB shows for April, so the focus was on getting the band up and running in time for those performances. Blondie had played CBGB a few times, before I joined the band. I wasn't aware how pivotal a venue it was about to become. None of us knew, in fairness. I didn't know where we were going, but I knew I needed to be in Manhattan to make it, and playing with Debbie and Chris was my entry into that world. Whatever they lacked in professionalism, I had the idea these couple of beatniks were already halfway there, so I told them, sure. Let's go. I quit Sweet Revenge and committed to Blondie.

Chapter 7

NEW YORK, 1975

My first show with Blondie was at CBGB on April 7. It was an eventful night, just not in the way I'd hoped. My girlfriend and I drove in from Bayonne in my dad's car and parked on the street out front, arriving unfashionably early. The Bowery was deserted back then, so there was plenty of parking. I got out of the car, full of excitement, but within hours, everything fell apart.

In a move that was almost comical in its timing, during the break between our two sets, Fred Smith announced he was leaving the group to join Television—a game of musical chairs instigated by Richard Hell when he quit to join the Heartbreakers. Debbie and Chris were understandably downtrodden. From their perspective, it was one step forward, two steps back. They were getting paranoid that the other New York bands were gunning for them and were talking about how this was the end of the band. Having just joined, I was having none of that and said we had to keep going. I knew the songs were good, that we could be great. I suggested we bring in my friend Gary Lachman to replace

Smith. He wasn't a bass player. He was more of a poet, but he knew a few chords, so I figured he'd be a good fit. At the time, Gary was at loose ends, still living in the abandoned storefront, so he jumped at the opportunity. Gary joining was a stroke of fortune for us all. He dropped the Lachman and adopted the stage name Valentine. More importantly, he and Debbie wrote "X Offender," the song that landed our first record deal.

In the wake of the Fred Smith debacle, we got a new band HQ. Debbie found a loft at 266 Bowery, just down the street from William Burroughs's place known as "the Bunker" and a block south from CBGB. Once Gary joined, he moved into Debbie and Chris's loft. It was unusual for New Yorkers to have cars at the time, but Debbie had this beat-up Camaro she used as a runaround. To avoid having it towed away by the city, she had to wake up at dawn and wait for the alternative side of the street parking to come into effect and move the car to the other side of the street for the next twenty-four hours. That was every day except Wednesdays, when the city just shrugged and let you park your car wherever.

The new HQ was decent sized, and it felt like a fresh start. It was spacious enough to accommodate our gear and for the band to rehearse whenever we pleased. The band set up in the living room on the first floor, and Debbie and Chris lived out back. A friend of Chris and Debbie's, Benton, lived above us on the second floor. He was a skinny, macho gay guy and dressed like a biker. Benton held the lease on the building and was around all the time. He sat in on our rehearsals and started designing backdrops for our shows. After Debbie started bleaching her hair, I remember Benton asking her to dye his hair blond—including his body hair—and him walking around the apartment with peroxide-white chest hair and a motorcycle jacket, stinking of bleach and leather. The third floor lay empty for a long time, until fashion designer Stephen Sprouse moved in, at which point, 266 Bowery became a real hub. It may have been spacious, but like most places in the area, it lacked amenities and was quite austere. There was no hot water, and the only toilet in the building was on our floor, so people were constantly passing through rehearsals whenever they needed to take a leak. If Benton was busy or tired, or if it was too cold, he'd piss in a bottle and bring it down to be emptied into the toilet later. Being New York, the winters were unforgiving, but we got used to the apartment being subzero half the year. There were shelters and flophouses up and down the Bowery and homeless people outside on the street. One morning, I found the frozen body of a homeless guy. The contrast between today and back then couldn't be more striking. You walk through the Bowery today and the whole area is so bustling and alive, it's like Disneyland for millennials and Gen Z.

With Gary on board, the band started to gel and, aside from the regular shows at CBGB, where Hilly would let us play anytime, we started to book a few low-key shows around town with the new lineup. One of the first places we played together was deep in the belly of the Financial District, nowadays known as FiDi. The place was called Whyte's Pub, where Debbie had a part-time job as a bikini bartender. She pulled a favor with the owners and persuaded them to throw a couple of hundred dollars our way for an afternoon's work. Whyte's was a watering hole for the Wall Street crowd— stockbrokers and speculators. Looking out on the audience, it was a sea of grey flannel suits and Egyptian cotton shirts. It wasn't quite *American Psycho* exactly, but you got a glimpse into that detached stockbroker, art dealer mindset. Just looking around, you knew none of those guys were finding any frozen dead guys on their front stoop when they walked out of their apartments to pick up *The Wall Street Journal*. They weren't our people, but we played there a few times.

We'd taxied up with our gear, Debbie would change out of her bikini and into something a bit more appropriate, and we'd play happy hour between 5 and 6 p.m. We were playing a lot of covers, songs by the Shangri-Las, "Lady Marmalade" by LaBelle, and Martha and the Vandellas' "Heatwave." I don't know that anyone was paying much attention to us. Probably, we were just background music, while these guys tried to seduce the waitresses or waited for their coke dealer to arrive. The place didn't have a stage, so the four of us just set up our equipment in the corner. Like a lot of the early gigs we played, it was just a case of show up and play. So that's what we did.

Overall, it was a cool time. We were picking up these low-dough shows around Lower Manhattan and constantly rehearsing. During the days, I wandered around Greenwich Village, stopping in Le Figaro Café or the Kettle of Fish Bar on MacDougal. Along the way, all the stores and stands pushed bad radio waves into the air. Having grown up on radio, hearing all this syrupy pop, album-oriented rock and prog rock was disheartening. Thankfully, I still had my vinyl, and soon the scene had Bleecker Bob's, which became the unofficial meeting place for the bands and a welcome respite from that onslaught of Top 40 radio.

Bleecker Bob's was set up by Bob Plotnik, a New York music industry legend and stereotypically grouchy record store owner. If you've ever seen the film *High Fidelity*, that's what Bob's place was like. The first time I visited Bob's, it was more of a specialty "oldies" store, but over time, as the new bands started to emerge, it became the destination store to buy their records. It was the only place you could find the British music papers like *NME* and *Melody Maker*. Crucially though, Bob's carried the best lineup of import records on the East Coast. Lenny Kaye, the guitarist from the Patti Smith Group, had a day job at Bob's as a clerk and was responsible for bringing a lot of great records to our attention. You'd read about the latest 45s happening across the pond, and maybe a week later, Bob would return from his latest trek to the UK wholesalers, and those records would be in the racks. None of those songs were on the radio, but we had access to them all. Once the CBGB artists started getting deals, Bob's was the place to go. I got the first Patti Smith record, *Piss Factory*, from Bleecker Bob's. It was probably the only place you could find a copy of the Television 45 "Little Johnny Jewel." A little later, Bob's was the place I picked up "Anarchy in the UK" by the Sex Pistols.

After the summer, the city scene was starting to get a little more traction. *Rolling Stone* ran a piece on CBGB's Top 40 Underground Band Festival, but as a band, Blondie's profile was still on the down-low. Despite getting on New Yorkers' radar, the places we could play were few and far between, and we were always on the lookout for a new venue to play. In the autumn of 1975, we found this club on West Twenty-Third Street, right across the street from the notorious Chelsea Hotel. It was a gay disco called Mother's, and we were turned on to it by the guys in the band the Fast. The Fast were a glam punk band hailing from Brooklyn. It was through our mutual friendship with those guys—particularly the three brothers, Miki, Armand, and Paul Zone—that we'd eventually wind up bringing our keyboard player, Jimmy Destri, into the group. His sister Donna was friends with them, so that's how we found Jimmy. Paul Zone was a good friend to us over the years. He used to cut our hair, and for a time, he helped Debbie with her styling. Plus, he took some great early portraits of Blondie. The booker at Mother's was Peter Crowley; he went on to do the same at Max's Kansas City, as well as to manage Wayne County. Peter was an early ally of the band, booking us at Mother's with the Fast and a few shows supporting the Ramones. Things were definitely starting to move.

One of Benton's friends was appearing in a production of *The Tempest* in a church basement in Chelsea, so Benton, Gary, and I went along. That was a scene: Benton with his bleached blond hair and motorcycle jacket, Gary wearing sunglasses at night, and me, dressed for a night out on the town. We got bored and decided to leave, so the three of us snuck out and onto the street to smoke a cigarette. We were standing around, smoking and talking, when a guy walking past gave us some NYC attitude. "Whaddayou punks doin' around here?" Benton and I just shrugged and carried on talking, but Gary was less easy going; he always seemed to have a chip on his shoulder. He shouted after the guy and told him to fuck off. Dumb move. The guy turned on his heel and started really going to town on Gary. Benton was stunned, too frightened to move, so I jumped on the guy's back in a bid to get him off. He was trying to throw me off, like I was a rodeo cowboy, so I tightened my grip around his neck. Gary was reeling on the floor, concussed, scrambling around trying to find his glasses, which the guy knocked off when he was pounding on him. Around us, you could see all the lights in the neighborhood going on and people coming out to see what was happening. It turned out the guy was the beat cop for the neighborhood, and someone dialed 911. Next thing we knew, more cops arrived. We were cuffed and carted off to the nearest precinct where we were booked for assaulting a police officer. After they did the paperwork, we got to make our one call. We called Debbie and Chris and hoped for the best. Meantime, the booking sergeant realized they had no room in the holding cells, so we were put in a meat wagon and taken uptown to the Tombs, the notorious Manhattan Detention Complex, a bona fide jail. On arrival, we were thrown into a holding pen with that past night's muggers and pimps and drunks. You know those movie scenes where the innocent guy finds himself in a cell filled with dozens of serious criminals? Well, that was us. The floor was just a mess of strung-out junkies and hoodlums drooling on the stone floor and trying to catch a few z's before they went up before the judge. I don't know that we slept too much, probably with one eye open. Benton, who'd been cowering through the whole sorry mess, was especially concerned, but in the end he was golden. Everyone assumed he was a tough biker dude and gave him a wide berth. This was Friday night, but a whole day passed while we waited to be arraigned. Saturday, nothing. Maybe the call to Debbie and Chris had been a waste of dime. Then finally, on Sunday, after spending forty-eight hours in the cell, a lawyer friend of Debbie and Chris's showed up and got us out in time for our show at Max's Kansas City that night. I understand the charges were quietly dropped, probably because Gary took a real beating. We went directly from jail back to the loft, took a cold bath, and went straight from there to sound check. Debbie made a little speech from stage that night, introducing us as fresh out of jail and now appearing on stage type of thing. It was the kind of strange shit that went down when you were with Gary, I guess.

The turning point for Blondie came in November, when we played our first headline date at Max's Kansas City, with support from the Martian Rock Band. I don't know if the Martian Rock Band even earned a footnote in rock history, but they supported Blondie, so they'll always have that on their resumé, I guess. The headline show came about after Peter Crowley, the booker at Max's, caught one of our shows at Mother's. He doesn't get a lot of credit, but Peter played a pivotal role in our ascent. Peter was the first one to see we were ready to step up from opening for other groups. Later, as our reputation started to grow, he had some aspirations to act as our manager, but it didn't pan out that way. Maybe a couple of weeks after the Martian Rock Band show, we played Max's again, with Mink DeVille, who were practically the house band at CBGB.

In the heart of this run of incredible shows, we found ourselves playing a place called Monty Python's, our first show with Jimmy Destri in the lineup. Monty Python's was a low-rent bar in the East Village, on Thirteenth Street and Third Avenue. That whole area had a seedy reputation. It was a debauched, broken-down neighborhood, like something out of a Velvet Underground song. Every other person you passed on the street was either a drunk or a junkie. Prostitutes were on nearly every corner, getting hassled by catcalling Johns while their pimps kept an eye on proceedings. In the summer months, it was like the city was in heat. The hookers got more brazen, touting their wares and turning tricks in the back seats of cars. The drunks were no longer drinking just to stay warm, so they grew rowdier and more dangerous. Drug dealers just went about their business, with no apparent fear of being arrested. The regular people who lived between Second and Third Avenues knew well enough to venture outside only during the daytime hours. What was going on in the streets at that time was just a backdrop to what was happening in our lives, so, personally, I never felt threatened. If anything, that wild side of New York life acted as fuel for our creativity. Besides, it wasn't as bad as other places. We all knew to never venture east of First Avenue and onto the waterfront. These days, Alphabet City—the avenues A, B, C, and D in Manhattan—is a cool, laid-back enclave in the East Village and one of the chicest addresses you can have now, but in 1975, it couldn't have been more desolate. The rows of abandoned tenements were just open drug marketplaces. I heard plenty of stories about people taking their lives in their hands and heading up a flight of stairs, stepping over the collapsed, wasted junkies, putting a few dollars through a hole in the wall and a baggie of heroin or whatever would come out of another hole somewhere down the corridor. By comparison, as degraded as it was, the area around Monty Python's seemed almost like a safe zone. The bar itself was just a block from a porno theater. Around the time we played, that row of tenements on East Thirteenth was used as a location in the finale of the Scorsese movie *Taxi Driver*, with Robert DeNiro and Jodie Foster.

I don't know that it was much nicer inside Monty Python's than it was out on the streets, but it was much the same arrangement we had at Whyte's. Just show up, tune up, and play. The five of us jammed our gear in one corner and rattled through a setlist of cover versions while the bar's patrons either wondered what was going on or didn't notice us playing at all. Jimmy's keyboards added a different dimension to our sound, and I think that was a real boost. We played Monty Python's a couple of times between 1975 and 1976. Occasionally, you'd get these characters down from the Upper East Side, slumming it for the night like they were on a safari or something. Well-to-do Manhattanites having a look at how the other half lived before jumping back into a limo and heading home to their comfortable Brownstone lives.

There wasn't exactly a scene going on, but one night at Monty Python's we got caught up with a group of well-to-do guys who were out partying with their girlfriends. I remember they became quite fascinated by us. We got to talking, and they explained they were all members of the same Manhattan equestrian club. They kept commenting on what we were wearing, paying particular attention to Debbie. Debbie was always the main door opener for us. She's impossible not to notice. The fact she became such an icon was no surprise to me. It was obvious she was going to stand out from the crowd, and in turn, that was going to make us stand out too. The rest of us would get our due, as far as personal acclaim and kudos went, so there was never any envy that she held that power. I always recognized that people would come around to us, and so much of that was down to Debbie's style and charisma. Even in 1975, when we were playing these dive bars, she always found a way to shine through. Like a lot of entertainers, Debbie's a little shy, but she had the stage presence of a Jim Morrison or a Nina Simone. It was always interesting how she'd interpret a song—we did some girl group stuff, but also songs by the Doors and Pop and David Bowie, or that Four Seasons song "Big Man in Town," where Debbie would sing it as a man. It took on some androgynous insanity although she was obviously very feminine, and her image was anything but androgynous. But those equestrians hadn't seen anything like it. I remember the crowning glory of Debbie's outfit that night was a pair of high-heeled fur-covered boots. After we finished our set, the equestrians asked if we'd come play this party at their town house on the Upper East Side in a couple of weeks' time. We all figured, what the hell, and agreed to come play for them. When they made the booking, they had only one proviso: "Just make sure the girl wears the same boots."

We went along to play for them a couple of weeks later. We didn't have a van, so we put all our gear in a couple of cabs. Cabs were our main form of getting around the city back then. The old Checker cabs that ran across New York used to have those jump seats in the back, so you could carry a lot of stuff. They'd bitch and complain, but cab drivers couldn't afford to be too discerning about who they picked up back then, so we arrived at a lot of shows that way. Just so long as they got the fare, the cab drivers were generally cool about having a band in the back. Once we made it uptown, we played the party and Debbie wore the boots, and it was a great night for us, hanging out with Manhattan's high-rolling equestrian community.

The punk scene still didn't have a name or much of an identity, and it had its roots in all kinds of different areas of the New York underground. In the same way London punk had its foundations in fashion, via Vivienne Westwood and Malcolm McLaren's shop on the King's Road, New York had similar ties to the arts crowd and gay culture. It was a cool, bohemian trip, and I was always thrilled we tried to do things differently. That was one of the great things about that time. You wanted to be an artist? Sure. You want to be an actor or theater director? Have at it. There was nothing going on, so you got the chance to make up your own rules as you went along. That was the mindset that led to us working on the revival of *Vain Victory*, the play by Warhol "superstar" and trans pioneer, Jackie Curtis. Debbie and Chris's upstairs neighbor when they lived on Thompson Street was this Brooklyn guy, Tony Ingrassia, a prime mover in the avant-garde theater world. More than that though, Tony was emblematic of that New York scene and its intersection among gay, theater, and music culture.

In the early 1970s, Tony directed *Andy Warhol's Pork*, which caused a real scandal in polite society. It was a notorious play, but hugely influential. When the production transferred to London in 1971, it caused a similar stir among the artistic cognoscenti over there. You don't need a history lesson, I'm sure, but the show was seen by Bowie, and that set off a chain of events that shook the world over the next couple of years. Probably I'm oversimplifying, but Bowie connected with Tony and Leee Black Childers and all those New York art scene people and facilitated the birth of glam rock in England.

Tony had an alliance with Bowie thereafter, and they worked together on David's *Diamond Dogs* project. Clearly, Tony loved working with artistic musicians, and he saw something in Debbie that set her apart from the crowd.

Consequently, he was always looking for ways he could help us get along. When the script for *Vain Victory* fell into his lap, he could see how music was going to be a key element, so he invited Blondie to work on the project. It being New York in the 1970s, there were a lot of guys called Tony on the scene, and the production of *Vain Victory* was overseen by Tony Defries and Tony Zanetta (or Tony Z) from Bowie's Main Man production company. Naturally, we were thrilled to be connected to our idol, even in a very tangential fashion. The play was so far off Broadway, we performed in someone's loft, with folding chairs set out for the audience.

Jackie Curtis was flamboyant and very cool to be around. At the time, he'd passed through his drag phase and had adopted his James Dean persona, but we were all completely starstruck to be in the company of one of Warhol's superstars. If you were hip to the Velvet Underground, as we were, Warhol cast a long shadow over New York at the time, and we embraced the association. Since I was in high school, I'd been a big fan of those Warhol movies—particularly, *Trash* and *Heat*. In the US, Andy Warhol is synonymous with Pop Art, and I think Blondie is in that same tradition. Even today, if you were to ask me if Blondie is pop or rock or whatever, I'd probably tell you we're neither. I think we're a Pop Art band. For me, there was always a through-line between the everyday and the glamorous in everything we did. And, obviously, we wanted to be famous for fifteen minutes. Although we did a little better, as things transpired.

Over time, we got to be quite friendly with Andy, so I think about that "famous for fifteen minutes" comment a lot. It's so profound, so prophetic. Everybody is famous for fifteen minutes today, thanks to the internet and reality TV, but in the 1970s, we were still a long way from the World Wide Web and *Jersey Shore*. As for *Vain Victory*, Debbie had a small role, and the rest of us "acted" as the band and we soundtracked the action on stage. I remember our performance generated one of Blondie's first positive press reviews. The writer Danny Fields, who had a regular column in *SoHo Weekly News*, gave us a great write-up. Danny, who worked for Elektra when they signed Iggy Pop and the MC5—and, famously, went on to manage the Ramones—was a real NYC tastemaker, so his word carried some weight. It was only a weekend run, but I got such a kick out of the play and the rehearsals; it felt like a great way to cap off the year. We were doing things our way, and people were starting to pay attention.

Chapter 8

CBGB

At the time of writing, it's the fiftieth anniversary of CBGB. One thing that strikes me is there's a strange cultural hindsight when people talk about that moment in time. Everyone speaks about it as a very glamorous place, but in truth, it wasn't. In a lot of respects, CBGB was a dump, but it transcended that. It was our little secret, and the coolest place to workshop all these great songs we were coming up with. You were free to make mistakes in public, with no consequences. At the time, the US was in its worst recession since the Wall Street crash of 1929 and New York was so debt-ridden, it was defaulting on its payments. Outside the rarefied air of Upper East Side Manhattan, New York was being slowly driven into the ground. Every week, some public sector workers went on strike for better pay or conditions, so even when things were working, nothing really worked right. On the Bowery, it was even worse—skid row essentially.

CBGB, even as the scene blew up, was never particularly violent, but the streets were another matter altogether. Usually, I was with a crowd of friends, so I felt safe, but you had to get in the habit of looking over your shoulder. Probably a good idea, because crime was everywhere. Across the city, David Berkowitz, aka the Son of Sam, was about to start up his rampage. Getting mugged was an occupational hazard if you wanted to carve out your own little niche in Lower Manhattan. Even so, the sociopolitical backdrop to what was happening in New York and the wider world was just subtext to our lives. Politics wasn't really in my orbit. In my senior year of high school, I campaigned for George McGovern against Richard Nixon. Vietnam was always on the nightly news, so it was definitely in the background of my thinking. McGovern was seen as the liberal, antiwar candidate, but the nation lurched to the right, and he was wiped out. When Watergate was exposed, for me and for a lot of people I knew, it just confirmed our suspicion that politicians weren't trustworthy. The draft ended the year I'd have been eligible, but by then I felt completely alienated from politics. It's like that line in the Patti Smith song "Rock N Roll N****r": "Outside of society is where I wanna be." That's where I felt I was.

In our little circle, I think we felt more of a kinship with the drug addicts, the gay crowd, and the so-called Bowery bums. We were underground, not plugged into what was happening in the straight world. Poverty wasn't an issue because we weren't concerned with money. We didn't need money to do what we were doing. If we got hungry, we'd pick up a bodega cheese sandwich for maybe twenty-five cents, and that would sustain us until our next adventure. In a perverse way, the city being at such a low point was a good thing. The fact that New York was seen as this rotten apple of day-to-day disrepair and misery acted as a catalyst and helped to lift us up. If anything, we thrived in that environment.

Like the rest of the area, CBGB was grubby and neglected. An unassuming place to start a revolution when you stop and think about it. You'd never have guessed by looking at the place that it would become such a phenomenon. Still, for us and the other bands in the city, there was nothing else going on, so we congregated there out of necessity. The club was at the east end of Bleecker Street on the Bowery, amid soup kitchens and broken-down walk-up apartments. Everywhere you walked, alcoholics and derelicts were staggering around or huddled in doorways, living rough on the streets, drinking whatever they could lay their hands on. Just a bunch of lost, tortured people with no place else to go. Right above CBGB was the Palace Hotel, an old flophouse where you could share a bed with a cockroach or two for as little as $2.85 per night. Broken men, home from the war and entirely discarded by society, were scattered around the streets and back alleys, a step away from sex-workers and hustlers. Sometimes, these locals seemed confused to find us in their neighborhood, but I think they got used to us hanging around, spilling out from CBGB and drinking beer on the sidewalk. Not all of them, of course. You had to watch out for disgruntled drunks dropping empty liquor bottles out of the Palace Hotel windows onto the curb below whenever we got too rowdy outside.

Inside the venue, the CBGB amenities were, at best, basic. Insofar as the underground scene at CBGB goes, there wasn't much of one in the spring of 1975. There was no mass hysteria, no CBGB T-shirts, and no one was calling themselves punks. We were months away from the press picking up on what was happening. The place was set up like a folk club or cabaret, with candles flickering on little round tables and waitress service. The audience was mostly made up of people from other bands, mostly rock and roll guys and very few women in attendance. Certainly, there was no mania—it was all very laid back and cozy.

CBGB's owner Hilly Kristal had some history booking cabaret acts, and his vision for CBGB was as an Americana venue—the initials CBGB stood for Country, Bluegrass, and Blues—so right from the start, Hilly was catering for a broad spectrum of music fans. I think that's why he opened his doors to people like us. So long as you weren't playing covers, he didn't care what you played. It was more a beatnik crowd, with everyone in sunglasses and leather jackets, standing or sitting around and nodding their heads in appreciation. The dressing rooms were nonexistent, and in the days before I moved into the city, if we weren't inside watching our friends play, the whole band used to just congregate in my dad's car and hang out until showtime. It became an adjunct dressing room for us. I have a lot of great memories of sitting in the car, laughing and watching the ongoing street theater. Usually, Johnny Ramone would be out sulking on the pavement, coming up to the car window and giving us a hard time for smoking weed. Johnny had been a staunch, pro-Nixon Republican since he was a teenager, and he always made it clear he disapproved of our pot-smoking ways. Obviously, Johnny's irritation just made it funnier for the rest of us.

The bar didn't have an ice machine, so at regular intervals they'd send somebody out back to fetch more ice to stop the beer from getting warm. As business and attendance picked up, Merv Ferguson, CBGB's longhair bartender and some-time bouncer, would be forced to navigate the crowd, dressed in a yellow hard hat, so he could be seen carrying the buckets of ice on his shoulder. As for the sound quality, well, that wasn't great, but then, the place had been set up with more acoustic music in mind. The sound system they initially had in place wasn't suited to a band like the Ramones.

A few months down the line the place became ground zero for the Ramones, Television, Blondie, Patti Smith, and Talking Heads. Hilly conceded to the growing presence of a real scene by building a bigger stage and putting in a new sound system, with the help of Brian Eno.

In contrast to what happened with the British punk movement, where the Sex Pistols were catapulted to fame, and then overnight, a hundred copycat bands followed in their wake, none of the core NYC bands had much in common musically. It was more like a shared sensibility. We were drawing from a diverse range of influences, trying to figure out what kind of bands we were going to become. CBGB was like a band workshop. Everyone playing a couple of nights, or a few nights straight, gradually honing their craft, while the world outside the Bowery went about its business.

Working the door was a photographer friend of ours, Roberta Bayley. Roberta was ever-present. As well as taking that iconic cover shot for the first Ramones record, she became one of the key chroniclers of the New York punk scene. As Blondie's star rose, Roberta was there with us, working for our manager and running our fan club. Her book *Blondie: Unseen 1976–1980* includes a shot of me that is one of my all-time favorite photographs, taken at the Philadelphia Spectrum in 1978.

I don't remember ever getting paid for those early shows. I think whatever money we made just went into the collective pot, paying our dues for the rehearsal space and funding Blondie's next move. Today, you can't get by a single day without money, but at the time, living in New York was very inexpensive. Unless you were a major junkie, you didn't need real money. Everyone else in regular society was focused on surviving from day to day, from paycheck to paycheck. If I ever did have any walking-around money, it must have been the last remnants of my college grant—basically a small stipend for materials and lodgings. But then, it wasn't money that got me out of bed every day. What was driving me was the energy of the city. Being on the scene and being around those bands. It was about the music.

The Ramones and Television were the ones everyone had their eye on, of course, but we were in the trenches at their sides. By the end of 1975, we were all propping one another up in a lot of ways. If not for those other bands, it's difficult to imagine we'd have had our success. By the same token, there were people who probably underestimated us. In the eyes of many observers, we were the least likely band to succeed, because our act wasn't fully together. It's not a stretch to say that my work ethic changed things for the better. We may have played our first show in April, but by August, the momentum was building despite us not being the critic's darlings. We became unstoppable. Our success went hand in hand with that of CBGB's. In the end, we were just as synonymous with CBGB as the Ramones, Television, Talking Heads, and Patti Smith.

Chapter 9

X OFFENDER

I'm often asked about my memories of hearing Blondie on the radio the first time and how it made me feel, but I always draw a blank. Possibly that's because it was a while before I heard one of our songs coming over the airwaves. The New York radio stations were still hesitant to play anything punk, so I'd have to bide my time on that front. What I do remember is hearing "X Offender" being played loud and clear on the jukebox at CBGB and feeling elated that someone had put their dime in the machine and chosen our song. It was a rare distinction to be included on the CBGB jukebox. The choice of local bands' 45s was limited to only a few: Patti Smith's "Piss Factory," Television's "Little Johnny Jewel," the Ramones' "Blitzkrieg Bop," along with such garage rock classics as "Psychotic Reaction" by Count Five and the Seeds' "Pushin' Too Hard." Initially, the recording of "X Offender" came about because Marty Thau saw us at CBGB.

Marty was the original manager of the New York Dolls, and he played a big role in Blondie's early career and setting us on a path to becoming recording artists. The story goes like this: I bumped into the Dolls' Jerry Nolan one night at Nathan's, and he told me Marty was working as a talent scout and might be a help to us. We persuaded Marty to come down to CBGB one night, and he immediately realized there was something brewing in the Bowery. In terms of our appearance, at the start of 1976, we'd started to distance ourselves from the glam rock aesthetic. It was a group thing. I was turned on by the British R & B group Dr. Feelgood. They were a great band, and they had a different look. Sharp suits, cropped hair, back to basics. Their album *Malpractice* was a signpost for us that the look of rock and roll was evolving. Gary took the leap first, then me, then Chris. Jimmy had a straight job working at a hospital, so he never had the glam shag cut. Not long after, I went to a friend's clothing store, and they were selling a "new old" stock of those 1960s-cut suits and clothes by the pound. I filled a couple of bags and went back to the rehearsal studio. I was just tossing suits, Sta-Prest jeans, and polka dot shirts to everyone. By the spring of 1976, we were locked in to the new CBGB style.

After Marty saw this new-look Blondie, he placed himself firmly in our corner. He had a long history as a record man at Cameo-Parkway and Buddah Records. He was a little older, in his thirties maybe, but he wasn't one of those record company cliché characters, stuck behind a desk and shouting orders. Well, he was a little, but he was also someone who had his ear to the ground. Marty was interested in music and sensed the way the tide was turning. He had all that record company history, but the real reason we looked up to him was because of his association with the Dolls and his track record working with bubblegum groups like the Lemon Pipers, who had a big hit with the song "Green Tambourine" in the 1960s. Everyone in Blondie was a fan of so-called bubblegum music. On our first album you can hear that influence right alongside our more garage roots on a song like "Little Girl Lies." No one talks much about the convergence of these musical styles, but it was a thing. We weren't the only ones who paid tribute to the bubblegum shrine; Talking Heads covered "1, 2, 3, Red Light" and the Ramones covered "Indian Giver," hits by the 1910 Fruitgum Company.

Marty understood we had some commercial potential that no one else saw at the time. Once he came into our orbit, he began informally acting as our manager. It was never made official, no deals were signed, but he started working as the band's fixer for a while there, and things started to move a lot faster. He introduced us to the producers Craig Leon and Richard Gottehrer. Richard had a long and fascinating career with the McCoys, the Strangeloves, and other 1960s bands. He'd also cofounded Sire Records with Seymour Stein, who'd recently signed the Ramones. Initially, Richard and Craig had been plotting a "Live at CBGB" album, with the Ramones, Television, Talking Heads, and us, but there was no interest from any of those other groups. Once the live LP fell through, Richard switched his focus to Blondie. He came to our rehearsal space on the Bowery, and we ran through a few numbers for him, with a view to maybe selecting a single and a B-side. He chipped in with a couple of thoughts, and at the end of the session, I think he had an idea of what he wanted to do next. Shortly after, we signed a production deal with his company, Instant Records.

The deal was for a single, with an option for an album. Now, a production deal is not a record contract; the production company still needs to persuade a label to release the tracks it owns. But it's a start. Instant was essentially a middleman, with all accounting and royalties passed from the label through the production company to the artist. It's not the most equitable of arrangements, but it's a foot in the door. Eventually, after a little shopping around, the single was licensed through Private Stock, an independent—mostly pop—label run by Larry Uttal. Larry ran with the Brill Building crowd and was formerly president of Bell Records, where he had a lot of success. If the single did okay, Larry said, there was a chance of an album. Private Stock wasn't the biggest concern, but they had a little kudos, with me at least, because they had Frankie Valli and the Four Seasons as a partner in the company.

For a band who'd only been heard live in places like CBGB, we set about showing what we were capable of in the studio. The result was "X Offender," released on June 17, 1976. It was Richard's idea to add the spoken word intro, a nod to his hit song, "My Boyfriend's Back" by the Angels. The B-side, "In the Sun," was a tribute to the California surf sound of the Ventures, with my signature two-bar drum roll serving as an introduction. Whenever appropriate, those drum intros were something I always tried to incorporate into our songs.

With the single in the can, we headed out of New York for the first time and played two shows at the Rathskeller (aka the Rat), a club on Kenmore Square that was like the CBGB of Boston. With the support of WBCN, the city's top rock station, the shows sold out and probably we could've played another week without seeing a drop in excitement or attendance.

Buzzing with post-show adrenaline, we loaded our gear and made our way back to New York via Interstate 95, arriving home in the early hours of July 4, 1976. We told ourselves we wanted to catch the fireworks and regatta in New York harbor, but probably we wanted to avoid paying for another night in a hotel. Money was still that tight. After sleeping for a few hours, I spent the afternoon on a friend's rooftop overlooking the harbor, with a perfect view of the Bicentennial celebration. As spectacular as the show was, I couldn't stop thinking about our first show away from our home turf, pondering what that success meant for the future. Also, I had a decision to make—I'd been rehearsing on the sly with the New York band the Mumps.

While things seemed to be moving along with the band, I'd been hedging my bets on Blondie's future. This wasn't the first time I'd looked at my other options. I tried out for the Patti Smith Group, who were a far bigger deal than Blondie at the time. I auditioned in our rehearsal space, me, Patti, and Lenny Kaye. Gary Valentine was there, wearing sunglasses, and when Patti saw him, she said, "Is that what you play? Sunglasses?" in that cool, disinterested way she has. While I was playing, Chris and Debbie arrived unexpectedly, scanned the room, and probably thought, shit, here we go again. Another New York band trying to steal away one of our members. Anyway, after I got busted by Debbie and Chris, Patti hired the Mumps drummer, Jay Dee Daugherty, and I was asked to join the Mumps.

Lance Loud, the Mumps' singer, was a household name, via his appearance on TV's first reality show, *An American Family*. He was the first genuine media star I ever met and close friends with Warhol and the whole Factory crowd, and I was fascinated. The band had some good tunes and a real manager: John Hewlett, an Englishman who managed Sparks and had a past life as a member of John's Children with a pre–T. Rex Marc Bolan. The gig with the Mumps was mine if I wanted it, but I left them hanging while I figured out what I was going to do. Would I leave Blondie and become a full-time Mump? For me, the decision rested on whether we'd get the go-ahead to make an album for Private Stock. Soon after the Boston shows, we got the green light. Once the album deal came into view, I had a couple of calls to make. First off, I quit college, and second, I called the Mumps and declined their offer to join. I had an LP to record.

Chapter 10

BLONDIE

We recorded our first album, appropriately titled *Blondie*, at the iconic Plaza Sound Studios, in the upper reaches of Radio City Music Hall in Midtown Manhattan. Radio City is obviously a celebrated venue with a long, storied past, so there was a real sense we'd traveled a long way from our Bowery roots. I'd seen Bowie at Radio City a couple of times, so for me, it felt like we were walking on hallowed ground. This was no Lower East Side studio, with everyone crammed into one tiny room, or someone's garage. The studio was a beautiful space with the best ambient sound I'd ever experienced. The studio floor was large enough to accommodate a symphony orchestra and had been used by the classical conductor Arturo Toscanini. Despite its legacy, Plaza Sound didn't get a lot of artists using it, and that was fine by us. It meant Richard got a great deal for us. And because New York wasn't so neurotic about security back then, we had the run of the whole building. We ate a lot of pizza and had the opportunity to experiment. There were all kinds of instruments lying around from the orchestra: timpani drums, tubular bells, glockenspiels, different kinds of keyboards. We'd spent the past year living in reduced circumstances, so it really felt like a new world was opening for us. The vibe was so relaxed, I always enjoyed working there. I'd turn up around noon for the day's session, walk in through a side door on Fifty-Second Street, and call an elevator. Usually, I'd travel up with half a dozen Rockettes, caught up in a cloud of their perfume and their Queens and Brooklyn chatter.

Recorded over the course of August and September 1976 with Richard Gottehrer at the helm, our first album reflects our live set, plus a couple of newer songs Jimmy brought to the party: "A Shark in Jets Clothing" and "Look Good in Blue." Another new addition was "Rifle Range," which came together closer to recording the album, with lyrics by my friend Ronnie Toast. Ronnie was a brilliant lyricist. He had an eccentric take on the world and was such a character. I think if he'd stayed the course, he would've been destined for greatness. When I first met up with Chris and Debbie, my little gang followed suit and would hang out with us on the Bowery, so Ronnie was with us from the get-go. Because he was around all the time, and we all liked him, we were always trying to champion him, so we had him write the liner notes for the record. He had so many brilliant ideas, and his lyrics were wonderful. If Ronnie hadn't been so super-dysfunctional, he could have been another Joey Ramone. A couple of years later, as Blondie was going from strength to strength, Ronnie was still living this chaotic lifestyle. He had no fixed address, and I tracked him down because I had a royalty cheque in his name for $25,000. I didn't realize at the time, but tragically, that money proved to be his undoing. He went on a crazy drug and alcohol binge until the money ran out. I tried to warn him and tell him it was "fuck you" money to be saved for a rainy day, but he didn't listen. Having that much cash on hand was the ruin of him.

Most of the songs on the first album had been aired at CBGB and around the city. "Love at the Pier," which was part of our set at the time, with a cool Debbie lyric about the West Village gay scene, was passed over, although it would eventually find a home on our second record. On stage, we used to fool around with "Man Overboard" and "The Attack of the Giant Ants." I don't know if we ever planned to record them, but Richard had a different perspective. Maybe the heavy drum thing on "The Attack of the Giant Ants" reminded him of his work with the Strangeloves. That neat cocktail piano outro is played by Marty Thau, incidentally. Listening back today, because we weren't overthinking anything, the album has a real innocent quality. The rich studio ambience yielded a great drum sound and allowed us to create an homage to the great Phil Spector Wall of Sound. We never tried that approach again, but the naivety contributed to its longevity. Additionally, having four songwriters pitch in material made for a unique sound and worldview. Save for "In the Flesh," they're not your average boy-meets-girl songs. "X Offender" is about a prostitute getting busted and falling in love with the arresting officer.

The recordings with Richard ran smoothly, I think because we didn't have particularly high expectations. Just being allowed to record an album was fulfilling. We were just happy to be making the record and to be in the studio. Richard didn't dwell on our shortcomings, instead offering a lot of guidance with song structure, arrangements, and production ideas. Richard's process was straight out of the

1960s tradition. He had a "hit factory" mentality. He listened intently to your repertoire and selected the best tracks, essentially the numbers he thought would sound good on the radio, and he'd focus most of his attention building those recordings. For the rest of the songs, well, if they were good enough, maybe you'd catch lightning in a bottle with a hot live take. The real focus, though, was on the key songs. That's the way the music business used to work. Everything was geared toward having a hit 45. Everyone at the time was fixated on being like Tom Verlaine or Patti Smith, but Richard understood popular music and the Brill Building element of our sound.

Rock critics loved the edgier side of Blondie, but there was another side to us, the commercial aspect of the band, that people like Richard just got. There was always that dichotomy with the pop thing. Like with Warhol, being a serious artist but achieving so much popular acclaim—that was a tightrope we wanted to walk: to have commercial success but also the credibility factor. In the end, the critics loved us regardless, but at the time it wasn't like that. We were uncool. I think maybe that displeased Debbie, but the way I see it, Lou Reed wrote a lot of pop songs. He just took them to a darker place. People always fixate on songs like "Heroin" and "The Black Angel's Death Song," but that first Velvets album has a lot of pretty music on it.

Prior to Blondie, Richard wasn't known as an album producer, but his approach was effective. He had it all in his producer's bag of tricks. There are some fine moments on the *Blondie* LP, and he'd repeat the trick with our second album. A few years later, when Richard produced the first Go-Go's record, he'd refined his style further and showed he had the ability to make an album where every number sounded like a hit. Richard doesn't get enough credit for what he did for us. He truly believed in the band and completely understood the assignment, always chipping in with ideas to reinforce our sound. He also did a lot of work on "In the Flesh," suggesting the tubular bells that Jimmy plays, and bringing in Brill Building songwriter Ellie Greenwich, Micki Harris of the Shirelles, and opera star Hilda Harris to add backing vocals. Richard coached Debbie on some of her vocals, but songs like "In the Flesh" had been around a long time, so she nailed those right from the get-go. It's a fantastic song, with brilliant production. It's in 6/8 time and reminiscent of a 1950s doo-wop number, simple but very poignant.

To this day, "X Offender" is one of my favorite Blondie songs. I love my drumming on it, kind of an homage to Hal Blaine and the Wrecking Crew. It's an atypical song. Gary, who wrote the music, plays guitar, so it has a different energy, with his aggressive guitar licks rounding out the sound. Gary's riff is reminiscent of "Born to Run," and I always felt, despite our musical differences, we were on the same path as Bruce Springsteen in some ways. Springsteen's music was more orchestrated and professional, but it was coming from the same place and had a lot of the same references: Phil Spector, Roy Orbison, the music from our childhoods. "Rip Her to Shreds," one of our earliest tunes, is one of our punkiest songs. Some of the lyrics are dated, but the song reminds me of the Velvets and the Modern Lovers, with that Farfisa organ sound. I always looked at Blondie in the same light as the Modern Lovers, David Bowie, even Sparks and Roxy Music, because of all the influences that are not necessarily punk, but also nowhere near the mainstream.

Sometimes, a band goes into the studio and the job is to simply capture the live sound, but that first record wasn't the sound of Blondie live, it was something new entirely. It's the sound of us using the studio as a tool to create something unique. As a musician, you're never completely satisfied with what you've done. Because of your muse or whatever, you're always sensitive to imperfection, so you're constantly striving for better and better results. For me, the first Blondie album has some imperfections, but it's still a great record. If I'm going to be self-critical, we weren't quite at the point where we could articulate our vision, so some of the ideas weren't fully formed. In terms of ideas and songs, we'd go on to do a better job on our later recordings, but it gets a lot of accolades now in retrospect, and that's pleasing to me.

Chapter II

NEW YORK, 1976

At the tail end of the year, I took a temp job as a mail handler at the New York Bulk and Foreign Mail Center in New Jersey. My student grant had run out, and I needed funds to support my nocturnal existence. It was the time of Patty Hearst and the Symbionese Liberation Army and the movie *Taxi Driver*. I was infatuated with that movie. So much so, I had Travis Bickle's name written on the inseam of my work gloves, rather than my own name. In the run-up to Christmas, I remember there was an announcement that came over the mail center PA telling all workers there was to be no leave granted for temporary employees. No exceptions. I had to plead with my supervisor to give me a pass because the next day we were shooting the photograph for the *Blondie* album cover. I guess my foreman must have had a good heart because he let me take the day off for the session.

Jody Uttal, whose father, Larry, ran Private Stock, was our promotion point person and was very hands on about it. We had a lunch meeting with her at a swanky Greenwich Village restaurant, One Fifth, to discuss the cover photo, to be shot by Shig Ikeda. In some ways, we were more nervous about the photo session than recording the album. The cover reminds me of a 1960s Rolling Stones LP: the minimal color, the arrangement of the figures, and the lighting. We all wore our own thrift shop clothes—mostly from an Army Navy store a friend of mine had in Jersey City. I brought stuff in for the band, but I don't know where Chris got the Rhythm Kings satin baseball jacket he's wearing on the back cover. I still have those red corduroy trousers and could probably squeeze into them if I had a gun to my head.

Because I was splitting my time between the band and work, I started staying at a friend's apartment in Jersey City. I was getting by on no sleep and barely any food, sustaining myself with this little bag of blue amphetamine pills. I'd crawl back from CBGB at dawn, take a pill, sleep for an hour and then the speed would hit my bloodstream and wake me up in time to go to work. As we approached the end of 1976, I realized I was going to need another bag of those blue pills.

Blondie were booked to play shows around New York right through the month of December and into January of 1977. Private Stock, our record label, had scheduled the record for release for the last week of December. It seemed a curious time to put out a record, but for whatever reason, I guess the executives at the record company felt there was some advantage to be gained from releasing the album in the wake of Christmas. Then there was the small matter of us getting away from the cold of NYC and taking the Blondie bandwagon to the West Coast in the New Year. There was a sense of momentum, but to my mind, our being branded in some quarters as a punk band felt like it was becoming an obstacle. I appreciate there's a synergy that existed among all the bands at CBGB and being associated with that initial explosion helped propel Blondie in that first year or so, but punk hadn't broken into the mainstream. At that precise moment, it was seen as a New York and London thing and wasn't deemed commercially viable. As a result, radio stations weren't playing punk records. That meant they weren't playing any Blondie records either.

I was proud of how our album came out. I felt that it set us on the path to where we were going to be eventually, and that was an exciting feeling, but I wanted people to hear it. I had 100 percent belief in the potential of my partners, particularly their songwriting abilities, but even then, I was questioning what I was doing and where the band was going. I genuinely didn't know if Blondie was going to be my final stop, or if my time with the band was going to be a stepping stone to something else. On some level, I still had the mindset I had before Blondie. I still had my antenna up for other opportunities, constantly wondering what was next for me.

At the start of December, we played a couple of shows at 213 Park Avenue South. Today, it is a nondescript deli. There's no sign to commemorate it, but between the years 1965 and 1981, it was the site of the legendary Max's Kansas City. Alongside CBGB, Max's was the epicenter of what was happening in 1970s New York counterculture. In many respects, Max's was a more glamorous setting than CBGB, but still steeped in pop culture history. Back in the club's early 1970s heyday, when the place was owned by Mickey Ruskin, it became an infamous hangout for New York's elite artistic crowd. They served hors d'oeuvres at the bar, so essentially you could get a bite to eat for the price of a drink. The first floor, with its famous back room, was where Andy

Warhol held court during the 1970s, with Edie Sedgwick, Candy Darling, and all the famed Warhol Factory superstars as his courtiers. That's the site of David Bowie and Iggy Pop's historic first meeting of minds. In the early 1970s, the place became a hip, glam mecca. Alice Cooper, Marc Bolan, the New York Dolls would all find a home there in the famous back room.

Upstairs was ticket only and exclusively given over to renowned national acts. Usually that meant artists with recording contracts. Everybody from Tim Buckley to the Velvet Underground played there regularly, and, one famous night, Bob Marley and the Wailers opened for Springsteen. Still, whoever was playing, Mickey Ruskin would command the door, and he acted as the self-appointed gatekeeper to the first floor of Max's, which was practically out of bounds for the regular Joes coming in from off the street. My friends and I could only get into Max's if we paid to see a show upstairs, but the first floor was a no-go. I remember paying to see bands I wouldn't normally have sought out. Just buying a ticket so I could enter the building and be close to all that history. It was also one of the first places I got to see the New York Dolls live.

Later, when the glam era was on its downturn, Mickey handed over the keys to new owner Tommy Dean Miller and his wife, Laura. Tommy hired Peter Crowley from Mother's as the new booker and things started to shift. Max's began promoting bands who were coming up on the New York scene. Bands like Tuff Darts, the Ramones and Blondie. By the time our turn came around, the scene had shifted entirely. The last remnants of the glam era were gone, and we brought our own crowd, with their own sensibilities. It was a cross section of underground society. Working girls, blue collar kids, gays, affluent people from Upper Manhattan, and a whole lot of starving artists. I later understood that a lot of the starving artists had a few dollars of daddy's money behind them, but we welcomed them into the fold regardless of who was funding their lifestyle.

It was the same faces as the CBGB's audience most nights because the nights would spill over into each other. It was easy walking distance or a very brief cab ride between the two venues, and because every band played two sets a night and we knew all the other bands, we'd often watch someone's first set at one place, then migrate to the other to catch another friend's second set. Television might have a show at CBGB, and the Heartbreakers would be playing at Max's, so we'd catch Television's set at 10 p.m., pick up a bodega tallboy to drink on the way, walk up toward Park Avenue South, and cross over to Union Square to see the Heartbreakers play their midnight set at Max's. You just had to avoid the park, which was a different animal after dark. A complete no-man's-land. Drug gangs and muggers had the run of the place, so we stuck to the familiar streets.

Even if we were playing, we'd still see that migration between venues. People arriving halfway through the night, and another crowd heading off in the other direction to catch the other band downtown. The dressing rooms at Max's were located on the top floor, and it was always quite the gathering place. By hook or by crook, our friends and hangers-on would always find a way up. The two-shows-per-night dynamic led to a lot of interesting goings on between sets. Particularly for me as the drummer, I'd be warmed up from the first show and hanging out in the dressing room, having drinks, meeting people, and preparing for the second set, before walking out on stage and doing it all over again. Then I'd head backstage to meet another group of friends who'd been at CBGB earlier in the night.

Those early December shows with Tuff Darts were completely packed out. Tuff Darts had been discovered by our producer, Richard Gottehrer, and were our label mates at Private Stock. Tuff Darts were more of a traditional 1970s rock and roll outfit. Probably, they'd have been forgotten by history, except they were fronted by this amazing-looking, super-charismatic vocalist, Robert Gordon. Robert was this incredible New York rockabilly tough guy. He had the 1950s stylings down to a T: DA haircut and black "wife beater" vest shirt and an onstage persona to match. The juxtaposition of Robert looking like a stone-cold rock and roll rebel thug fronting this shaggy-haired, straight-down-the-line rock and roll—almost glam rock band—was a striking visual dynamic. They seemed to all of us as if they were going to step effortlessly into the big leagues, but ultimately Robert decided to change direction and left the band to go his own way.

As we approached New Year's, Blondie had two nights lined up with the Dolls. Not the New York Dolls, you understand, but almost. The Dolls, as they were briefly known, was the band formed in the wake of the New York Dolls, by David Johansen and Sylvain Sylvain. This new incarnation rose from the ashes of the New York Dolls, following the departure of Johnny Thunders and Jerry Nolan, and featured New York Dolls former tour manager Tony Machine on drums. We all knew Tony Machine from when he was the doorman at the Gramercy Park Hotel. Completing the Dolls lineup was Peter Jordan on bass. Peter was drafted in to play bass after Connie Gripp, Arthur "Killer" Kane's girlfriend at the time, badly slashed Arthur's thumb and left him unable to play. It could've been worse. Originally, Connie planned to cut his thumb off so he couldn't play bass anymore.

Connie became one of the prototype rock and roll women who hung out around CBGB and later became Dee Dee Ramone's girl. She and Dee Dee had a similarly tumultuous relationship to the one she'd had with Arthur. To those of us who regularly attended CBGB, seeing Connie and Dee Dee fighting and breaking bottles in the street outside CBGB became a familiar sight. These weren't your garden variety lovers' spats; they were real toe-to-toe brawls. CBGB was a real grungy place and something of a boys' club, so she always stood out in my memory as one of the female pioneers, along with Joey's girlfriend, Linda Ramone, and Johnny Thunders's former girl, Janis Cafasso. They had a unique style. Linda was quite diminutive, and Janis was tall, but they both dressed in the same Raggedy Ann style, with bright red hair and a lot of rouge. Like the rest of us, they were huge Dolls fans. In fact, Janis was the original inspiration for the New York Dolls song "Chatterbox." At turns, they were wild, funny, and interesting people, and they all got caught up in CBGB's folklore in some way or another. Whatever was going on, those women managed to hold their own at the heart of a tough, macho New York scene.

One time, following a wild late night at Max's, on a whim, a group of us decided we wanted to go to the Staten Island Zoo. We were hanging out with Janis and Linda and some good friends of ours from the Fast. It was around 6 a.m., and we were either wired, still drunk, hungover, or maybe a combination of the three, but it seemed like a cool thing to do. We caught the earliest ferry across the bay to Staten Island, and I suppose we all staggered off in different directions to see the monkey house or whatever. Janis and I just lay around in the grass and made out to the sound of zoo animals waking up around us.

The Blondie shows with the Dolls took place on December 29 and 30, 1976, at Max's Kansas City, right at the height of New York's festive season. Like in any major city, be it London or Paris, the run-up to New Year's is an exciting time, but I was a little apprehensive about the shows. The original line-up of the New York Dolls was so revered, I think we were all a little dismayed they were trying to carry on without three of the band's mainstays. But the shows were a complete sell-out, and the New York crowds were in a mood to have a good time. They were very late nights. There was a lot of hanging out and a lot of fun.

I was spending 90 percent of my time in Manhattan, but life was moving at such a pace, I still hadn't moved out and found an apartment. Following the show on the thirtieth, I somehow made it home to my dad's house in Jersey because I distinctly remember waking up in Bayonne and trudging through the snow in the early evening of New Year's Eve to make it back to the city for our final show of 1976. Once I made it to the station at Journal Square I met up with Frank Infante, a Jersey friend of mine. He was generally known as the best guitarist in town, and via our friendship, he'd become close to the band. Probably, he was the only one of my Jersey friends who was interested in the CBGB thing as it started to take flight. For my part, I was always trying to encourage people in our circle to come along and check out the scene, but most were reluctant. Either they didn't want to go to the Bowery, or they didn't want to be walking the streets at four in the morning or whatever.

Frank had a bit more of an adventurous spirit than most, and once he clocked what was happening in the city, he became a regular on the scene. He and his girlfriend offered me a ride, so we headed into Manhattan together through the heavy snow and drove up to Central Park, where Blondie had a show booked at the band shell. Infamously, New York was practically broke, but I've since read that the city still owes us $500 for our performance. We weren't doing the show for the money, of course. If anything, as naive as it might sound, at that stage in your career, you're doing it for the notoriety, for the fame. You're doing it because you want to become a rock and roll star. Traditionally, the fame always came a long time before you saw any money, and that was the case with Blondie, for sure.

In contrast to the heat of those two prior nights at Max's, we saw in the New Year with an outdoor show in Central Park under a blanket of snow. They'd set heaters up to blow warm air onto the stage, but it being December in New York, it was still cold enough that you could see your breath in front of your face. We played at the stroke of midnight. I don't remember any of the CBGB crowd making it. It was hard to imagine the cool people we usually hung around with braving the freezing cold when they could be elsewhere in the city at one of the usual clubs. In any case, unless you lived nearby, Central Park wasn't exactly a New Year's destination. If someone wanted to see in the New Year, they'd congregate in Times Square. Still, we played the show and stayed for a few drinks. I jumped back into the car with

Frank, and we headed back through the snow to New Jersey in the dead of night.

The following night was memorable for different reasons. We got to play a show with John Cale at My Father's Place in Roslyn, Long Island. Like the other venues who sensed the changing tide, My Father's Place took to promoting shows from upcoming CBGB bands quite early on. The Central Park show was just another gig, so to play the next night opening for John Cale was a real badge of honor. Coming from New Jersey, most of my friends were Grateful Dead fans, but when I first met Debbie and Chris, the Velvet Underground had been one of our shared touchstones. At the time, it felt like only a select group of people appreciated their brilliance. We went on to play with John on a few occasions, and it was always thrilling. He was, and still is, such a great musician. It felt very significant. At the time, people still characterized us as a novelty because we were pigeonholed as this band with the beautiful girl singer. When we started to land these choice gigs with people like John and the Dolls, it felt like acknowledgement of our legitimacy as a band. The next big question was, how was the rest of America going to take to us?

Chapter 12

LIVE ON THE SUNSET STRIP

Before we flew out to Los Angeles at the start of February 1977, we had some loose ends to tie up on the East Coast. There were a couple of packed nights at Max's with the Cramps as our opening act. That was a great bill to find ourselves on. It was the Cramps' legendary original line-up with Lux Interior, Poison Ivy, Brian Gregory, and Miriam Linna on drums— Miriam was also president of the Flamin' Groovies fan club.

The Cramps created their own world around them, which is why they were so wild and so much fun. Link Wray meets Boris Karloff is how I think of them. It was a unique style, totally out of step with what else was going on at the time. Even in the context of our CBGB scene, they stood out as complete outsiders. Naturally, we took to them immediately. Both backstage and onstage, they were incredible. The shows, like all our New York shows by this point, were a complete sellout, but those nights really stand out. It was in the back of our minds that in just a few short days, we'd be taking the Blondie bandwagon out to California, so we really let off some steam.

The flight to LA was only my second or third time traveling anywhere by plane. I was met at LAX by our publicist, Toby Mamis, this cherubic, bespectacled, red-haired guy and just an excellent human being who doesn't get enough credit for his part in the Blondie story. In a past life, Toby had been one of the Students for a Democratic Society, the political group that blew up big on college campuses during the civil rights and antiwar movements in the 1960s. We strolled through the terminal, flagged down a cab and drove into the sun and low-lying smog. Toby ran through the itinerary: we had a day or two of West Coast press and rehearsals lined up before the shows at the Whisky a Go Go.

Toby was cool, unflappable. He was called "Famous Toby Mamis" because his list of clients read like a roll call of twentieth-century pop culture legends: John and Yoko, Alice Cooper, the Hollies, the Dolls, Lynyrd Skynyrd, and practically anyone else you care to name. Toby entered the picture in 1976. He was one of the first people in the business with a little bit of vision, and had the idea we could break out of the new wave CBGB scene and into the mainstream. Whatever was going on, whatever we were trying to achieve, Toby was always there in the background working his ass off. He became our gatekeeper. He didn't mind stepping on anyone's toes when it came to his clients. If anyone can claim credit for the successful promotion of Blondie, it's Toby.

We were booked to stay at the Bel-Air Sands Hotel, a relic from a bygone era, several miles from all the action on the Strip. The Sands was one of those 1960s motor hotels on the outskirts of Brentwood, at the intersection of Sunset Boulevard and the 405 freeway. It was an alien environment for me. I'd never been to Los Angeles; compared to New York, with its defined neighborhoods, LA felt like a set of random, sprawling suburbs without a defined city center. The key difference between NYC and LA is that LA is a city you get around in by car, so we never had the chance to find our bearings on that first trip. We were either in our hotel room, performing our shows at the Whisky a Go Go, or driving in a station wagon back and forth between the hotel and the shows or whatever happened afterward.

In addition to the Whisky shows, the main reason for us being in Los Angeles was to play a promotional concert on a boat for KROQ radio, hosted by DJ Rodney Bingenheimer. An arrangement was made with KROQ: They'd cover our hotel expenses while we were on the West Coast in return for us playing the boat concert. Ultimately, the boat show didn't happen. Nobody seems to know why, but we got a couple of weeks' free bed and board out of the deal.

After checking into our hotel, Toby took me and the band on a guided tour of some of the places we'd be haunting over the next couple of weeks. First up was the Rainbow Bar and Grill on Sunset, adjacent to the Roxy Theatre, just a block or so from Toby's office. It was a deliberate choice of Toby's. One look inside the Rainbow Bar and you could see right away that LA was completely detached from what was happening in New York City. We really were outsiders. Everywhere you looked, the regulars were knocking back their drinks still dressed in the clothes we used to wear back in our Club 82 days. It was like an early '70s time capsule. Up and down the bar, everyone was decked out in bright-colored satin shirts, velvet flares, and Rod Stewart–style feathered hairdos. By contrast, to those Rainbow customers,

I guess we probably looked like we'd beamed in from another planet or era.

Aside from our shared love of the style of the Beatles and the British Invasion groups, Blondie was influenced by the 1950s biker aesthetic and movies. We entered the place looking like a gang, essentially. The guys in the band all had short haircuts and were dressed in black leather motorcycle jackets and wore sunglasses. Living on a budget in NYC, we'd all learned that Ray-Bans were too expensive, so we used to get old-style black-framed glasses from Cohen's Fashion Optical on the Bowery. We used to ask the clerk for discontinued stock and have them made into our own custom sunglasses. We were fascinated by all that iconography, and by the mythology surrounding James Dean in particular. The shock effect of these rough New Yorkers, clad in black, was incredible. Within a month of us and the Ramones arriving in LA—the Ramones were set to play with us during the second week of our residency—that whole satin-bellbottoms-and-feather-cut-hair scene would go the way of the dinosaur, just as it had done in New York a few years earlier.

After a minute surveying the scene, we got a table and ordered one of the famous Rainbow Bar and Grill pizzas along with drinks. Toby was bustling around, introducing us to every LA scene maker he could find. Bruce Johnston from the Beach Boys came over and asked if he could join us. He and I talked for a while, and he was engaged and interested in what we were doing musically. He was one of the old guard, the first in a long line of LA musicians we'd meet on that trip. Still, like everyone around us, he was puzzled by the CBGB image. "Why," he wondered, "are you guys all wearing sunglasses inside?"

After a couple of drinks at the Rainbow, we were whisked along Sunset Boulevard to the Whisky to check out the venue. The place was full of LA music scene faces. This was a couple of years on from the Whisky's late 1960s, early 1970s heyday, and the place seemed a little old-fashioned. The place still had table service. The wall behind the stage was decorated with strips of silver foil, like tinsel on a Christmas tree, and it shimmered in the background. The air was thick with the stink of hamburgers and French fries being served at the bar and yesterday's beer. I was caught up in the moment. I'd read so much about the place, all the iconography and history. As soon as we strolled in, I headed straight to a booth at the back of the venue. There was a photo I'd seen in a magazine about the Beatles' first trip to the US, taken in that same booth, of George Harrison with the Hollywood starlet Mamie Van Doren. Disgruntled George was hurling a drink at the photographer.

While we were taking everything in, Rodney Bingenheimer came over to our booth and introduced himself. He was dressed to the nines in the Rainbow Grill uniform of the time, with the feathered hair and bell bottom trousers. You could tell the music industry people from a mile away. They all wore satin baseball jackets with the corporate logo (Warner Brothers or Capitol, or whatever) on the back, the go-to look for the record executives of the day. Like the glam rockers at the Rainbow, Rodney was really taken by our appearance. I'd changed into a black suit and tie, and the first thing Rodney said to me was he thought I looked like Tony Hicks from the British band the Hollies. It was an obscure reference, but I got it immediately. Much as I appreciate the Hollies, I told him I was going for more of a Paul McCartney look.

The late actor, Sal Mineo, one of James Dean's *Rebel Without a Cause* costars, had christened Rodney the Mayor of the Sunset Strip. Rodney had his famous English Disco between 1972 and 1975, and was ahead of the curve when it came to championing new music. He knew all the LA producers, all the rock stars and songwriters. Anything you needed, it was in Rodney's phone book, essentially. He was the first DJ to play a Blondie record in America, on his KROQ, "Rodney on the ROQ" radio show. KROQ was one of the key California radio stations, and always supportive of us. They picked up on the NY underground groups way before anyone else.

None of us knew what to expect from Los Angeles or our shows at the Whisky, we were so out of our element. Captives of geography out in Brentwood—in a bubble of promotion and rehearsals—and then suddenly, we were on stage performing, two sets a night, at 8 and 10 p.m., much earlier than our usual midnight and 2 a.m. New York showtimes. I knew it really meant something to be appearing on that stage—all of us were aware the place was soaked in history. As a young kid, I'd read about these residencies by Trini Lopez, a hero of mine, and the American rock and roll singer Johnny Rivers, not to mention bands like the Doors and Love. Being on that stage felt like a privilege. On our opening night, after the first set, a friend and I went across the street from the Whisky to check out the front of the famed record store Licorice Pizza. The store had a huge painting of our album cover on the wall outside, to tie in with the residency. It was still a surreal experience to see our band on a painting like that. It didn't occur to me that seeing my face on posters and signs would be something I'd have to get used to.

Walking back across Sunset to play our second set, I fell afoul of LA's traffic laws. A couple of passing LAPD officers wrote me a ticket for jaywalking. Coming from New Jersey, I had no idea you could get a citation for crossing the street in the wrong place. Because I was without a fixed address, I had to give my dad's address in New Jersey, and he graciously paid the fifty-dollar fine while I was on the West Coast. Debbie made a joke about me getting a jaywalking ticket from the stage during our second set and got a big laugh from the audience.

Our opening act that first week was this gang of long-haired guys from the South, Tom Petty and the Heartbreakers. It's funny to think about it now, but the name, the Heartbreakers, was a red flag to us at first. As far as we were concerned, there was only one group called the Heartbreakers and that was Johnny Thunders's band. I don't know who came up with the name first, but both sets of Heartbreakers seemed to coexist on opposite sides of the country at around the same time. Anyway, we were a little cagey when we first met Tom and the guys. Our dressing room was alongside theirs, and we were eyeing each other, trying to make out what this combination was going to be like. There was our band, with our short hair and black leather, and Tom and his guys, still in a long-haired-rocker time warp. We definitely had an attitude and felt a rivalry, like, we're going to show them.

When they took to the stage, they dispelled our cynicism— they were great. These Heartbreakers had come to LA after signing a record deal, and while they initially came across— at least to us—as naive Southerners, they clearly were not that at all. Their style was different from ours and what was happening with the whole CBGB scene, but for lack of a better term, they were also playing a new wave of rock and roll. Listening to their set, I realized they shared some of the same roots as us and loved a lot of the same garage rock 45s—bands like the Seeds and Count Five—that were on the CBGB jukebox, so we had a shared DNA in that respect. And they were better acquainted with the whole Los Angeles music-business milieu than we were. Every night there was a procession of stars, like Roger McGuinn from the Byrds, showing up to see them play and to hang with Tom after the show.

I don't know if Tom and the guys felt any of that initial rivalry between us. A decade later, I was briefly involved in the recording of Tom's first solo album, *Full Moon Fever*, and played on some sessions with Heartbreakers' guitarist Mike Campbell. Mike didn't mention any friction when we reminisced about those days at the Whisky. I had to laugh when he reminded me that one night after a show, he found me passed out drunk backstage. He said he wondered whether I ended up spending the night in the dressing room. Maybe I did—I have no idea.

I really enjoyed having the chance to test our sound in front of a new audience. Back in Lower Manhattan, we were a safe bet. Much as we loved it, we were a known quantity to the New York crowds, so it was interesting to play for these LA audiences and to try to win them over—while staying true to our provocative NYC roots. One night, Debbie donned a wedding dress for our performance of "Rip Her to Shreds," which she tore apart while she sang. The following night, we arrived in the dressing room to find that Tom had written the initials "TP" on the wedding dress in black spray paint, proof that any frostiness between the two bands had thawed.

Over the course of the residency week, a cast of characters began to assemble around us. Night after night, people who'd go on to stake a claim to notoriety started popping up in the audience. All of us made a few lifelong friends. LA was the place we first met Joan Jett and her band, the Runaways. Jeffrey Lee Pierce, later of the influential LA band the Gun Club, was one of the first people to take us to his heart. At the time, he was just this LA kid who got entangled with us and became an obsessed—bordering on stalkerish—Debbie fan. He got a peroxide-blond makeover in the image of Debbie and became the president of the Blondie fan club. Kid Congo Powers, who went on to be a member of the Gun Club and, later, the Cramps, was a fixture at the Whisky most nights.

At the onset, we met up with Kim Fowley, the legendary LA rock Svengali. Kim was a real bellwether when it came to music trends in LA, and having his seal of approval was extremely helpful for us. There was LA punk scenester Pleasant Gehman, someone I still see around from time to time. At the time, she lived in an apartment building that she and her roommates dubbed "Disgraceland," and it became a punk flophouse for visiting artists. She was good friends with Belinda Carlisle and the girls who formed the Go-Go's, and another LA band, X, who would spring up in our wake. X was a band that didn't get the appreciation they deserved. They started in 1977 and toured with us several times in later years. Like Blondie, they were fronted by a couple of beatniks, from the Venice Beach poetry scene, John Doe and Exene Cervenka.

The important thing for us was that the people showing up were all kids. I began to see we were influencing the style of the Whisky's clientele. Amid the sea of satin and feather haircuts, kids started to show up in the crowd in black leather jackets or black skinny ties and shades. Some of the LA longhairs had gone home after the first night and cut their hair short, while the girls were starting to mimic Debbie's style. Whatever metric you want to use to measure these things by, we were leaving our mark. Probably, we imagined it was all down to us, but those shows in LA were packed out because Toby Mamis got everyone in LA talking about us. Every night, he filled the guest list with radio and record people, and because they liked Toby, they all came.

After that first week, we'd acclimated to our new surroundings and found our feet on the Strip. We had our small coterie of friends with us and were getting rave notices. We spent our days by the hotel pool, and every night, we inhabited that Sunset Boulevard area between the Whisky, the Rainbow, the Roxy, and, a little further down the Strip, Gazzarri's, the home of LA's hard rock bands.

Gazzarri's was a whole different scene. One night a guy with long blond hair and dressed in a striped jumpsuit wandered into our dressing room and we got to talking. To me, he looked old-fashioned, but he was telling me how his band was going to be one of the biggest in the world and he was going to become the world's biggest rock star, and I should come see him play Gazzarri's. I was humoring him, telling him, yeah, sure, okay. The guy was David Lee Roth, and his band Van Halen had a residency at Gazzarri's at the same time we were playing the Whisky.

We were used to the bars staying open until 4 a.m. in New York, but LA clubs closed their doors at 2 a.m. We'd play our second set and decamp to the Rainbow for drinks, and when the Rainbow closed its doors, everyone would congregate in the parking lot for an hour or more before splintering off into factions to track down the best parties, where we'd stay until dawn. Word would inevitably get around about some after-hours shindig in the Hollywood Hills or wherever. A lot of times we'd head over to Joan Jett's apartment across the street from the Whisky to carry on the party at her place.

The Rainbow parking lot became quite a scene, usually involving drugs or alcohol or both. Coke hadn't found its way into our circles yet, so it was quaaludes mixed with booze, which can be a lethal combination. Lethal, but fun. We had Debbie fronting the band, but we were young, good-looking guys, and we didn't mind causing a little mischief and trouble. It didn't always go down well with the local crowd. One night, Jimmy Destri stole Danny Wilde's girlfriend out from under his nose. Danny was a member of one of Kim Fowley's bands, the Quick. Jimmy and Danny had a fight that started in the bar of the Rainbow and dramatically spilled out into the parking lot, like something out of an old Western movie bar fight. Another parking lot scene was the late-night record swap meet at the Capitol Records Building on Hollywood and Vine. We'd cram into the station wagon and head there, a unique LA hangout for the bands and kids on the scene, lasting through to Sunday morning.

In the gap between residencies, we recorded a show for Rodney Bingenheimer; when it aired, practically everyone in LA was listening. We knew the second-week run was going to be even better, when Blondie was going to open for our friends the Ramones. We'd ended our week with Tom Petty in a place of mutual respect, but it was great to have the Ramones with us.

With the arrival of the Ramones, a lot of the CBGB crowd flew across from New York, so suddenly playing the Whisky felt like we were playing on home soil. There was a friend of Debbie's from back in the Max's Kansas City days, Sable Starr. Sable was once Johnny Thunders's girlfriend. By the time I met her, along with Lori Maddox, she'd become known as the queen of the LA groupie scene. The word "groupie" carries a lot of baggage these days; it's a terrible, outdated term. They were just chasing the excitement of being around cool bands and musicians, but for a while, Sable and I became very close. She was extremely charismatic, very precocious, and so full of life. I liked her company and she seemed taken with me, so over the course of my time on the Strip, we began a little affair. She was nineteen, I was twenty-two, so we both knew what we were doing. Sable ended up moving into my

hotel room for the duration of our stint in LA. I'll just say it was a fun couple of weeks.

Those times felt really uninhibited, but certain behaviors could still attract judgment. Society has moved on, thankfully. Today, people can be what they want to be, without all the stigma. Sable was an infamous character, and to sleep with her was almost like a badge of honor. I guess on some level, our fling legitimized my so-called sex appeal, but I wasn't thinking about it that way. I was young enough that I just enjoyed our time together. I mean, we took a few quaaludes along the way, but I like to think I saw a different side of her. She had a real innocence. She'd led this storied life, probably not that far removed from the Penny Lane character in the movie *Almost Famous*, but there was more to her than her reputation.

Gary, me, Sable, and Debbie at the Tropicana (Chris Stein)

Sable came from a place called Palos Verdes, an upper-middle-class suburb on the California coast, and during our downtime between gigs, she took me under her wing and became my personal LA tour guide. We visited all the cool boutiques on Melrose Avenue and spent our afternoons in the bars along Santa Monica Boulevard. One morning I told Sable I hadn't seen the Pacific Ocean, so we traveled west up Sunset Boulevard to Gladstones, a tourist spot overlooking Malibu. Another day, I went to her family home on the Palos Verdes Peninsula to meet her parents. I recall they were both quite conservative, but I got the idea they were trying to be tolerant of Sable's lifestyle. Or maybe they'd just given up trying to control her. Probably, they just realized that neither Sable nor Coral—Sable's sister, who'd been involved with Iggy Pop—was going to be bringing home a Republican boyfriend anytime soon. After I met her folks, Sable and I walked down from her parents' house to the beach and lay on the sand and drank in the warm Pacific air.

"Why are you hanging out with me?" I asked, and she thought about that for a minute. "Because you're gonna be famous," she said, smiling. "And you're a babe. And you're great."

I was a little older, but during our brief time together, I still felt like an impressionable kid, only pretending to be a rock star. Sable was so sweet and kind, and unlike me at the time, she knew the rock and roll ropes. She was blessed with a generous spirit and gave me a lot of positive reinforcement. Though it was never built to last, it was a beautiful time we spent together.

Whoever had the idea to put the Ramones and Blondie on a bill in LA—it was a masterstroke. Both the first Blondie and

Ramones albums were newly released, and the world seemed ready for a changing of the guard. No one thought we were going to re-create the NYC scene in LA. What happened at CBGB was still underground, and every night you could feel the sense of excitement building. Somewhere like England, you can become nationally known in a heartbeat, but in the United States, you need to tackle every territory on a city-by-city basis, like a military campaign.

We might have been sequestered away in Brentwood during the days, drinking by the pool and enjoying the LA sunshine, but leaving the hotel and driving east through Beverly Hills and seeing our name in lights on the marquee outside the Whisky, with lines of people snaking around the block to see us, was a real buzz. Every night, I'd see more girls in the crowd with Debbie's blonde look, and more guys with short hair and skinny ties. We shared a dressing room with the Ramones for the week, so there were all kinds of comings and goings and antics before and after the shows. Just as a snapshot, one night we were all backstage with Arturo Vega, Connie and Dee Dee Ramone, and Roxy Whitney, who was Johnny Ramone's longtime girlfriend, as well as Malcolm McLaren, the Sex Pistols' manager, who somehow found his way backstage. I remember Johnny Ramone was pissed with Malcolm for some reason. An altercation followed, and Johnny threw him out of the dressing room.

It was in LA at an after-show party that I met Peter Leeds, our new manager. Until Peter, our management was in the hands of Chris and Debbie. The release of "X Offender" in 1976 built a groundswell of momentum, but it was clear we needed professional help to keep it going. We'd met some helpful people along the way, but none of them stuck—they were minor characters. A few contenders played bigger roles. Alan Betrock, a NYC record collector and music writer who published *The Rock Marketplace* fanzine, produced a demo that had several originals: "Thin Line," "Puerto Rico," "Platinum Blonde," and "Once I Had a Love," also known as "The Disco Song." Yes, that one, which was later recorded as "Heart of Glass" and became one of our biggest hits. We also took a swing at the Shangri-Las' tune "Out in the Streets" in the hopes of impressing the song's cowriter, Ellie Greenwich. Alan went on to start the seminal magazine *New York Rocker*.

Then there was Marty Thau, who brought Richard Gottehrer to our door, who in turn introduced us to Peter Leeds. Richard was so convinced we were a good fit that he invited Peter to a cocktail party at his home knowing that Debbie would be there, hoping something would spark. Peter had helped Debbie when she was in her late 1960s psych-folk band Wind in the Willows by securing them a deal with Capitol Records. Anyway, after seeing Debbie at the party, Peter came along to CBGB, threw his hat into the ring, and got the job. More than anyone else, even us, Peter saw that Blondie was going to be a major success.

Initially, the deal was done on a handshake, but once we were presented with an official contract, not everyone was so willing to sign on the dotted line. I thought the resistance was weird, because Peter struck me immediately as a serious guy and a good fit for the band. I found him to be a calming presence, but Chris and Gary seemed to have an innate distrust of him. Rather than seeing Peter as someone who offered welcome guidance and who had our backs, they viewed him through a different lens.

While we were on the coast, hanging out at the hotel between sold-out shows, we got the heads-up about our imminent next step. Owing to some wheeling and dealing from Peter and Toby, word found its way to the band that we'd been invited onto Iggy Pop's tour when it reached North America. Not only would we be playing with Iggy, but we learned David Bowie was on keyboards. Bowie had recently released his album *Low*, but he was taking a back seat to Iggy and enjoying a little "anonymity" as a member of the band. Bowie's presence in the lineup made the step up we were making seem even more significant. We were still broke, but we were elated and it felt like such a good omen for what was to come. Only a few weeks prior, we'd been playing in front of a crowd of our friends in Lower Manhattan. Whoever you cared to ask in the band, all of us wanted to break through. We wanted fame and we wanted to hear our songs on the radio. People were talking about the band, about Debbie, and about the album. It was a curious feeling. Blondie and the rest of the CBGB thing had been an isolated, insular experience for the first couple of years, basically a microcosm of the bohemian New York intelligentsia, but finally, it was starting to make waves in the wider world. Still, the idea of us playing a national tour with Iggy and David seemed unreal.

The gradual shift in the makeup of our crowds from old glam rock fans to young West Coast punks just seemed to catalyze with us and the Ramones on the same bill every night. At first, it was a modest-sized contingent of waifs and strays; then, out of nowhere, it was a full-fledged punk scene.

It was surreal. It had taken two years for us to make a name for ourselves in New York, but by the end of that run of shows at the Whisky, we were solidly established in Los Angeles. Next up was San Francisco.

Chapter 13

SAN FRANCISCO

After our triumphant run at the Whisky, I was still hanging out at the hotel in Brentwood. We had a few days to kill before we were booked to play the promotional boat show for KROQ. The head of the radio station who arranged the concert was still footing all our hotel bills, and I understood he wasn't happy. Maybe because I usually had three people staying in my room, all of us ordering endless room service and making calls home while we hung out. The hotel bill started to spiral out of control.

In the interim, we had appearances lined up in San Francisco and a couple of venues around the Bay Area. After three or four weeks holed up in our hotel rooms overlooking the 405 freeway, it was a breath of fresh air to find ourselves back in an urban setting. Our hotel had been converted from a homeless shelter, what they used to call a welfare hotel back in the day. Coming from Manhattan, it seemed a much more natural environment. Instead of being shuttled around in a station wagon from our hotel to the venue and back again, I was happy to find my bearings and just stroll around and take in a bit of the local color and history. Socially, the boys in the band would tend to go one way, and Chris and Debbie would go off and do their own thing, but we tagged along with Chris to check out Haight-Ashbury. A lot had changed since the times he'd spent there in the 1960s with the free-love crowd, but there were still a few hippie casualties on the scene.

During our downtime, we got to see Chinatown and Little Italy firsthand. Exploring these places on foot, walking among the local people, was a blast. There were cool art galleries, and if we needed a taste of home, there was David's, a New York–style deli and hang spot. We'd wander down to North Beach and into City Lights, the famed bookstore, and the Vesuvio Café, the legendary Beat generation hang for people like Allen Ginsberg, Jack Kerouac, Neal Cassady, and Lawrence Ferlinghetti. We were all fascinated by the place, particularly Chris and Debbie, who were still beatniks at heart. We had the benefit of being an enlightened generation, but that probably stemmed from the generation before ours, the hippies and beatniks of the 1960s breaking down a lot of social barriers.

Being turned on to John Lennon, Allen Ginsberg, and David Bowie and living around New York influenced the ideas that seeped into my consciousness. They were my role models. Today's role models are more likely to be tech billionaires, so my generation were lucky in that regard. Punk was partly about creating a sense of chaos, but we still had the virtue of being more interested in peace and love than in material things. None of us saw sexuality or gender as an issue—since our earliest days, Blondie had a strong bond with our gay audience. Our policy was live and let live. We played one of the earliest Pride events in Lower Manhattan after the Stonewall riots, so San Francisco immediately felt like familiar ground. Harvey Milk, who would soon become the first openly gay man to be elected to public office in California, was spearheading what would become a revolution in gay rights. Everywhere, the gay movement was out and proud. We spent our days wandering up and down Polk Street, stopping at cafés and bars, soaking up the culture and vibes.

The backdrop of the Beat poets and the gay movement made San Francisco really feel alive, in the same way things were back home in Lower Manhattan. And it's worth remembering that some of that punk style was derived from gay culture. We all shopped at places like the Leather Man on Christopher Street in the West Village for our accessories and wound up sharing a lot of the same imagery. The link was obvious to us, but from the outside, people didn't pick up on that until later. It seemed strange when hard rock fans saw Rob Halford from Judas Priest and didn't make the connection. He was decked out like a mannequin in an S and M shop window, but it was like they couldn't see it. I guess that's why it was so subversive.

The same goes for disco. Alongside Philly, New York was the birthplace of disco, and I've always felt the disco movement in NYC in the 1970s was a lot more rebellious than punk ever was. It was much more of an underground scene, and there were way more sex and drugs and illicit goings-on. By comparison, the CBGB scene was quite innocent. Eventually, I had an apartment on Christopher Street, which was kind of New York's gay equivalent of Main Street. While we were in New York at that time, my friend Gary Valentine's girlfriend, Lisa Jane Persky, was appearing in an off-Broadway play, *Women Behind Bars*, at the Astor Place Theatre. The real star of that show was John Waters' muse, Divine, whom we got to hang out with during the play's run.

Our first San Francisco shows were at the Mabuhay Gardens on North Beach, just down the street from the Vesuvio. By day, the Mabuhay Gardens was a Chinese restaurant and bar, but it quickly evolved into a key venue for the Bay Area punk and new wave scenes in the late 1970s. As East Coast interlopers, it was curious to see this new scene evolving so quickly around us and bands like us. The Mabuhay Gardens was a little like a couple of restaurant venues that emerged in LA's Chinatown around the same time. Places like Hong Kong Gardens, which catered to LA's punk contingent with acts like the Germs or the Weirdos, and Madame Wong's, which became more renowned in new wave circles.

We had a small entourage who traveled with us, but I was aware that everywhere we went, we created a new hotbed of followers. That still holds true. Wherever we go in the world, we have a contingent of local friends we can call on. One of the things that distinguished our time in San Francisco was meeting and hanging out with more musicians who were active on the local circuit. One of our new friends was Jonathan Postal, who went on to be the leader of the band the Readymades. Jonathan took some iconic photos of the band while we were in SF, including some great shots from the Mabuhay dressing room. Because the Mabuhay Gardens was such a new venue, I remember the walls of the dressing room were pristine, with no graffiti whatsoever. If you head into any punk rock dive today, there's graffiti everywhere you look, so obviously we all took the opportunity to christen the dressing room walls. Ronnie Toast, our friend from New York, was in our thoughts, so we scribbled "Toast is the most from coast to coast" on the clean white walls.

The San Francisco scene was more hardcore than the scene in LA. Compared with the Whisky, the SF crowds were more readily identifiable as punks from the outset. Some of the fans and bands were flirting with Nazi imagery, and the music had a harder edge. I think the San Francisco punks were taking a lot of their cues from what was happening in London at the time—not necessarily musically, but a lot of the California bands were trying to emulate that snotty English "fuck you" attitude. It was in stark contrast to what we created at CBGB. In New York, it was about art and culture, bohemianism, beatniks, Lenny Bruce, William Burroughs, Warhol and the Velvets—all this stuff that was part of the city's DNA.

Word had spread from LA, and San Francisco was primed for our arrival. News of our shows at the Whisky in the California press and the whole CBGB thing had started to filter through by now, so we made an immediate impact. Our LP had been out for a couple of months and had gotten some great reviews, including a brilliant write-up from renowned rock critic Lester Bangs, so we were preaching to the choir from the get-go.

We played two nights at the Mabuhay Gardens with a couple of bands; one was local punk band Crime. They were a gang of sinewy, snot-nosed guys who used to get on stage dressed as cops. They had this one tune I remember, "Hotwire My Heart," which was covered much later by Sonic Youth. There was another band, the Avengers. Their lead singer was Penelope Houston, and she and I became quite friendly. She was still attending fashion school and became a big presence on the scene. After I returned to the East Coast, Penelope and I used to write letters back and forth for a time. We also played with the band the Nuns, featuring Alejandro Escovedo on guitar. Alejandro is a dear friend of mine to this day.

Infamously, both the Nuns and the Avengers would go on to open for the Sex Pistols when they played their ill-fated final show at the Winterland Ballroom in 1978. The Nuns were fronted by Jennifer Miro, who was this incredible, statuesque albino woman. Jennifer was an exceptionally talented piano player and singer, with a totally unique operatic style. We became great friends and would meet up whenever Blondie was playing on the West Coast. For many years we had such a strong connection, and I think she was maybe in love with me, but our relationship never progressed beyond friendship. She moved to New York, probably following me there, and got an apartment next to the Dakota building. Jennifer went on to be an icon on the NY underground club scene.

After a show with John Cale at the Keystone in Berkeley, we played our final gig on the West Coast at the Keystone in Palo Alto. Today, Palo Alto is the heart of Silicon Valley, but in 1977, it was just a typical Northern Californian suburban town with very little going on. The setlist provides an interesting snapshot of where we were at the time. We played "Little Girl Lies"; "Look Good in Blue"; "(I'm Always Touched by Your) Presence, Dear"; "Man Overboard"; "In the Sun"; "Rip Her to Shreds"; an early unreleased original, "Evil Friends"; "Poets Problem"; "Flight 45"; "Platinum Blonde"; "Kung Fu Girls"; "I Didn't Have the Nerve to Say No"; "Rifle Range"; "Fan Mail"; "A Shark in Jets Clothing";

"Star Beast" (another unreleased Ronnie Toast original); "X Offender"; a cover of John Barry's James Bond theme song "Goldfinger"; Martha and the Vandellas' "Heatwave"; the Freddy Cannon hit "Palisades Park"; the Doors' "Moonlight Drive"; and Ronny and the Daytonas' "Little GTO."

I remember the Palo Alto gig being well attended, but I have also heard that no one promoted the show and we played two sets to practically no one. Maybe I blocked that out—whatever the attendance was, we loved the Bay Area, and I guess the feeling was mutual because we built a strong following in San Francisco, and we returned many times.

Chapter 14

IGGY POP

Beyond continuing as a band, I never knew what our aspirations were. The goalposts kept shifting. At first, we wanted a record deal, any record deal. Then, once we had a contract, we weren't thinking about any big success because that seemed such a distant prospect. We carried on, show by show, song by song. It didn't happen all at once, we climbed higher incrementally. As the landscape changed, I went from having modest ambitions to believing anything was possible. With each new success, we grew, and so did my ambition. In 1973, I considered the Dolls to be a band who had "made it," but in terms of quantifiable commercial success, they were a failure. They didn't nudge the needle in terms of record sales, but they inspired a lot of people. We were following in their footsteps, we thought, so it seemed a logical step for us to play with Iggy Pop and David Bowie, two of our musical heroes.

Between the West Coast shows and the dates with Iggy, we returned to NYC for two homecoming gigs at Max's. The second night, we played two sold-out shows, at midnight and at 2 a.m., before climbing in the back of an RV and heading for the border to Canada. We joined Iggy Pop's *Idiot* Tour on March 13, 1977, at Le Plateau Auditorium, in Montreal, and headed directly to our dressing room, where we all crashed. Minutes later, the door swung open and there stood Iggy Pop and David Bowie, coming by to introduce themselves. As if they needed an introduction.

"Call me Jim," Iggy said, going around the dressing room, addressing everyone by name. "We're gonna have a great time," he said, and he wasn't wrong. Bowie was everyone's idol. His records changed my life. The Stooges were one of the first bands Debbie, Chris, and I bonded over. Now here we were, in the same room and about to go on tour together. Also in the band, on drums and bass, were brothers Hunt and Tony Sales, along with Ricky Gardiner on guitar. Tony would later go on to join me in the band Chequered Past.

Blondie played more than twenty shows with our heroes. If this book were a movie, we'd drop into a montage right now, the endless road, and every marker along the way: Montreal to Toronto, Boston, back into New York for the Palladium, on to Philly, and Cleveland, hometown shows for Iggy in Detroit, then Chicago, Pittsburgh, Columbus, Cincinnati, Milwaukee, Portland, Seattle, Berkeley, Santa Monica. The film cuts to us, exhausted but delighted, taking our bow at the final show in San Diego on April 16. Calling it a whirlwind doesn't do the experience any justice. That time in my life has become blurred around the edges, but I'll never forget this positive upward momentum, like a wave, carrying us from city to city. This palpable sense of having arrived and these vivid memories of David and Iggy. Soaking up every moment, whether it was sound check or David hanging out like one of the guys, showing a keen interest in everything. He was always so curious and engaged, no distance, just being a part of everything. At sound check, David would have his elbows perched on the edge of the stage, checking out Jimmy's new Polymoog keyboard or watching Debbie closely during a run-through. Every night, I watched their show from the side of the stage. Once, I was waiting for the set to start and David came and stood next to me. I was surprised to see his hair brushed forward instead of his usual combed-back style. He turned to me and said, "What do you think of my Tom Verlaine look?," making me laugh. The whole tour was everything. Seeing how they treated us was an object lesson in how to act toward our own opening acts down the years: with grace and kindness.

In Seattle, the people from the fanzine *Back Door Man* held an aftershow party. Chris, Gary, Iggy, and I showed up to find a makeshift stage in the living room with a local punk rock band playing. About fifty people were there and were treated to the coolest jam they'd probably ever see when we took over the band's gear and played a few songs, including "I Wanna Be Your Dog" and "Gloria." People still bring up that legendary party every time I go through Seattle on tour.

After the show with Iggy in San Francisco, Jimmy Destri and I bumped into Penelope Houston. We'd gotten word of a party being held for David and Iggy nearby, at the apartment of one of the Tubes, the SF rock band. We decided to crash the party. Once we were there, we started ringing the buzzer to be allowed through the glass lobby door, but they wouldn't let us in. Being turned away didn't go down well. Maybe it was adrenaline more than anything, but Jimmy picked up a trash can and hurled it through the glass. In the ensuing chaos, we all ran off into the night. We'd forgotten all about it, but soon after, the Avengers were playing a gig at the Mabuhay, and poor Penelope paid the price when some guy went onstage and bit a chunk out of her arm in retribution for Jimmy smashing the door. Ever the gentleman, Bowie later smoothed things over by paying for the damages his punk tourmates had caused.

A few days after we finished the Iggy shows, we had a few headline dates at the Whisky and invited Hunt and Tony Sales from Iggy's band to open for us. I was thinking about my first meeting with Blondie and Chris asking if I could sing and me saying, "Yeah. I can sing like Iggy Pop." Well, on our final night, a little worse for wear, and still high from the tour, I showed everyone what I was talking about. For an encore, Hunt and Tony took over drums and bass. Joan Jett grabbed a guitar alongside Chris, and even Rodney Bingenheimer jumped in on the action, getting behind Jimmy's keyboard to pound one note. Even with this chaos, the crowd couldn't have guessed what would happen next. I entered as the band started ripping into "I Wanna Be Your Dog," holding a leash with Debbie on all fours at the other end of it. I had the mic in one hand, singing like the best of them, and the leash with Debbie in the other. We gave them an unforgettable encore; it was as wild and punk and rock and roll as it gets.

The legendary LA photographer Donna Santisi documented the whole crazy thing with pictures that conveyed the action just as it happened.

Onstage with Joan at the Whisky (Jenny Lens)

Chapter 15

THE DREAM CONTINUES

When I was a teenager, a cold, rainy night could bring to mind dreams of England. I'd imagine strolling down to the Marquee to catch the Who or the Yardbirds' set. Or maybe I'd find my way to the Cavern to see the Beatles in all their ragged post-Hamburg glory. I had a growing collection of British Invasion 45s beside my record player and on my nightstand, a stack of paperback books—the story of the Beatles and Merseybeat. The floor was littered with imported copies of *Rave* and *Fabulous* magazines. I was more tuned into whatever Ringo Starr and Keith Moon were getting up to in their day-to-day lives than to anything that was going on locally. I'd never heard the word "Anglophile" when I was fifteen, but that's what I was fast becoming. I wasn't the only one. I imagine if you talk to anyone my age who was in a band, at least half will tell you the same thing. The dawn of the Beatles and the subsequent British Invasion was a seismic event. It changed all our lives.

I spent way too long in front of my bedroom mirror trying to get my hair to look like a Beatle's. In the mid-1960s, young guys growing out their hair was the cause of some consternation in polite society, but I made the leap just the same. Older cousins of mine, kids raised on a diet of doo-wop music, dressed like greasers and hot-rodders, used to muss up my hair and ask me what the hell was I thinking walking around like that? They took offense to my Beatles style, but they were also pissed these longhairs from the other side of the Atlantic were ripping off Buddy Holly, Chuck Berry, and other American rock and roll artists from a few years before.

When I first heard the Beatles, I was ten years old, so I didn't know what my cousins were talking about, but yeah, so what? The Beatles and the Stones were bringing our music back to us. They didn't exactly make a secret of it. They were doing us a service. I'd been too young for Elvis, so he held no appeal to me. Meantime, the early rockers like Chuck Berry and blues artists like Howlin' Wolf and Jimmy Reed had been swept away by all these prefabricated singers called Bobby this or Bobby that—Bobby Rydell, Bobby Vee, Bobby Vinton, and so on—with a watered-down take on rock and roll. They'd taken all the rock and all the roll out of it. They sang songs about sweet girls with apple blossom complexions and uncomplicated lives. They were commercially successful for a couple of years at the turn of the decade, but they weren't cool. It was too sanitized. We still had Motown, of course, which was the only US music that appealed to me in my teens, but otherwise we had to look beyond our borders to find something good. Something with a little more edge to it.

Obviously, by the time the Beatles arrived on our shores, Brian Epstein had polished away their rough Hamburg image. Then the Stones followed them over; they were the antithesis of the Beatles, more streetwise, rough, and rowdy.

Both bands had a real appreciation of rock and roll and where it came from. It was like they'd come over to jog our memories. Their first albums were composed mostly of cover songs of American artists.

The Beatles were charming and funny. The Stones were wild and sexually ambiguous and, philosophically, they were in the business of upending the status quo. Both bands had this attitude: things they said in interviews hadn't been vetted and prepackaged by some record company guy. Anybody with sense just said goodbye to the saccharine pop singers and embraced the new British bands. Naturally, if you asked me then if I'd be able to someday reverse the tides and make it in the UK, it would've sounded like a crazy notion. At that point in time, the love affair I had with Britain was one-sided, but eventually I'd find a warm welcome on the other side of the Atlantic with Blondie.

I traveled to England for the first time in November 1975. Despite my years' long love of the place, I had no idea what to expect. Blondie was happening to some extent, but I still had my antenna up for new possibilities. My girlfriend, Diane, had transferred to a London college, so I decided to head over so we could spend some time together. Her college was in London's East End, around Petticoat Lane, but her student digs were in Egerton Gardens in South Kensington, a short walk from the Victoria and Albert Museum. I didn't know much about the city, but that's quite a well-heeled area of London, so I just figured that's what England was like. It was Christmas, and we did the tourist thing, visiting Harrods and those places. For a few days, I assumed everywhere in the country was moneyed and had these grand museums and department stores at the end of every street. While I was in town, I made a pilgrimage to London's West End to Anello & Davide shoe store and had two pairs of Beatle boots custom made for us. One for me, and the other for Chris. Because he wasn't with me, I'd made a drawing of the outline of his feet to ensure they got the measurements right. By day, I made sure to visit Carnaby Street, browsing through the boutiques. At night, I'd mess with the radio dial until I landed on the John Peel show on Radio 1. It was like another world, being able to tune in my transistor radio and hear records by David Bowie and all these artists who didn't fit in with US Top 40 radio programmers.

Every day, I scanned the listings in *NME* to see which bands were playing where and went to a show whenever I could. I didn't fulfill my adolescent fantasy of seeing the Who or the Yardbirds at the Marquee, but I saw Be Bop Deluxe open for Bad Company at the Olympia in Kensington. I saw Gong play the Roundhouse. I caught a Dr. Feelgood show at the Hammersmith Odeon. I went farther afield to Brunel University to catch the Kursaal Flyers with Eddie and the Hot Rods and even managed to get a ride back to London with Barrie Masters, aka Eddie, and the band. Punk was just beginning in London, but Eddie and the Hot Rods were in that pub rock tradition that was a precursor to punk in the UK. Straight away, it was clear we had a lot in common. They were a garage band, and we talked a lot about those 1960s garage records and the band I had in New York.

I had no idea London and England were caught up in an economic downturn. It was a lot like New York in that sense. Inflation was spiraling ever upward, there were strikes, rolling power cuts, and a three-day workweek. I didn't pay much attention to the sociopolitical backdrop because I had more pressing matters on my mind. I didn't imagine the streets were paved with gold, but part of me was thinking I might find my musical fortune on the other side of the pond. The guys in Blondie were still a few months away from getting our hair cropped short, so I still had my glam rock hair. I had the idea I could come to England and audition for the band Sparks. I think that stemmed from reading about how the Mael brothers from Sparks had come to England and found success.

Before flying to the UK, I'd met up with my photographer friend Leee Black Childers. Leee was part of Bowie's MainMan organization and was just the loveliest person. Being the sweet Southern gentleman he was, Leee wrote me ten letters of introduction to various people in London. In essence, the letters said, "This is my friend Clem, from New York. He's in a brilliant band, Blondie. He's going to be a big rock star. By the way, he's not gay. Can you look after him and show him around?" One of the letters led to me having a meeting at RCA Records' London offices. I chatted with some English record exec awhile, while he played the new—at the time unreleased—Bowie record *Station to Station*. Some of the letters Leee wrote for me went undelivered, including a letter of introduction to Marianne Faithfull, which I still have.

Eighteen months later, there's Toby Mamis, picking me up from my dad's house in a JFK Airport–bound limousine, creating a flurry of excitement around the neighborhood. I'm heading to London, and it feels like the fulfillment of the dreams I'd had as a kid, fantasizing about being in England. Blondie were sharing a bill with Television. The two bands played together at CBGB a few times before I joined, but my first shows with them were in the UK. Television and Blondie were friends, but after the warm welcome we got from David and Iggy, they seemed a little standoffish with us. We'd made our mark on the same turf, but we represented two distinct New York styles. *Marquee Moon*, Television's remarkable debut, had just been released, and they were generating a lot of heat in the UK music press. The weekly music papers, primarily *NME*, *Melody Maker*, and *Sounds*, were still playing catch-up with the New York scene, but they really took to Television. Compared with Blondie, they were seen as a virtuoso guitar band. In that way, Television had the jump on us. They played the kind of music the rock press respected. We still weren't on the critics' radar, but we were grateful to be there.

Our first LP was in stores, but we were still an unknown entity going into those dates. If anyone was talking about us at all, I think we were pigeonholed as a pop band. Certainly not as serious as our friends from the Lower East Side. Ultimately, that worked in everybody's favor because we each provided a neat counterpoint to the other. We knew it was a big break. We were playing actual bona fide theater shows, but our ascent from opening act to headliner in the UK was so swift, we'd headline many of those same venues before too long.

A few days prior to the Television dates, we played our first show on English soil, in the seaside town of Bournemouth, down on the south coast of England. It was at a venue called the Village Bowl, with support from Squeeze, an up-and-coming London band. In the van, we'd relegated our Private Stock A&R guy, Dinky Diamond, to sitting on an upturned bucket at the back. We struck up a conversation, and I couldn't believe it when I realized he was actually *the* Dinky Diamond, the drummer from Sparks. It was a jolting glimpse of the ups and downs of showbiz. Arriving at the venue, we spilled out of the back of our tour van, all of us the worse for wear from jetlag, rubbing our eyes in the spring sunshine. We were a bare bones unit without a big entourage. It was us, Peter, and two roadies: a redheaded Yorkshireman called Keith Crabtree, along with our friend from New York, Michael Sticca. Keith hailed from Bradford, and I think I caught maybe every third word he said. Keith was the guy who indoctrinated us in the ways of British culture, like which side of the road to drive on and the pubs to go to after a soundcheck. I still remember my first taste of that heavy English beer being a real shock. I have a vague memory of it knocking me on my ass after a couple of pints and Keith laughing it up at my expense.

Michael was the roadie for pretty much everyone from the Dolls to the Ramones. He stayed around long enough to travel the world with us. But Michael is probably most remembered as the roadie for the Dead Boys, the US punk band out of Cleveland, Ohio. In 1978, he landed in serious legal trouble when he was out with Dead Boys drummer Johnny Blitz and got in a shouting match with some guys in a car on the Lower East Side. The car came to a screeching halt, and a bunch of angry Puerto Rican guys piled out. It escalated quickly: one of the Puerto Ricans pulled a blade and left Johnny bloodied in the gutter. He was rushed to the hospital with life-threatening wounds to his chest.

When the NYPD arrived, the Puerto Ricans had split the scene. The cops jumped to the wrong conclusion, and Michael was arrested on suspicion of attempted murder and wound up on Rikers Island. Everyone on the scene was shocked to the core, but we took care of our own. CBGB held a Blitz Benefit to cover Johnny's medical bills and raise Michael's bail money. Arturo Vega, the Ramones lighting man and artistic director, who made up the Ramones' presidential seal–style T-shirts, made special Blitz T-shirts. Blondie played with Robert Fripp from King Crimson, and *Saturday Night Live*'s John Belushi played drums for the Dead Boys in Johnny's place.

Our first English gig was a joyous blur. The room was heaving with bodies—young kids pogoing and vying for position in front of the stage. Everyone there was either a Blondie fan, or about to become one. The upcoming Television tour would be great, but because they were—understandably—a big deal, we'd be playing to a mixed crowd—mostly their audience. By contrast, the Bournemouth show had a level of intensity from the crowd that none of us had ever experienced. We were so energized by the reception we got, it was like we ingested their enthusiasm and used it as fuel to carry us onward and upward through sold-out shows. During May and June, we hit Glasgow, Newcastle, Sheffield, Manchester, London, and Bristol and then hit the continent to Amsterdam, Brussels, Paris, and Copenhagen. We forged bonds that would last a lifetime. It was beyond my wildest expectations. The culmination of half a lifetime's dreaming, coming true.

Chapter 16

PLASTIC LETTERS

When we touched down on US soil, we were due to start recording our second album, *Plastic Letters*, immediately. That was the plan anyway. The sessions went ahead, but maybe not as smoothly as originally envisaged. That's because our lineup was set for a further shuffle. This time, it was Gary's turn to leave the fold.

It was clear to anyone paying attention that Gary was becoming tired of the band, but he said he'd stay long enough to record the new album before making it final. From Gary's perspective, he didn't want to leave us in a bind, but it didn't sit well with everyone. I did my best to persuade him to sleep on the decision, but his mind was made up. The bad blood that existed between him and Peter meant Gary was out of the band before a note was played. A vote was taken, but I was outnumbered; the first of many occasions I found myself pulling in one direction while my bandmates were dragging just as hard in the other. That's my memory of the situation, but I spoke to Peter Leeds, and he's dead set he fired Gary.

There was a show at the Village Gate, just before we entered the studio, and Gary was pogoing around the stage and almost took Debbie's eye out with his bass. According to Peter, that was the final straw. I don't know who's right and who's wrong, but the result was the same. Gary was out of the picture completely. It was an unsettling time; I'd brought Gary into the fold, so I felt I had a lot at stake personally. I liked the energy he brought on stage, the way his stage moves were reminiscent of Wilko Johnson from Dr. Feelgood.

Once the battle lines were drawn, there followed a brief Mexican standoff when I threatened to quit. It was one of those, "if he goes, I go" situations, but it didn't last long. Ultimately, I decided to stay in the band and Gary left. Gary was young and impetuous, full of attitude. He had his heart set on a full-time move to Los Angeles to be with his girlfriend. He had a vested interest in the band and I wished he'd put up more of a fight. I thought it was a hot-headed decision, but he always followed his own path, and in the coming years, he gained a little notoriety with his band the Know. Later, he reverted to his given surname of Lachman and carved out a successful career writing numerous books on esoterica, music, mysticism, and the occult.

In the meantime, the album sessions were approaching, so we had to move fast. I had an instinct that what Blondie needed was Frank Infante, a friend of mine from Jersey City. Frank had a band, World War III, but it seemed like a natural progression for him to step in as a session player to help us. He was already hanging out and knew everyone and was more than capable of covering bass duties. He also conjured up a couple of standout guitar parts on the songs "Kidnapper," "I'm On E," and "Detroit 442."

Once again, we recorded at Plaza Sound Studios, on the rooftop of Radio City, with Richard Gottehrer at the helm. Behind the scenes, Peter was shopping the band around to various record labels in the hope of extricating us from the Private Stock arrangement. We were aware of that, but it was background noise more than anything else. Our focus was on making a good record and enjoying our time in the studio. We were so fortunate to have a hit songwriter in the studio with us in Richard. He was completely on point when it came to working on arrangements, with a neat understanding of songcraft and where a song might require a chord change or a middle-eight, or whatever. Whenever I finished laying down a drum track, I'd sit back on one of the sofas, listening while he built the song from the foundations up, layer by layer. It was a great learning experience for me. If we had a break from recording, or if some of our friends called by to hang out, we'd congregate on the roof, smoke a cigarette, and talk as the traffic passed by below.

We were really into the recording process, and the vibe between us was cool. We'd listen to the playbacks and go back and forth with Richard over what needed to be changed. Debbie was always in a quiet corner, scribbling down lyrics and last-minute song ideas. If it was raining and the roof was a no-go, we'd gather behind the Radio City movie screen and watch the movies, with the image turned back on itself, like we were on the backside of a mirror. Generally, we clocked off at midnight or later, and Debbie and Chris went their way and, because things didn't get going in Manhattan until midnight, the guys and I would head downtown to Max's or CBGB to see the night through. That building conjures memories of making those records every time I'm near it.

Blondie never actually got to play a show at Radio City, much to my regret, although we did perform at a Bowie tribute, many years down the line, after David passed away. The minute I walked in, it was like nothing had changed and time stood still, waiting for me to come back.

Our musician friends came by to check on our progress: Alan Vega and Martin Rev from Suicide, and Marty Thau, the former Dolls manager, who had moved on to signing Suicide to his Red Star label. Marty was still part of our inner circle, along with Ronnie Toast and Paul Zone from the Fast. Central Park was a short walk away, and we were only a couple of blocks from Manny's Music on West Forty-Eighth. We had a band account there, and sometimes, I'd go with Chris to check out the guitars. Manny's had a wall of autographed black-and-white photographs of previous clients —Hendrix, Cream, Del Shannon, the Young Rascals. If you were somebody and passed through the city and needed a guitar string, your picture was probably on the wall somewhere. I was pleasantly surprised to walk in one day and see Blondie's photo on that famous wall.

Plastic Letters wasn't a giant leap forward from our debut, but Frank brought more musicality to proceedings. He really should get more credit for his work on the record. He's billed on the album as Frank "the Freak" Infante, but if you want to be pedantic, more correctly, he was known as Frank Freak. He will correct you if you get it wrong, I assure you. *Plastic Letters* has songs on it we still play to this day, so they've stood the test of time.

We had several writers in the band, but we never had much leftover material. A lot of times, especially in the early years, we just came up with enough songs to make an album.

Everybody was open to everybody else's ideas, and we went with whatever transpired in the rehearsal room. Somebody would come up with an outline, and I would try to support the writing, helping shape the arrangements. At this point, none of us understood the economics of songwriting. That may have been a universal thing. Tom Petty told me when he initially signed his deal, he thought publishing meant sheet music. Artists might have been unaware, but old hands like Richard Gottehrer, a genuine hit songwriter, understood the benefits of publishing. Jimmy had a hand in writing six of the thirteen tracks, and overall, I think of it as our Jimmy Destri album. Jimmy's tune "No Imagination" carries a strong Procol Harum influence. One of the things Jimmy and I first bonded over was our love of Procol Harum. I loved their drummer, B.J. Wilson, and tried to channel his style on that number. Jimmy's song "Kidnapper" was written with Robert Gordon in mind. It's kind of a rockabilly song, and he thought it might suit his style. Good songs were at a premium though, and we kept it for our LP instead. Many musicians have been through the sophomore slump, the challenge of coming up with a second album's worth of material mere months after using up all the songs that took years to develop. The album would have benefited from a couple more Debbie and Chris songs. I'm still surprised we didn't include "Platinum Blonde" because that was a live mainstay for us. Still, Chris wrote and co-wrote a few choice numbers, including the dirge-like, Velvets-sounding "Cautious Lip," with lyrics by Ronnie Toast. There's "Love at the Pier," Debbie's song held over from the first record, and two others she cowrote. "Youth Nabbed as Sniper," which sounded like a *New York Post* headline. Like the first record, there's a lot of cinematic ideas on the record. Titles of movies that never got made.

Quentin Tarantino has gone on record stating that "Contact in Red Square" is his favorite Blondie song. I think Debbie's lyrics and poetry don't get enough credit. As far back as our first demo, the thing that drew me to the band was Debbie's original material. Numbers like "Puerto Rico" and "The Thin Line" proved she was in a field of her own. She never got writer's block. It was like a sort of alchemy watching the process; she'd conjure these extraordinarily vivid words, turning the most basic song into something special. She could apply her art to anyone's music. Anyone can play a few chords and hum along, but coming up with interesting lyrics is a real art. To me, she's like Bowie. Debbie has so many brilliant ideas, one being for us to cover the song "Denis." "Denis" was our first big hit in England, going all the way to number two on the charts in 1978 and landing us on our first appearance on *Top of the Pops*.

In the end, the record was touched by Gary's presence even though he'd been shown the door. Part of our live set before Gary left was an exceptionally great number of his: "(I'm Always Touched By Your) Presence, Dear," that I really wanted to keep. Fortunately, Richard sided with me, and the song found its way onto *Plastic Letters*. It was also a top 10 hit in the UK, the follow-up to "Denis." If we didn't have "Presence," I'm not sure we'd have kept our momentum in Britain, so it was a crucial song for us and a great swan song for Gary.

Plastic Letter's success was still a long way off, though. The backroom deals Peter was striking meant the record wouldn't see the light of day for many months.

Chapter 17

ENTER NIGEL AND CHRYSALIS

In 1977, the middle of the USA was still uncharted land for us, but in the same way we'd gotten a foothold in New York and Britain, we felt like we were starting to make inroads on the West Coast. Despite Frank stepping in for a few club gigs in NYC, the band was a little lopsided: Frank was filling in on bass and doing a fine job, but he'd always been a guitar player first and foremost. Despite the skewed band setup, we had a run of shows at the Whisky that had been in the tour diary for some time, so we had to make do for a while. Our second LP was in the can, awaiting a release, and we were touring as a makeshift five-piece. When we returned to New York, we were a six-piece. The "classic" Blondie lineup, gearing up for a world tour.

We didn't have the benefit of KROQ bankrolling our stay this time, so we stayed at the notorious Tropicana Motel on Santa Monica Boulevard. We'd partied there a few times with the Ramones when they were staying there during our first trip to Los Angeles. For those who don't know, the Tropicana has a similar reputation to New York's Chelsea

Hotel, synonymous with wild parties and bleak comedowns. The place has a ton of musical and countercultural history. It was Iggy Pop's base while the Stooges were recording the *Fun House* album, and the Doors' Jim Morrison used to party all night and sleep off his subsequent hangovers there for days at a time. I remember seeing Tom Waits, who was living in one of the Tropicana bungalows around the back of the motel, just shuffling about the place, like a character from one of his own songs. We got a kick out of being there.

The Tropicana had a restaurant, Duke's, where we used to grab breakfast, and it became our de facto headquarters and informal hang spot while we were in the city. All the LA artists and musicians would come by, and we'd hold court in Duke's or out by the pool. As well as being a cool place to socialize, it was a good place to conduct business. The Tropicana was where we held a breakfast meeting with Runaways tour manager Bruce Patron, to size him up for the same job for Blondie—a role he'd make his own in the coming years. As with our first trip, our publicist, Toby Mamis, was ever present, buzzing around, tirelessly hustling. He was always doing way more than a publicist should do. When we arrived, he said he'd found a new producer for us, an Australian named Mike Chapman. Mike had made his name in the UK producing hits for bands like the Sweet, Suzi Quatro, Mud, and Showaddywaddy. Toby had invited him to one of the Whisky shows in February, and during the show, Mike scrawled a few words on the back of a napkin and handed it to Toby. It read "I have to produce this band," but Toby had to pass. Peter was working behind the scenes to get us out of Private Stock, but we still had an exclusive deal with Richard Gottehrer. Same thing happened with Phil

Spector, although that was probably a bullet dodged. Now, months later, we met with Mike at the Tropicana, and although nothing was set in stone, it was clear we had our new producer.

A lot was happening, all at once. We still had a problem with the balance of personnel, but again, Toby came to the rescue. Toby had been speaking with a bass player in LA, Nigel Harrison, who was working with Doors organist Ray Manzarek's current band, Nite City. We arranged for Nigel to come to the next day's soundcheck to play a few songs. Nigel was this curly-haired Englishman with the glam rock persona of Marc Bolan. He hailed from Stockport, on the outskirts of Manchester. Immediately, he gave off a positive vibe. Nigel had made a few records with the English glam rock band Silverhead, featuring singer Michael Des Barres. It was also cool that he'd played with Iggy Pop when he staged his first solo concert at Rodney Bingenheimer's English Disco, a performance he dubbed "Murder of a Virgin." In terms of the business, Nigel seemed to have everything figured out. The rest of us were finding our feet, while he'd had experience working in the British music business and understood how to work within the system. He had a lot of connections in and around the LA scene, including our mutual friends Kim Fowley and Joan Jett. In fact, Nigel played bass on the first Runaways album.

In a smart move, Nigel attended the previous night's show with a portable cassette recorder and taped our entire set. I later learned that Nigel had a tape recorder with him wherever he went and a set of binoculars as well. Later, when we were on tour, I'd find him sitting in his hotel room with his binoculars pointing out the window. After recording the show, Nigel went back to his place and must have spent all night woodshedding all the bass parts. He had every song down. Obviously, he aced the audition, and we told him to pack his bags and meet us in New York. I felt we clicked straight away and made a great rhythm section. Nigel charmed us all. He had great musicality and style, and being English, I think he brought a different energy to the group.

The Whisky shows were a level up from our last trip to the West Coast. They also illustrated the crossover between our music and the visual arts. It was on this LA trip that we were approached by photographer and director Sam Shaw. Sam was a New Yorker who made his reputation with a clutch of iconic photographs of Marilyn Monroe in the 1950s. Maybe he saw a similarity between Marilyn and Debbie and that piqued his interest. He came over to meet with us at Duke's one afternoon with a pitch for a Blondie documentary built around our shows at the Whisky. We said we were interested, and the wheels were set in motion. Sam's collaborator and camera operator on the project was the Hollywood maverick John Cassavetes. I don't think any of us really appreciated what a privilege it was at the time. I wish I'd interacted more with Cassavetes, a missed opportunity on my part given the high regard I held for his films.

John made a point to blend into the background, but he shot some candid interviews with us at Sam's house in Laurel Canyon one day. John and Sam were tapping into that fly-on-the-wall cinema verité aesthetic. Just be yourselves, play, and we'll capture the moment. I loved seeing Cassavetes at those Whisky shows, contorting himself into all these weird positions, lying flat on his back and crawling on his belly to capture the best shots of our performance. Frustratingly, the documentary didn't see the light of day. I never even saw a rough cut of the whole movie. So much was happening around us at such a rapid pace, it just fell between the cracks. Occasionally, clips surface in various Blondie retrospectives. It's become a real enigma in our career. I'd love for it to be seen and to find a wider audience someday.

Once we got back to New York, there was no more downtime. Living in the city, being the toast of the town, was something else entirely. As a music fan, I looked at everything from that perspective. Every time we released a new record, I'd make a point of filing it on the shelf alongside my Beatles records because it meant so much to me. Nothing I'd ever done had made me so proud. I saw our success as an opportunity to give other musicians a leg up and started producing and collaborating with emerging artists—bands like the Colors, who were managed by Hilly Kristal. Because we had the line of credit at Manny's Music in New York, I was able to walk in off the street and supply up-and-coming groups with equipment.

We were all night owls, so even if we weren't playing or doing the promotional rounds, there was always a place to go or some show to take in. Every night melted into the next day—it was easy to keep going with Max's, CBGB, or one of a dozen after-hours clubs, like the Nursery, Mudd Club, Area, and Limelight, that were springing up across the city. I think I was handling success quite well—but the coke era was creeping in. Everywhere I went, people were offering me a toot, but for the most part, I was just high on the city.

The only prerequisite for living such a fast life in New York at the time was a pair of sunglasses. You had to have sunglasses because it was always such a shock to the system to see the daylight when you emerged from whatever dive you'd ended the night at. It was a crazy time.

During the day, my life didn't reflect any big new status, although I'd moved into a better apartment with my girlfriend, Diane, on West Twenty-Second Street in Chelsea. There wasn't much money, and my lifestyle was the same. But at night, I could really feel it, the edge of big success, being acknowledged wherever I went. It's like in the song, if you can make it there, you'll make it anywhere.

On the business side, Peter was working to get us out from under the Private Stock deal. We didn't hate Private Stock—we wouldn't be here without them—but they weren't ambitious, and the relationship with them was sometimes fractious. During a photo call for the first album cover, Debbie arrived at the shoot wearing a sheer black blouse and no bra, so her breasts were exposed through the material. She was persuaded to keep that outfit for the shoot, with the promise that the photo would be cropped and wouldn't reveal anything. After the album was released, Private Stock got the original full photograph blown up and plastered them all over New York. Debbie was absolutely devastated. Peter rushed over to Private Stock in a fury and had it out with Larry Uttal, the label head. Larry was old school and didn't give a shit what the band or management thought. Peter wound up taking reams of posters and all the chromes from the photo shoot and stormed out.

When the dust settled, he went back to try for another meeting regarding promotion for *Plastic Letters*. Larry told him it was none of our business. That was the final straw. Peter was certain Private Stock didn't have the vision to take Blondie where he saw us going. Our break into the business had tied us to a deal that could take us only so far. Peter was positive that Blondie was an international band, and his belief in us made us see ourselves in that light too.

Ultimately, Peter found the money to buy us out, which, of course, we had to pay back—half a million dollars. It was an expensive lesson about signing production deals without proper representation. Toby Mamis had a conversation with the head of Capitol Records saying he thought Blondie could be as big as ABBA and got laughed out of the room. Peter approached other record companies, who all turned us down. Deciding he needed to get creative, Peter orchestrated an elaborate campaign to get the attention of Terry Ellis, the head of Chrysalis Records. Chris Stein is a great photographer and was always bringing Peter photos of the band and Debbie. Peter got Terry's home and office addresses, and for several days a week, he'd send an envelope containing one of Chris's Blondie photographs or a Blondie newspaper article, with no return address or note. He never attached his name. After a few weeks of this, the mystery envelopes piqued Terry's interest, and he looked Peter up. Soon after, he flew out to New York to see the band. He didn't tell us he was coming, just walked into CBGB with Peter, and after a handful of songs, the pair of them left and went to a hamburger joint to talk about Blondie.

There's a lot you could say about us leaving Private Stock for an international label like Chrysalis, but it really comes down to clout and vision. At the time, record companies were deep in a mid-1970s mindset, doubling down hard on metal and prog rock bands like Kansas and Styx. In spite of that, Terry Ellis at Chrysalis saw something in us. Before Chrysalis, Blondie had a small-time, strictly East and West Coasts worldview. Before Blondie, Chrysalis had built its success on Jethro Tull. Terry saw us, and he saw Debbie—this amazing, iconic frontwoman—and knew we had the potential to explode on a global stage.

To get the deal finalized, we found ourselves locked in an attorney's office on Fifty-Seventh Street, New York's music row. As we shuffled in, one of the Chrysalis lawyers told us no one was leaving until the deal was signed. There was the band, our attorney, Chrysalis and their legal team, and the representatives for Private Stock. The negotiations dragged way into the night, with hamburgers and cartons of Chinese food brought in at regular intervals, while the details were thrashed out. Meanwhile, we flew paper airplanes out the window. By nightfall, we were bouncing off the walls, pacing around, picking up the office phones to make long-distance calls just to cut through the boredom. Terry made a futile push for us to base ourselves out of Los Angeles. You couldn't get Chris and Debbie out of the Village, let alone persuade them to move away from New York entirely, so that idea went down in flames.

Finally, in the early-morning hours, a deal was struck. When we emerged from the office building at sunrise, I was twenty-two and about a quarter mil in the hole to Chrysalis Records. Even so, almost as soon as the ink was dry on that contract, you could feel the difference between a record label with global reach and one with the more modest ambitions we'd come to expect at Private Stock.

Of all the record labels, Chrysalis had the best artist development, promotion, and marketing in the business. On paper, they were independent, but they were a big organization. We celebrated the new deal with the "perk" of being VIPs at the

Jethro Tull concert at Madison Square Garden. As the label's new celebrated acquisition, we were invited to the post-show party at the posh Indian restaurant Nirvana, located on West Fifty-Ninth Street and Central Park South. I was taken with the surprise of exiting the elevator on the penthouse floor to this full-on Raja temple décor, ornate and opulent, with a view of Central Park. This was also my first time tasting the culinary art of Indian cooking.

It seemed like we'd gone from being CBGB's least likely candidates to succeed to being the most likely. Compared with the other CBGB bands, we were about to be on another level. No one in the Ramones or the Television camps had their eyes on the prizes the way Peter had. In fact, Peter didn't want Blondie identifying too closely with punk rock. He didn't want any categorization diluting our appeal. Peter put the kibosh on my attending the *Punk* magazine awards show where I was to be named "Punk Drummer of the Year." We were steered away from being on the bill of punk rock line-ups. He thought punk was becoming toxic in the mainstream and wanted commercial success. It was helpful in terms of the band's identity; without any strong identifiers, we were able to bring something else to the party, helping Blondie to shift between genres without any punk rock baggage. While other punk bands on major labels struggled to get their records played on the radio, we broke through.

For the kid who once gazed across the river from Bayonne wondering what it would be like to be a success in the city, it felt amazing. It felt like I was in a movie. If I could go back, the only thing I'd change about that time would be to tell myself it would end one day, because at the time, I thought it would last forever. Or at least until I retired at thirty.

Probably, I should have had a more objective view, but you can't help but look at the world subjectively when you're in your early twenties and someone hands you the keys to the city.

Chapter 18

FIRST WORLD TOUR

A world tour was the first phase in Chrysalis's plans for the band's ascent, largely due to Peter's vision to get us in front of a worldwide audience. We were booked on a six-month tour of the world: Europe, Japan, Thailand, and Australia. I'd spent my formative years plotting a similar path for myself, so I was happy to put in the work. With Frank and Nigel rounding off our new lineup, it was an opportunity to get serious and to really get the band tight. We started out a pretty good outfit, but when we returned from the tour, we were on the road to becoming one of the biggest bands in the world. It cemented our friendships, and the chemistry between us was there for all to see. With the new members, essentially, we were a new band, but with the advantage of a back catalog of two albums' worth of material. There were a lot of contributing factors, but we wouldn't have had our eventual success without the groundwork we put in on that world tour.

Over the course of those six months, we lost touch with a lot of people. Being on the other side of the world meant you were out of sight, out of mind. I know my girlfriend was bummed out I'd be gone so long and had to get by with occasional postcards and expensive long-distance calls. The world wasn't as interconnected as it is today, so it was difficult. I'd send an airmail letter telling her to be by a certain pay phone at a certain time on a certain date and hope the letter got through so I could make a free collect call—it was a scam because back then there was no way to trace the reverse charge. I was making the effort, but I really wasn't homesick—there was too much happening day to day. There were, of course, odd moments I felt a longing for my New York home. I used the pay phone strategy to call the CBGB phone booth just to hear what was happening in the city. Mainly, it felt like the world was opening every door for us, and I was thrilled to be there for all of them. One day, the Great Barrier Reef in Australia celebrating Christmas, the next, Bangkok. It was a phenomenal, unexpected circumstance. A true once-in-a-lifetime experience, and none of us had time to dwell on what we'd left behind. We were focused completely on creating our success.

Three weeks after the Whisky shows, we headed for Europe. There was a lot of work ahead of us, but optimism was high. We'd had a few rehearsals in Manhattan with Nigel on bass and Frank on guitar, and then—it seemed like minutes later—we were landing back in the UK for our own headline shows and our British TV debut. That's right, TV. On November 7, 1977, we appeared on Granada TV—the station that covers the northwest of England—on Tony Wilson's *What's On*.

As well as being a regional TV personality and news journalist, Wilson was the maverick Svengali behind Manchester's

Factory Records label—the home of Joy Division, New Order, Happy Mondays, and countless other bands in the post-punk era. We played "Rip Her to Shreds" and shared the bill with the Liverpool comedian Ken Dodd. Dodd was an old-time vaudevillian comic, basically a joke machine, who also enjoyed a run of schmaltzy easy-listening hits in the 1960s. I remember his hair more than his jokes. He looked like he'd fallen down an elevator shaft, unkempt hair all over the place, which was a bit punk, in a way. Someone wiped the tape of that performance, but there's a scratchy VHS transfer you can find online that shows the first signs of our new lineup starting to fall into place.

If we were worried England had forgotten us, we didn't have to wonder too long. We opened our UK tour at Barbarella's, the Birmingham club where all the punk and new wave bands earned their stripes. Tickets for the show had been oversold, the walls were dripping with sweat, and it was as if we'd never been away. I heard after the show that Robert Plant from Led Zeppelin had been trying to get in but couldn't get past the doorman. Sorry, Robert. Maybe call ahead next time?

The band immediately noticed the heft of Chrysalis's support because we didn't get a moment's pause. I was nearly breathless at how quickly things were moving. We played a handful of shows across England, ably supported by the psychedelic new wave band XTC, climaxing at London's prestigious Rainbow Theatre, before heading over to the continent for whistle-stop club dates in Paris and Munich, and then witnessing the drug culture firsthand at Paradiso, a converted church and legendary venue in Amsterdam. We stayed at Amsterdam's American Hotel, a place I've returned to many times and a noted stop for visiting musicians and people in the business. Amsterdam is a wonderful place to lose yourself. It's half sin city and half high art and culture.

Four days later after Amsterdam, we arrived in Australia. Australia isn't usually such a quick touchdown for an up-and-coming band, but synchronicity was at work and "In the Flesh" had been a number-two single and our debut album was in the top 20. Australia gave Blondie our first real chart success anywhere in the world. It was kind of an accident, and the circumstances were a little surreal. After recording the first LP, Peter Leeds funded a video shoot with our friend famed photographer Bob Gruen and Richard Robinson, editor of *Rock Scene* magazine and the husband of rock journalist Lisa Robinson. We recorded three primitive promo videos in one day: "X Offender," "In the Sun," and "In the Flesh." Officially, "X Offender" was intended as the record's A side, but according to legend, Molly Meldrum, the host of *Countdown*, Australia's weekly pop TV show, announced "X Offender," only to have someone in the control booth roll the tape for "In the Flesh." Presto, new unexpected hit single.

When we arrived to play our first show in Perth, the audience—and the Australian media—were expecting a straight pop band, performing this sweet ballad that was on the radio everywhere.

We hit all the big cities—Perth, Adelaide, Sydney, Brisbane, and Melbourne—and a bunch of smaller towns. We had backing from the record label, but our transportation wasn't luxurious. There were no Learjets or air-conditioned tour buses with all the bells and whistles. In fact, Ray had arranged for us to travel across the Australian Outback—along with

The style started early

My mother Antoinette

My father Clement Sr.

My first gig

Me and Diane

Early days at the Bowery loft, New York, 1976

New York City, 1976—we never took Raideen the Brave on the road

Helen Reddy is . . .

Two blokes on the bus

CBGB days

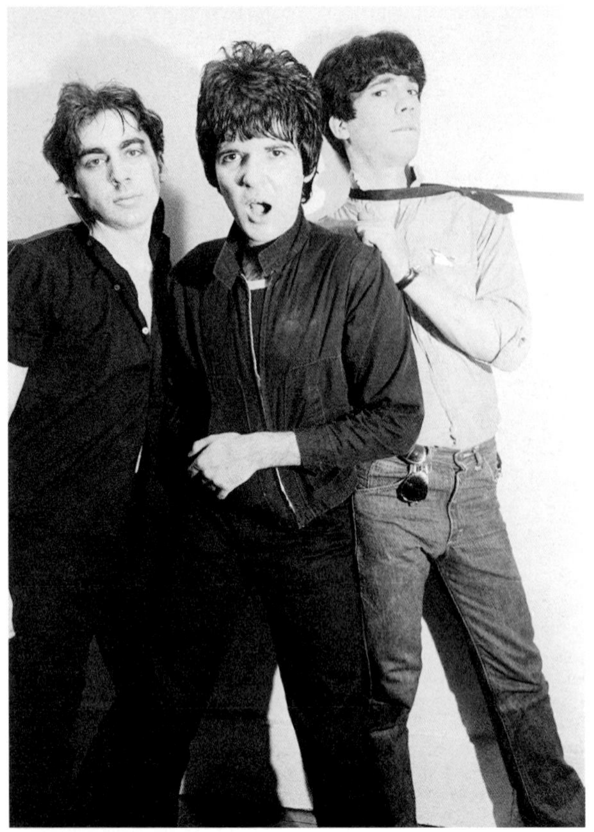

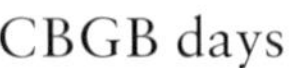

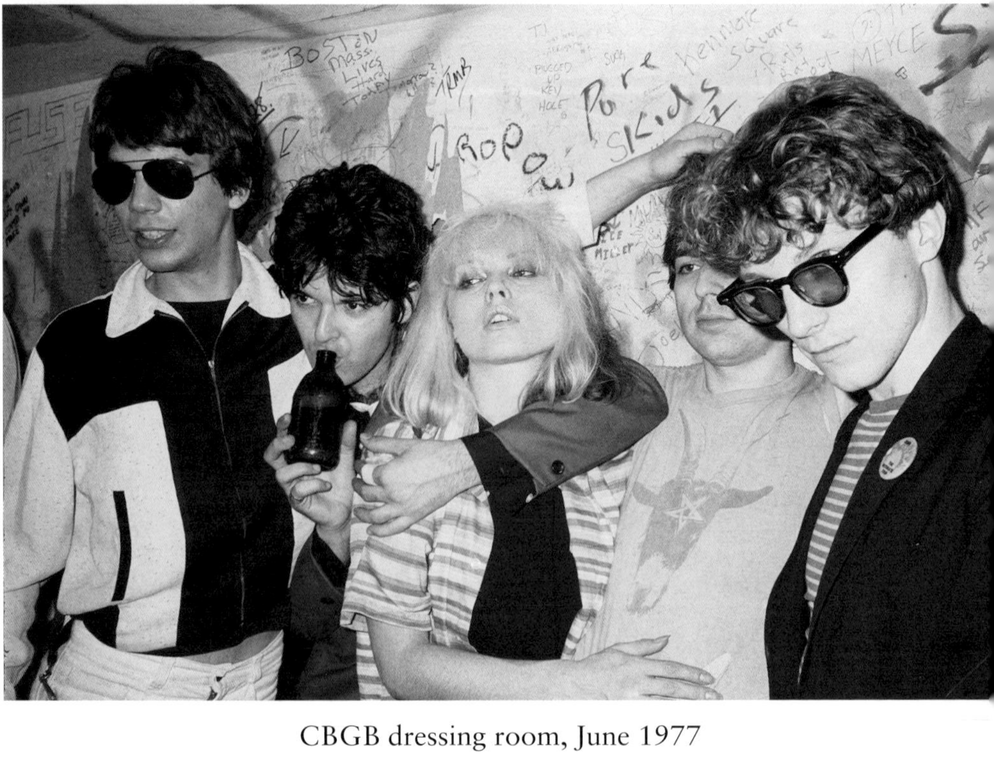

CBGB dressing room, June 1977

First time to Los Angeles, February 1977

On a Los Angeles wall sitting next to two CF-570s that we got in Tokyo in 1978

On the road

Holding a cardboard cutout of Debbie
at the *Making Tracks* book launch,1982

Hair is key

Enter Nigel and Frank

From stage to box

High from a show

On top of the kit

Poolside with the band at the Sunset Marquis

Boys in the band—Edo Bertoglio's *Parallel Lines* cover shoot

our support band, the Ferrets—in an old school bus. If you've seen the film *The Adventures of Priscilla, Queen of the Desert*—it was a bit like that. We'd stop off somewhere in the back of beyond, and Blondie and the Ferrets would kick a football around for an hour or so. It was a strange combination. The Ferrets were more of a straightforward rock group—we weren't a good match musically.

We worked our asses off, playing something like twenty shows on the mainland. The shows were promoted by Michael Gudinski, Australia's answer to Bill Graham in the US. Michael would go on to establish Mushroom Records. The hard work laid a strong foundation with our Australian audience that continues to this day. Debbie got sick at the end of the tour, attributed to some bad cherries—well documented in the press. We had to cancel our final show at Her Majesty's Theatre in Brisbane, causing riotous scenes with angry fans breaking the windows of the venue. It was like Blondie-mania, and even though I was caught up in the excitement, it also felt matter-of-fact, like everything was going to plan. I was getting to where I was always meant to be going.

Following the mainland shows, we packed our gear onto a barge and set sail for Great Keppel Island, off the Great Barrier Reef. Our agent Michael had booked us to play a holiday resort for three shows over Christmas, alongside some well-deserved rest and relaxation between shows. The holiday camp was no-frills, the most basic accommodations. Stepping outside the cottage, though, I found myself in paradise, and we all went wild for a few days over the holidays. Between shows, we snorkeled in the Pacific, started campfires, and caused more than a little dismay among the other guests. Maybe a bunch of urban New York rockers weren't the best suited to island living, but we were giving it our best shot. Keith Crabtree, our fair-skinned, redheaded roadie, turned as red as a beet in the searing sun.

Then came the day of the Great Keppel Island Shipwreck. We were all hanging out on the beach, when Chris pulled up in a tiny dinghy with an outboard motor. Frank and I jumped in back, and we headed out to sea. Chris steered us past the reefs, and before I knew it, we were adrift on the high seas: two guitarists and a drummer, floating in this endless expanse, with no idea how to get back to land. The ocean had its own ideas about where it wanted to take us, and the tides kept pushing and pulling our dinghy until we were stranded on the edge of a reef, stuck banging against the coral. I had a lot of plans about how I was going to make it. I'd been strategizing half my life, but there's nothing in the playbook telling you what to do when you get shipwrecked in the Pacific Ocean in your bathing suit.

We wound up having to abandon the boat and walk the top of the reef in our bare feet until we reached a remote and deserted part of the island. We had no idea how we were going to get back. The rest of the band and crew had finally figured out we were in trouble and sent a rescue boat for us. When it came into sight, we'd been gone for hours. Frank and I, lobster red from sunburn, climbed aboard, but Chris was told to stay on the dinghy, tied to the back of the boat. The captain seemed like a man of few words, but he did offer one insight to Frank and me as he steered us back to the resort. "There's nothing worse," he said, "than cunts at sea." We landed to the cheers and welcomes of the others, except for Debbie, who was sobbing tears of relief.

I rang in the New Year in Thailand, starting December 29, with a run of four shows in Bangkok over ten days. We played two sets on New Year's Eve at the Ambassador Hotel, literally half a world away from Central Park, where we'd seen in the last New Year. After the tranquility of Great Keppel Island, you could sense immediately there was something in the air. We asked the local promoter why the mood was so celebratory. He explained that the curfew that had been in place since the Vietnam War was coming to an end at the stroke of midnight, and Bangkok was set to become a twenty-four-hour city once again. Consequently, the nights were crazy. We weren't playing for the local Thai audience so much as for the international jet-set crowd, and the setting couldn't have been more appropriate.

The hotel was like something out of a James Bond movie. Relaxing by the pool one afternoon, world renowned pedophile Gary Glitter, accompanied by several young Thai girls, came over to say hi and tell us how much he loved Bangkok. At night, everyone was dressed to the nines with half a mind on getting to a casino. They weren't our people, but we met some cool tour friends anyway. During our downtime, we visited the city and found a tailor who made us all bespoke suits for pennies on the dollar. We all picked up a couple of custom pairs of trousers with zippers all over.

One night, we met up with an Australian who introduced us to a couple of local customs. He brought us a few Thai sticks: hash oil or resin on a bamboo skewer layered with cannabis leaves to form a sort of marijuana cigar. On our final night in Bangkok, he invited us to his house for dinner. It was a weird scene. He had a coterie of Thai women at his side all night, rolling neat, potent joints and handing them around the table between courses. We didn't really need them because every course he served us contained marijuana. At the end of the night, we were so wasted, we were all face down in our soup, unable to move or speak. I still don't know how we got back to the hotel.

Bangkok left us red-eyed and nursing sore heads for our arrival in Japan on the fifth of January, ready to embark on our biggest year to date: 1978. This was like landing on another planet, a wild collision of old and new. Flashy neon signs, quiet temples off the beaten path but just steps away from millions of people rushing about their everyday lives. We were taken out to dinner every night and treated with kindness and generosity everywhere we went. Japanese fans surrounded us, bowing their heads and shyly offering gifts to Debbie and the band. I did tons of shopping, but that was a given wherever I went in the world. Checking out clothing stores and shoe stores was a top priority whenever we visited someplace new. I quickly learned a men's size medium in Japan is not the same as it was back home.

The audiences were more reserved than we'd been used to, but in their unique way, very attentive and saving their enthusiasm for the end with applause and multiple encores. Musically, Blondie had transcended being a punk band, but we had kept the attitude, and it made us interesting to the Japanese audiences. Coming from New York was a cool calling card for us, because everyone in Japan found NYC fascinating. After the break of Great Keppel Island and our stay at the luxurious Ambassador Hotel in Bangkok, I felt newly energized. It felt like a given we'd win over the Japan crowds, with six sold-out shows at the outset. We crisscrossed the country on bullet trains, visiting Tokyo, Osaka, and

Nagoya, performing at a series of grand Japanese theaters that normally hosted the great opera and ballet companies of the world. It was a great time, and the perfect repose before returning to England and the notorious Battle of Dingwalls.

Chapter 19

DINGWALLS

Leaving the neon of Tokyo sparkling in the rearview mirror, we landed into a much less colorful, drab, gray London for a Blondie showcase at Dingwalls, a club in Camden. The place only had a capacity of five hundred people, so it wasn't Wembley, but the show was a big deal. A showcase is a one-off gig, usually arranged by a record company, with press and media invited along to help raise an artist's profile. There would be a full tour of the UK to follow, but the idea was to generate a little hysteria out there and to launch the band into the nation's consciousness. Copies of *Plastic Letters* were being sent out with the album and accompanying single "Denis," arriving in stores in just a couple of weeks.

It was all sorts of cold and miserable. For those of us who braved the New York winters though, it should have been a cakewalk. The Dingwalls showcase was a sellout. Our following was growing from the Television tour, so I had high expectations it was going to be a great show. Before the show, Chris complained he felt sick and feverish. Some killer Japanese strain of flu, maybe, and he didn't think he was going to make it. Given that most of the UK's press were in attendance, he was persuaded to soldier on. The show must go on, right? How hard could it be? Well, pretty hard, as it turned out. The band sound-checked without Chris, while he was at the hotel getting a B-12 shot. In the meantime, while we're waiting for him to show up, the venue is steadily filling up. We started receiving guests and well-wishers backstage and doing interviews on the fly. Most of the day we'd been caught up in a storm of activity, doing various press and radio, lining up for photographs. It was a glimpse into our future: everyone wanting a piece of Debbie and the band. Aside from Chris being sick, the mood was good.

Some faces from our trip before came by and despite the English cold we were getting a warm welcome. Alan Edwards knocked on our dressing room door and asked to represent us with the UK press. He was quite charming, and based on that optimistic approach, he was given the shot to become our UK publicist. I think Debbie was taken with Alan. He looked like a young David Essex, the British pop singer. His tenacity served him well, and he must have done a good job, because he's still our publicist to this day. Meanwhile, the B-12 shot kicked in and Chris was back on his feet. We just had to make it through the next hour.

When we hit the stage, we were met with an anxious crowd awaiting our show. It was crazy loud, a lot of feedback, but we sounded tight. After the more reserved audiences in Japan, the British fans seemed extra wild. I put my head down and drove the pace to keep the energy level high. One song would end, catch a breath, and then 1-2-3-4 straight into the next number. It was pissing off Chris, who was barely standing, leaning against the wall or his amp for support. Seeing the crowd's reaction, I was having too much fun to care. I might've looked up once or twice and saw he was getting riled up, but I'd just count the band into the next song. As it turned out, Chris had a temperature of 104 degrees, but in that moment, I wasn't buying that he had the flu. Whatever the case, he was furious with me. At one point, he was tuning up, but I didn't notice and just kept driving the set, all cylinders firing—and then it happened. Chris lunged at me with his guitar and the showcase descended into chaos. I thrashed my kit and knocked Jimmy out of the way trying to get at Chris. Once I caught up to him, Chris and I started going at each other. Debbie made a kind of "Uh, so goodnight then" statement. The show was over.

The houselights went up and the fight tumbled out of the side door of Dingwalls and onto the courtyard behind Camden Market. The brawl continued, and Debbie was screaming at me to stop. Actually, she did more than stand by her man, she started kicking the living shit out of me. Dennis Sheehan, our tour manager, scraped me off the damp cobblestones and put me in a car back to the group's hotel. Despite the adrenaline and still being pissed off, I went to sleep. The next thing I knew, I got a call from Dennis for the lobby call and airport ride. Back to business as usual. Dennis went on to be U2's longtime tour manager and confidant. Every time we crossed paths, he'd say with a smirk, "How are you and Chris doing?" Nowadays, when I'm asked about the fallout from Dingwalls, my usual reply is "Ah, the good old days."

We had a flight to Amsterdam for some big TV spots, and another couple of sold-out shows at Paradiso, where Blondie-mania was full on. When our car pulled up to the venue, we were surrounded by a mob of maniac fans; it was like something out of *A Hard Day's Night*. This became more and more common as the tour swept across Europe, playing every cool capital city club venue. All the while, we're hearing from the record company that the single is on the radio in Britain and across Europe and we have our first hit. Peter Leeds had to carve out time for us to go back to London to appear on *Top of the Pops*. So much for having a day off.

The single was "Denis," a cover of Randy and the Rainbows' "Denise," dropping the second *e* and switching the gender to "Denis," and that song became our breakthrough hit in Europe. The original was more doo-wop, but I like how our version sounds like the Bay City Rollers. It captures that Phil Spector Wall of Sound type of thing that Richard was so good at. It's immediate, catchy, innocent power pop. In the UK, "Denis" sold a lot of records and peaked at number two on the charts. In one of those "dreams fulfilled" moments, we found ourselves all over the radio and appearing on TV in front of millions of British viewers.

Britain was so different from the US. For a start, there were only three television channels, BBC1, BBC2, and ITV, so being broadcast on a national show meant you were guaranteed an audience of millions. Getting *Top of the Pops*, which had more than ten million viewers, was huge for us, but you didn't just hit the stage and play your song. We had to mime to a backing track, but because England was this weird Orwellian nightmare of regulations, with hundreds of years' worth of arcane rules, you couldn't just lip sync to the record that was in stores. In the 1970s, it was the policy of the British Musicians' Union that any song performed on the show had to be re-recorded in advance. To be fair, no one really did it, but you had to appear to go through the motions so someone could check a box on a form.

On the day before we appeared on *Top of the Pops*, we were taken to AIR Studios in Oxford Circus, and the chap from the Musicians' Union was sitting in the control room. As crazy as it may sound, we simply pretended to record the song by using a copy of the master recording on the tape machine. Sequestered behind a gobo, a movable acoustic panel, we were handclapping and foot stomping along with the track. The engineer stopped us: "This is all out of time. Can we try that again?" Since it was all miming and pretend, it was pretty funny because what would have been out of time was already recorded and on the master.

At some point, one of the record company people took the union guy to a nearby pub, and when he returned, we just told him the remake was finished so he'd sign off on it. In the end, it didn't matter what version we mimed to, because on February 11, 1978, we appeared on the show and, in the UK at least, everything changed for us. That show let the rest of the country in on the secret, and we took our first steps into the mainstream. I'm often reminded by longtime UK fans that their first life-changing encounter with Blondie was seeing us beamed into their TV sets. Hearing that means a lot to me because I always noticed how many viewers reported having their minds blown after seeing David Bowie performing "Starman" in his first *Top of the Pops* appearance. To think that I was in a band that had a similar effect on people is incredible.

Three months later, "(I'm Always Touched by Your) Presence, Dear" would follow "Denis" into the top ten. We were back on *Top of the Pops*, and from that moment on we were an established band in the UK. *Plastic Letters* went into the top ten and was awarded a platinum disc. We were still chipping away at the US market, but in the UK, Blondie had landed in style. We moved up from the club circuit to the university and college shows, without catching a breath, a dozen shows, culminating in a prestigious headline show at London's iconic Roundhouse that felt like a homecoming to us.

They say timing is everything, but our arrival on British shores couldn't have been orchestrated better. The punk and new wave scene was breaking across the nation in the aftermath of the Sex Pistols and the Clash. At the start of 1978, we were aligned with that scene, but our music and commercial success set us somewhat apart. We were on *Top of the Pops* with Abba and these established mega-selling artists, and the people in the UK just accepted us immediately. I often felt the English public was looking for its next Marc Bolan or David Bowie, and Debbie, with her combination of glamour and the streets, was the one who fit the bill.

In terms of awards, I don't have much stuff on display, but my set of UK Gold and Silver discs for our run of 45s holds a place of pride in my home. Not to detract from people's success today, but in the days before streaming, where every song is a swipe away, each of our records was a hit because of someone hearing it on the radio, walking into a shop, handing over some cash, and buying the record. I never took it for granted, and this is something I still cherish in the UK. I love how we've endured in that country. It's not an easy thing to permeate another culture like that. Today, we can still play vast arenas or outdoor shows and it's standing room only. Even with one of the biggest-selling albums of the era and four number one singles in our canon, we really don't have that kind of success in the States. I see us as having more of a cult status in the US. In the UK, though, Blondie's place in the pop firmament looks like it's a forever deal. And I can live with that.

Chapter 20

PARALLEL LINES

In the run-up to recording our third album, Diane and I moved to an apartment in Chelsea on West Twenty-Second Street. The place was a little more upmarket, but I wasn't exactly living like a king. I had a little money coming in from Blondie, and we had a few accounts set up in a few stores around the city, so we had a new TV and a new stereo system. Still, it was more a place for sleeping than anything else, like a slightly more upscale crash pad. Most of my resources were focused on conserving enough energy to make it through the night, to roll in after dawn, and to start the process again the next day. When Blondie wasn't on the road, I was meeting up with friends and going to gigs. The biggest chunk of my day was still the nighttime. When I did see daylight, I'd wake up late, make a coffee, smoke a cigarette, put on a record—all my old favorites, the Beatles, the Stones, and the bubblegum pop 45s I loved, had been joined by all the new British punk records—and I'd kill a few hours, maybe do nothing for a while before heading up to the studio.

It goes without saying that Chelsea in 1978 isn't the place it is today—with all the art galleries and coffee shops—but maybe the contrast isn't as stark as it is with some places. I'd moved up in the world, but only incrementally, I suppose. Compared with the Bowery, it was a nice neighborhood. It was still New York, of course, and it was still the 1970s, but there wasn't that same sense of danger in the air. The back of our apartment looked out on the back of the Chelsea Hotel. We were living there around the time of Nancy Spungen's murder, but wherever you were in the city, looking out the window and seeing a bunch of NYPD detectives standing around a crime scene wasn't so uncommon. It wasn't as tough as the Lower East Side, more of a mixed, semi-gentrified neighborhood, but just as vibrant. A blend of tenements, apartment blocks, city housing projects, townhouses, and row houses, with a diverse population.

From my apartment, I could walk down to the West Village, a straight shot down Seventh Avenue, maybe duck into a restaurant and grab a bite to eat before heading uptown to the Record Plant. I'd spent a lot of my youth wanting to be living in Manhattan, and I'd become so used to New York City living, I hardly ever left the island. The band was on an upward curve, the toast of New York, and I was optimistic about the new record. In the context of the band, Frank and Nigel were initially outsiders, but from my perspective, I had another two friends I could relate to and hang out with, along with Jimmy, when Debbie and Chris retired to their shared universe. The four of us would head out into the night to do our own thing, and we developed a genuine bond.

Before we settled on New York, there was some back and forth between the band and Chrysalis about where we'd record. Mike Chapman, our new producer, wanted us to relocate to the West Coast, but that idea was never going to fly. We'd spent a lot of time on the road and were adamant we wanted to work in NYC for a while. Mike wasn't happy. He was comfortably settled in Beverly Hills—essentially the antithesis of the Bowery—equally not wanting to switch coasts, but eventually he was persuaded to relocate and start work on the new album in June 1978. Mike grew to love the city. We got down to preproduction, followed by recording sessions at the Record Plant on West Forty-Fourth Street, where the New York Dolls recorded their first record. After the sessions, Mike and I, along with Jimmy, Frank, and Nigel, spent a lot of evenings together in the restaurants and bars around the West Forties and the Theater District. One of our favorite haunts was Cafe Un Deux Trois at 123 West Forty-Fourth Street. Mike was a real fish out of the water at first. He referred to women as "sheilas" and had all this weird Australian vernacular and these tough guy mannerisms. It wasn't until a few years later, when the movie came out, that I realized Mike was basically Crocodile Dundee.

In contrast to working with Richard, where the focus was on the two or three strongest numbers, Mike wanted every song to be a hit. He didn't want to make a punk or a new wave album. He didn't want to be limited by those labels. He approached everything from the standpoint of wanting to have success. That was his mandate: to make the perfect pop album. The idea of us having a massive hit record seemed like it was beyond our reach at the time, but we grew to believe in Mike's vision. We wanted our songs played on the radio. The new batch of songs were strong, like crazy strong. There was a bunch of originals and a couple of covers, including "Hanging on the Telephone," originally recorded by the Nerves and written by their frontman, Jack Lee. Jack even came down to the rehearsal studio and pitched and sold us on another song of his, "Will Anything Happen." The Nerves never managed to make it, but *Parallel Lines'* success meant Jack did OK.

As for Mike, his reputation preceded him, and I had an instinct he was going to be a good fit. He was proactive, always coming down onto the studio floor to get his point across. Prior to Jimmy being called in to overdub his keyboards, the basic tracks were always recorded by me, Frank, and Nigel, usually with Mike acting as our conductor. We always worked from the ground up. My drums were the foundation, my little Ringo Starr riffs and Hal Blaine homages thrown in, leading the arrangement. Once we were satisfied with the drums, Frank and Nigel would lay down their tracks. I don't think the record would've been the success it was without Frank and Nigel in the fold. Nigel's song "One Way or Another" was developed from a jam session he, Frank, and I had with Robert Fripp, from King Crimson. It happened spontaneously, while we were waiting for the other members of the band to show up. We'd met Robert at the Johnny Blitz benefit, and he joined us on stage for our Palladium show in May, when we played a cover of Donna Summer's "I Feel Love." It was a groundbreaking moment for us. We were all admirers of his work on Bowie's *Low* album. It was incongruous and cool that Robert Fripp made time to play with a new wave band. It was one of those curveballs we liked to throw, and I think it really characterizes Blondie's out-of-the-box thinking.

Unlike our recordings with Richard, which were usually live takes, Mike was the master of the edit. Often, we'd finish a take and he'd tell us, "Yeah, that was great. Now do it again, only better." He understood arrangements perfectly and would hear something in one take, something in another and look to combine the best elements of the two. He had such a keen ear and could make the edit in his head. This was still the predigital age, so there was no dragging a section of a recording across a screen and dropping it into place on the track in two seconds flat. Editing was far more laborious. Mike would take a razor blade to the tapes and assemble the finished track by hand. I found the process endlessly fascinating.

When it came to recording "Heart of Glass"—a song that had been in our set for a couple of years and had gone through various permutations, we were faced with a few challenges. Today, you'd use a midi-interface to link the synthesizer with a drum machine. I recorded the bass drum piecemeal, a classic disco quarter-note kick drum pattern, four on the floor, playing along to an arpeggiated synthesizer track to create a custom click track. I recorded the rest of my drum part over the top of that. Mike built the rest of the instrumentation to the drums. It's all stuff that can be done with the flick of a switch today, but at the time, you had to come up with these creative methods, and Mike was a master. In terms of attitude, he disparaged our musicianship a little and got very demanding. "You're going to make a great record," he said. "And that means you're going to start playing better." Personally, I didn't take offense. Not to that, at least. Of course, Mike was quite egomaniacal and prone to exaggeration, but he might have had a point in some respects. We could have been better, and we needed a hard taskmaster sometimes. I appreciated that the record would be better for it. He didn't pull any punches with us.

There was some friction between Debbie and Mike during the vocal recording. She didn't like being coached—she had a unique style that had worked just fine for two records and more than a couple of hits. He also bumped heads with Chris, who spent a lot of time working in isolation to get his guitar parts just right. The fact was, Mike wanted us to make a great album, and I was completely on board. Mike has since gone on record saying the band members hated one another, but he's wrong—that wasn't the case on *Parallel Lines*. There were times later, and we'll come to that, but these times were good for the band; we were more unified than we'd ever been.

In the years following, Mike has said a few negative things about me and my playing. He said I had all the right ideas but felt I was trying too hard. I mean, that might be true. I was prepared to work. On *Parallel Lines* and all the subsequent sessions with Mike, I tried to give everything to the recordings, so I don't see that as a detriment. Whatever anyone thinks or says, there's no getting away from the success we had working together. We made a great record.

Chapter 21

HERE COMES SUCCESS

At the time of writing, *Parallel Lines* has just been selected for inclusion in the National Recording Registry at the Library of Congress. The registry is a list of sound recordings deemed "culturally, historically, or aesthetically significant" and is quite an honor. Commercially speaking, *Parallel Lines* is Blondie's crowning glory, but it would take a while for us to get there in the States. Unlike the UK, where the album soared to the top of the charts almost instantaneously, in the US, the album took a long time to take off.

There's a distinction in perception between people in the UK and in the US regarding our rise to fame, because in England our success was almost immediate. A lot of our UK success was driven by our access to television. In 1978 we scored a couple of early hits and appeared on *Top of the Pops* a few times, and everyone in England just assumed we were huge stars back home. They were ahead of the curve, because US fame would take a while longer for us to achieve. For much of 1978, it was like we had two separate careers on the burner at the same time: one in the US, where we were mainly

169

known on the coasts, and one in the UK and Europe, where we were fast becoming ubiquitous. I think the people at Chrysalis in the UK had a better handle on what would make a hit record. When *Parallel Lines* came out in the US, it was more of a slow burn. The American public didn't know what to make of us. Apparently, neither did the record company in Los Angeles, because they went with a curious choice of single to head up the campaign: the Buddy Holly cover "I'm Gonna Love You Too." It wasn't a hit, and consequently, our progress was stalled.

Meanwhile, the UK label released "Picture This," which went top 20 after being launched on *Top of the Pops*. For that appearance, I had ordered a suit from this guy Colin Wild, who had a shop called Carnaby Cavern. Colin was well known; he'd made clothes for Marc Bolan and all these people, so I commissioned a red suit. I thought it was going to be ready the day before, but it wasn't, so after the first rehearsal, I snuck out and took a cab to go pick it up. The thing is, you're not supposed to leave the studio. It was something like when Ringo goes missing in *A Hard Day's Night* because apparently, back at the studio, the *Top of the Pops* people were panicking. I was still being measured and having last-minute fittings, but it was getting late, and I had to get back to the BBC. Finally, it was done and I put the suit on and went back, where they were getting ready to have Rick Buckler from the Jam take my place and mime the song. The show went on, but a bit later, I was in the cafeteria and Paul Weller was there and said, "It wasn't worth it, mate"—I guess causing all that confusion. I was eating a sandwich and burped, and this cafeteria lady said, "Who's the pig in the red suit?" For a while, I was known thereafter as the pig in the red suit.

After "Picture This," we returned to the top 5 with "Hanging on the Telephone." Those singles sent the album to the top of the charts. The promotion in the US didn't get off the ground until January, when we released the third single, "Heart of Glass," practically four months after the album hit stores. There was a lot of negativity from new wave purists about disco, a kneejerk reaction to the success of the Bee Gees and other artists that would lead to the whole "Disco Sucks" sideshow later in 1979. We came at it from our own angle. The rise of punk in New York ran parallel to the disco scene, and we were caught up in both. The early days of disco provided the backdrop to the Club 82 era, so working in that genre didn't feel like we were betraying our roots at all.

In the meantime, we toured, and we toured. Leading up to the album's release, we hit the road with the Kinks on their US tour. Ray Davies and company were one of my favorite bands. It was a dream come true for me to be in their orbit for a few weeks. I'd faithfully watch them every night from the sidelines and enjoyed hanging out with them. They were a wild bunch. There was only one rule you couldn't break: no one touches Ray's bottle of Moët champagne. One night, we were all in the dressing room, and Ray was checking the rider and noticed his champagne was missing. "Who's been in my dressing room?" he demanded. Everyone in the room looked to me, the only non-Kink. I pleaded my innocence, but to no avail. I felt the wrath of Ray and was ejected from the Kinks' inner sanctum. Eventually, all was forgiven, but the bottle—which I didn't take, honest—never turned up.

Tom Petty and the Heartbreakers joined the tour for one night in Atlanta. There was some animosity between the

Kinks and Petty—some issue with their respective managers—which made for an uncomfortable few hours as they bickered over soundcheck times. All that pent-up aggression came out onstage, so ironically, it was one of the best nights of the tour. There followed a wild after-show party at the Kinks' hotel. Kinks bassist Jim Rodford was explaining how Dave Davies slashed the speaker cones of his amplifier to get that nasty sound on "You Really Got Me" as a hotel lamp flew past my head. Jim and I looked across the room to see Dave and Mick Avory wrestling each other to the ground before falling into the bathroom tub to continue fighting. I thought I was the punk rocker in the room, but those guys made me look tame.

With the Kinks tour at an end, Jonny Podell, our booking agent, lined up a New Year's Eve show for us at the Oakland Coliseum. I guess a polite way to describe some of Jonny's career choices for Blondie would be "wacky." Also, wacky is a polite way for me to describe Jonny himself. So, that New Year's Eve we found ourselves supporting the rock band Journey. Mostly it was a Journey crowd, although I remember a banner being held up in the crowd bearing the legend "Blondie Is a Group," so thanks, whoever did that.

Parallel Lines hadn't crossed over—"Heart of Glass" had yet to be released. After everything we'd gone through, shifting labels, replacing Richard with Mike Chapman, and touring the world, the weird Journey show made me feel frustrated, like we'd been passed over in the US. After the concert, I went to a party at the Jefferson Starship house. I don't know how I wound up in that crowd, but it was New Year's Eve and I had a lot of excess adrenaline to burn off. John Belushi was there, the life of the party, generally acting like his Bluto character from *Animal House*, putting on a show for the crowd of guests: the distinguished members of Jefferson Starship and several Grateful Dead guys and their entourages. Meanwhile, I was in a corner with Toby, pressing him as to why we were being asked to play with a band like Journey. As I made the point, I realized Neal Schon, Journey's guitarist, was standing behind me the whole time, shooting me daggers. Belushi, who was passing us in the corridor, broke the tension by biting into a beer can and tearing it open with his teeth.

These incongruous support slots were happening a lot; for example, we soon found ourselves opening for Rush at Philadelphia's Spectrum Arena. I guess the thinking was to just get Blondie in front of enough people and they'll cut through somehow. As if it couldn't get more incompatible, we ended up playing to precisely the wrong crowd opening for REO Speedwagon at the Winterland Ballroom in San Francisco. Also on the bill was our friend from the San Francisco days, Jonathan Postal and his band the Readymades. It seemed insane for us to be opening for REO Speedwagon, an AOR band. However, the show was promoted by industry legend Bill Graham, so it was made clear it was a big deal, regardless of my opinion. Back in my teenage days, my friends and I would go to the Fillmore East because Bill was known for putting on these esoteric bills, with eclectic, left-field bands or artists, so maybe he saw Blondie and the Readymades opening for REO Speedwagon in the same way he saw a lineup of Miles Davis and Procol Harum. I don't know. I just thought it was a bad fit for us. We were coming up, and they were an established band with a string of hit records behind them.

We didn't get media training in those days, none of us were housebroken. As far as I was concerned, there was a line drawn in the sand between us and the bands of the old guard, so when I was asked about the upcoming show on KSAN radio, I looked across the studio at the host and said, "We don't like REO Speedwagon at all. I hope everyone walks out after we finish our set." At the exact moment I was making my proclamation over the airwaves, REO Speedwagon were setting off in their limo for the venue. The radio, obviously, was tuned to KSAN, and they heard the whole thing. By the time we arrived at Winterland, the band and their management were up in arms. When Bill Graham caught up with me, he was red with rage. Bill was a real trailblazer in the business and had a reputation as a tough guy. If you were Bill Graham, you needed to be tough. His Fillmore venue was in a bad neighborhood. I doubt it would've survived if he hadn't had a tough streak. He was quite menacing. Veiled threats and the like. It wasn't quite "You'll never work in this town again," but he came close. He was up in my face, hollering, "There's no way you're getting an encore." I didn't have any regrets. We may not have got an encore, but we still got to play, and the crowd loved us. Fast forward to 2007, and there we were, once again opening for REO Speedwagon, this time at the NFL party the night before the Superbowl. Thirty years older and wiser, we realized we had more in common than we'd ever thought.

We started to see signs that things were moving along for the record. There were a lot of radio and press interviews, but in the pre-internet age, appearing on TV was the only surefire way into the world's hearts. I was watching with my parents when the Beatles appeared on Ed Sullivan and could physically feel the impact it had on me. I always knew that if I was going to achieve anything, television was going be a part of it. To put this into context, today's stars can announce a new record to fifty million social media followers on Thursday and be number one on Friday. In the 1970s, the music industry landscape was still only half formed. You recorded a record, someone put it out, and then you toured your ass off, territory by territory, and hoped the record connected with a big enough audience for you to do the same thing all over again.

A lot of credit goes to the record company for their perseverance, but also to Toby Mamis and Peter Leeds. Peter always said one of his greatest achievements was to work us like dogs in those early couple of years. I can see what he meant. That cycle of relentless hard work reached its apex during the promotion for *Parallel Lines*. The album wasn't a hit in the US yet, but by increments, it was building. Debbie's face was looking back at us from the newsstands, and radio was finally picking up on our records. The live touring didn't take a back seat, but there was a shift in perspective and focus to getting us on television.

In January 1979, we were asked to appear on Don Kirshner's *Midnight Special*. This was a coast-to-coast live musical variety show broadcast from Los Angeles. Don was the man who developed the TV show *The Monkees*. The *Midnight Special* producers, like a lot of the old guard, hadn't caught up with the new music yet. They weren't booking the Ramones or Television and British punk music barely made it to US television at all. Usually, these shows had no idea how to present us, but as I always suspected, point a camera in the general direction of Debbie, and you'll probably be okay. Still, there were always weird moments, like Kirshner's deadpan introductions and the incongruous cutaways to the audience disco dancing while we're playing "Dreaming" or "Hanging on the Telephone." It was a curious blend of us being slightly out of place but also in exactly the right place at the right time. And the right place was everywhere.

In the same way I felt about playing live or recording, I took to TV. I was never nervous, never anxious. Just excited.

My generation had grown up with television, and I was mindful that every performance could be another step navigating Blondie into the mainstream. Walking into a TV studio and knowing you're about to be transmitted direct into the nation's living rooms, suddenly it felt like we'd come a long way from playing the Bowery at 2 a.m. Those crowds at CBGB were a home crowd—friends and associates and faces from the New York scene—so finding our way into these strangers' homes seemed like an act of subversion almost. We still had the same street-tough New York attitude and the music press took us seriously as musicians, but now we were part of, for lack of a better term, showbiz, and we got to straddle both worlds in a way few of our contemporaries managed to do. Being in a band wasn't a nocturnal thing anymore. We were Blondie 24/7, and I had no problem with that. If we had an LA show, inevitably we'd lose a day off to a TV show or two, but it meant more people were getting to see and hear us.

More television, more success: in April 1979, we took the train to Philadelphia to prerecord our second appearance on *The Mike Douglas Show*. During the interview, Mike mentioned we'd cleaned up our act a little bit since our first appearance. By then, the album was riding high. Usually, unless we were in the UK or Europe appearing on *Top of the Pops* or some Euro chart TV show, we performed live on TV, but we'd mimed an appearance on *American Bandstand*. It's something we all did as kids, miming to your favorite records and imagining yourself onstage. I never had a problem with lip-syncing. When we first played to a backing track, the playbacks were very low, but once we got the audio tech to crank up the sound, it became easy to fake it. Another bonus of lip-syncing is knowing that the performance is going to sound good—there's no pressure; we could have some fun fooling around. Sometimes, the ending could be a little awkward if the recording had a fade on it. Wherever you were in the world, be it *Top Pop* in Holland or *Top of the Pops* in England, we got to meet a lot of other artists on the shows. That's where I became friends in 1978 with Ian Dury and the Blockheads and the Boomtown Rats. TV broke the band and by the spring of 1979, "Heart of Glass" had made its way to the top of the *Billboard* charts, and Blondie was a cultural phenomenon.

In the wake of "Heart of Glass," Middle America had woken up to us and the *Parallel Lines* Tour was an overwhelming success. Our support band was Nick Lowe and Dave Edmunds's Rockpile—go figure, let's put someone on before us that could blow us off the stage on any given night. They were the greatest musicians and the most fun to tour with. Hanging out with Dave and Nick and the guys from Rockpile was a complete joy. Watching them every night was beyond inspiring, playing rock and roll with such intensity. One day off in Florida, Blondie and Rockpile chartered a boat, got drunk, and hit the open seas. I dove in the water and got stung by a bunch of jellyfish, which everybody except me thought was hilarious.

Jake Riviera, who became a good friend of mine, was Rockpile's manager. I always found Jake to be good company—he helped me secure my first-ever drum endorsement deal with Premier Drums—but sometimes, he could be just as prickly as those jellyfish stingers if you got on his wrong side. One day backstage, completely out of nowhere, he had an altercation with Bruce Patron, our tour manager. I stood there dumbfounded as he grabbed Bruce by his nose and started screaming, "Blondie is just a poxy little pop group." I still don't know what that was about, but it was over before it started. The occasional light assault notwithstanding, the spirit between the two camps was good. Nick and I got on well and we'd hang out a lot. He was telling me to just keep doing what I was doing, because I was on a righteous path, and that meant the world to me.

We had a homecoming New York show at Central Park's Wollman Skating Rink in the summer of 1979. I remember thinking, this is it. I was on stage at the same venue I'd seen Led Zeppelin with my buddy Dan a decade earlier. The night was incredible, one of the greatest of my life. Nothing could ever spoil it. Making things more exceptional was having my family, especially my dad, there to share in the moment. Ever since I was a kid and my mom got sick, I had to balance my career with my family life, but the two sides rarely intersected after I started in the band. That's just regular life, I guess. My dad had gone into his own world after my mother passed. As I grew older and fell headfirst into the New York scene and my nocturnal life, he was only vaguely aware of what was happening. I'd roll in at dawn, sleep until noon, maybe get up to fix us both some food, and then head back to the city after night had fallen. It was meaningful to me for him to experience what was happening in my professional life and to celebrate my success.

After the show, as we were whisked away to an after-party, the car couldn't get through the crowds—hundreds of ticketless fans had congregated outside the venue to listen to the show and showed no sign of heading home. The fans were hammering on the roof of the car as we tried to navigate through. Having watched my musical heroes from a distance, to be on the inside, experiencing success like that made me realize I was finally living my dream.

Chapter 22

EAT TO THE BEAT

In April 1979, with "Heart of Glass" at number one in the charts and the world at our feet, the band reconvened to start work on our next record, *Eat to the Beat*. It should have been a breeze, but the record wasn't exactly at the forefront of our minds. That's because the relationship between our manager, Peter Leeds, and Debbie and Chris had broken down entirely. It was a situation that had been simmering away in the background for some time, even going back to our 1977 world tour. Just before we took off, Peter took Debbie on a short promotional tour. I don't think he was looking to sideline the other members of the band; he just saw Debbie's charisma as a way for us getting our foot in the door with radio and promoters. I see why he thought it was a good plan, but it wasn't the best decision. The tension between Peter and Chris had never gone away, and I think Peter underestimated the power of the bond between Chris and Debbie. Separating Debbie to promote our band on her own widened the wedge, a big straw for the camel's back.

Another time, after a show in Manchester, an argument Chris had about something or other turned into a showdown, with Peter saying "If this happens again, I'll put you out of this fucking band." With the brilliance of hindsight, even Peter will tell you that was really stupid: On the one side, there's the business guy who just threatened to fire our guitarist/founding member/songwriter and singer's boyfriend. And on the other side, there's Debbie and Chris, a solid team and force, who are just going to go back to their room and get in their bed together.

The final blow-up couldn't have happened at a worse time because it coincided with our breakthrough into the mainstream. I didn't always see eye to eye with Peter, but I had a special bond with him—probably why I hadn't allowed myself to see what was coming. When he'd first started with us, I had no idea how the publishing side of the business worked, but Peter set up our publishing company, Monster Island Music, and we all got a fair share. Making sure I got a break, without me having to ask, or even know that I could, made me feel like, in his eyes, I was a valuable, essential part of the band. I mean, I knew I was, but for a business guy to validate that meant a lot.

When the end came, it felt like a bolt out of the blue. Debbie, Chris, and I were in a car after a show with Bruce Patron, our tour manager. Chris said they had something to discuss with me—I thought he meant the usual gig post-mortem, but instead, they told me they wanted Peter and Toby gone. They thought Peter wasn't a good manager. I tried to change their mind, reminding them that only two years ago they were living on the Bowery and now they'd had a number one record. Peter had been our manager the whole time;

clearly he'd done something right. Debbie and Chris were unmoved. It was either Peter or them, and I had to choose. If I didn't back them up, it would be the end of the band.

I was pissed at the decision, but I wasn't waking up every morning thinking, shit, we shouldn't have gotten rid of the manager. It was more of a nagging voice in the back of my head: Is this going to work out okay? Already it was looking like it would be an expensive judgment call since Peter had to be bought out of his deal. Frank and Nigel were less invested in whether Peter stayed or left than I was; they were caught up in the band's success. They had a couple of songs on the new record, so from their perspective everything was rolling along just fine.

We were recording at the Power Station on West Fifty-Third Street, in Hell's Kitchen, with Mike Chapman producing again. Hell's Kitchen is a cool neighborhood with a lot of history connected to the Irish mafia. We were still young and had a little more money, and our lives were better, but all the band members were in a different headspace than we had been during *Parallel Lines*. As the sessions went on, sometimes the business side of things was overpowering the creative, musical, actual being-in-a-band part of things. And the legal bills were piling up. There were times we'd have to cancel the studio at the last minute to go into a meeting or have a business discussion, so the studio costs were spiraling too. It was at the Power Station that Debbie met Nile Rodgers and Bernard Edwards from Chic, and I can't help but wonder if all the upheaval led to some initial discussions about Debbie making a solo record with them.

When we were in the studio, being the band we were supposed to be, making music, I could forget some of that background noise. It still felt like Blondie. After the success of the last record, Mike gave us free rein, and we turned out a pretty great rock record. The negativity hadn't managed to negate the success we'd achieved. The band and Mike hit the town every night to blow off some steam.

Mike was like an additional member; his ideas and creativity were a part of the sessions, but we also looked to him for guidance. His great skill was as a "viber," setting the mood of a song while we were working and dispersing any tension that arose. It seemed to me like Blondie had gotten under a cloud that kept moving over things, making our success more difficult than it needed to be. Mike was the adult in the room, distracting the kids from getting into trouble with the creative process. He was completely tuned in to everyone's emotions during the recording. This is a skill that isn't talked about a lot, but nearly always crucial when a producer is working with a band of highly creative, strong-willed, and opinionated artists. I credit Mike for keeping us on track during all the business chaos and for making sure there was no drop in songwriting or musicality. *Eat to the Beat* contains some of our best work.

I will always be proud of my studio work with Blondie. During *Parallel Lines*, I accepted Mike's view that every song needed to be polished. I think he used reverse psychology on us, because now we were recording in a far more direct way. "Dreaming" was captured by the first or the second take, a spontaneous performance between Nigel, Frank, and me in the studio with Mike. Thinking we were just running it down, I intentionally overplayed, throwing in over-the-top Keith Moon–type fills, just having fun and showing off. Once it was played back though, everyone agreed that we'd nailed the track. If we'd recorded a bunch of takes, I probably would have held back and refined it more, but as things happen sometimes, totally unplanned, it's become one of my signature tracks. Joey Ramone once told me that as a Keith Moon fan, "Dreaming" was his favorite Blondie song.

On Chris's song "Shayla," I went for a much more stripped-down, simplified approach, something more like Moe Tucker from the Velvets style. When Nigel was going through his demo of "Union City Blue," he was trying to capture something that referenced John Lennon's "#9 Dream." We fooled around with it for a while, and I came up with my drum intro, coming out of the drone at the beginning of the song to create this tension to draw you into the lyrics. Before recording a song, in my mind's eye I'd always try to reference the style I was looking for, or the vibe of a certain drummer. On "Union City Blue," I was harking back to Procol Harum's B.J. Wilson, with those offbeat, asymmetrical drum fills. The chord changes are quite basic, but with the drums acting as an orchestral counterpoint, it lends a certain majesty to that song.

Once again, Mike Chapman seems to look back with a very different perspective than I remember. I'll never get over what a weird thing it is to have people who were in the same place at the same time have completely different takes on an era. In a 2001 re-release album notes diatribe, he admits the music is good, and he is right that the band had more "wear and tear" than before, but he goes on to say things were "a mess" and to ask if the record was "just the waste of seven sick minds."

However our producer saw things, I was unaware that we'd entered the era of doom and gloom that would grow until it consumed us. I thought this was an incredible time for the band and that the future held nothing but more and better. *Eat to the Beat* is a contemporary pop record with a lot of diverse influences and a harder edge than *Parallel Lines*. It was always going to be hard to follow a runaway success like *Parallel Lines*, but *Eat to the Beat* was a success by any standard. There was still an ongoing disagreement between the UK and US record companies regarding strategy, so in the US, we released "The Hardest Part" as a 45, but in the UK, the single "Atomic" would go on to be a huge hit, yet another number one. "Dreaming" too only just missed the top of the charts over there. Chrysalis in the US took their foot off the gas when "Call Me," the single we made for the *American Gigolo* soundtrack, was released in early 1980. Because that became such a huge hit, it overshadowed the singles from the album.

As a collection of songs, our fourth LP showed we were still willing to be adventurous. It follows the Blondie template of changing things up, trying something different, and covering a lot of different stylistic ground: everything from pop to new wave rock, disco, reggae, and funk. We had Judy Garland's daughter Lorna Luft singing backing vocals on Jimmy's Motown-sounding "Slow Motion," which could easily have been another single from the album. That was a missed opportunity, but by the same token, we were so prolific at this point, it's understandable how it fell through the cracks. I don't know who came up with the idea of splitting up the band for the sleeve, three on the front, three on the back. It doesn't make any sense. I guess if you wanted to get a laugh out of it, you could say the cover had (say it out loud and slowly) Frank and Stein on the front cover with

Debbie. To this day, whenever I see a copy in a record store, I make a point to flip the cover around so it's Jimmy, Nigel, and me staring out at you from the racks.

We were showing the way to a lot of artists who would follow in our steps when we released a long-form video album to accompany the record. A lot of the clips were shot on the soundstage at Studio Instrument Rentals—most famously, the promo clip for "Dreaming." There was some snobbery about making promo videos in some new wave circles, but we always enjoyed the process and understood it got us seen by a bunch of people who probably wouldn't have seen us before. It was Terry Ellis at Chrysalis who suggested we take the leap and make an entire video album. To my knowledge, we were the first band to do this. There probably was a financial reason behind the idea. Making an album's worth of promos over a couple of days was going to be more cost efficient than recording individual videos over the course of the album campaign.

The only problem with the idea came when the video album release was delayed over a rights issue. Video was a new frontier, and we were making the rules up as we went along. It's frustrating because we were ideally positioned to become an iconic MTV band. Videos were the perfect vehicle for us. Debbie is visually stunning, and generally we were all easy on the eye. I was young and handsome, although with the passing of years, I gotta admit, I'm just as handsome these days. We should have pressed our advantage here. Later, when MTV approached us to work together to promote our 1982 tour, for some reason we didn't play ball. Then we broke up, just at the advent of MTV changing the course of pop music. MTV made the Police and Duran Duran, putting their music into millions of homes across America, while we were in the process of putting ourselves out of the game. It's such a missed opportunity. We'd been ahead of the curve, spending hundreds of thousands of dollars on videos, but we wound up not reaping the rewards.

Prior to taking the album out on the road, we had an album release party at Fiorucci. There's a song on the album, "The Hardest Part," about an armored-car heist, so naturally, we wanted to arrive at the party in an armored car. It's not that easy to rent an armored car in Los Angeles—probably for good reason—so we settled on a tank. We made quite a scene on Rodeo Drive.

Back in New York, when the album hit stores, we headed up to 30 Rockefeller Plaza and played "Dreaming" and "The Hardest Part" on *Saturday Night Live*, right at the show's height, with Steve Martin as the host. It felt like the pinnacle of our hometown New York success, and people still talk to me about that moment, me in my Keith Moon mod target shirt, jumping over the drums at the song's climax and managing to not fall on my ass. Unbelievably, I'd never seen the show before—I was always out on a Saturday night—but I knew it was a milestone for us. At the end of the taping, when the cast gets called out for the curtain call, I was standing with Garrett Morris, the comedian. Steve Martin is going through his thanks-for-watching shtick and glad-handing the rest of the cast and Garrett is standing next to me, joking that he couldn't get Steve's attention. He's all like, "Hey, Steve," and muttering, "Motherfucker" under his breath every time Steve ignored his outstretched hand.

Following the show, we went downtown to Tribeca to Dan Ackroyd and John Belushi's bar on Hudson Street for an after-party. Belushi was working the bar, getting everyone drinks. After *SNL*, we played the Palladium and spent time filming a movie, a pet project of our new manager. Then we flew back to the UK for a huge tour, seeing in the New Year with one of two shows at the Glasgow Apollo, which went out live on the BBC. There weren't the arenas in place that exist now, so in practically every big city, we played two nights at these four- and five-thousand-seat theaters. We played eight nights at the Hammersmith Odeon and probably could have added another two nights and still sold them out. The business side of the band was in disarray, but somehow, we were in the throes of Blondie-mania. We could have played every night of 1980, but right after January, we didn't play another show until 1982. If you want to pinpoint the precise moment things started to go south for us, that was it.

Chapter 23

CALL ME. OR DON'T.

While we were touring with the Kinks, we got word that legendary German producer Giorgio Moroder wanted to collaborate on a track. He had a song for the soundtrack of "American Gigolo," his new Paul Schrader–directed movie starring Richard Gere and Lauren Hutton. Originally, he'd pitched this new song to Stevie Nicks—her pass was our gain. Following the run of perfect disco records he'd made with Donna Summer, Giorgio was the hot producer du jour. We were all fans of his work—Donna Summer had been one of the key inspirations for our hit "Heart of Glass," so it seemed like a good match. Giorgio's song was called "The Man Machine," but after seeing a rough cut of the movie, Debbie penned a new set of lyrics, written from the perspective of Richard Gere's male hustler character. "Call Me" would go on to be one of our most enduring songs.

In August 1979, we decamped to the Record Plant in NYC and recorded the backing track for "Call Me" in one day. I came up with the triplet drum roll as the introduction to the song, and we built the track from there—or at least, that's what we set out to do. Giorgio's recording process was completely different from the open, collaborative approach we were used to. He had a coterie of session musicians and his usual engineer, Harold Faltermeyer, whom he was used to working with in the studio. Before we even set foot in the session, he'd prepared a prerecorded synthesizer track that we had to play along to. He seemed genuinely puzzled that we wanted to play on the record at all. That method of recording has become standard in the industry, but at the time, it was a very modern approach.

I'd only experienced working from a "click track" on a couple of occasions because I always acted as my own click track, but I had no difficulty doing what was asked of me. The synthesizer track prompted the sixteenth-note hi-hat pattern I play, so the new technology inspired my own creativity, and I put my individual stamp on the recording. Everyone contributed to the arrangement of the song; I know Frank is rightly proud of the guitar riff he came up with. None of those little signatures were on the original prerecorded track. It was a quick session, but we all brought our A game. If there was one slight grumble, it was an interpersonal thing. Giorgio had already enjoyed great success and had our respect as an innovator, but he was very distant with us. I don't recall him coming down even once from the control room to the studio floor to interact with the band. Maybe he only knew how to relate to studio session players and the idea of an actual full-fledged rock and roll band made him uncomfortable. It made for a strange experience for us after the enthusiasm of the producers we'd made records with. It's likely he was more interested in working with just Debbie as a vocalist, but that wouldn't have been Blondie, and it was Blondie that made "Call Me" a hit, so too bad. If he wanted a new muse, he could work on a solo album with Debbie, which probably would have also been a great collaboration. We all rose to the challenge of working in a whole new way, even without any camaraderie with Giorgio.

After we finished recording, Richard Gere and Paul Schrader stopped by the studio, and we posed for a group photo together with them and Giorgio. At the time, Richard was on Broadway playing the lead in *Bent*, a play about homosexuality in a German concentration camp. He may have come from rehearsals, half in, half out of character, because he couldn't have looked less like the suave American gigolo character from the movie. He was a cool guy, and he made sure we all got tickets for that night's performance. As for Schrader, I was a big admirer of his films, *Taxi Driver* in particular, and a little starstruck in his company. *Taxi Driver* was the quintessential New York document of its time. It's a movie that's close to all our hearts, because it perfectly captures a moment and place in our lives, alongside the rise of Blondie. That area below Fourteenth Street and around the Bowery had been our stomping ground when we were coming up.

I'd totally forgotten about "Call Me" and our day in the studio with Giorgio. It was only when I was in a limo riding home from Newark Airport the following February and heard something vaguely familiar on the radio. My memory was stirred, and I asked the driver to turn it up. I heard "Call Me" and it sounded great, like a hit. I'd love to tell you I got goosebumps, but in truth, it seemed par for the course. We were at our peak, and I'd come to expect nothing less when hearing Debbie's voice and our sound coming out of the radio.

Still, I don't think I anticipated the impact the record would have on our careers. Blondie was on autopilot in a funny way, almost blasé about our successes. When the song was finally released as a 45 in the spring of 1980, it went on to be our biggest single, hitting number one in the UK and spending six weeks at number one in the US. *Billboard* named "Call Me" single of the year. It was only then I realized that this one-time, unique, and uneasy alliance between Blondie and Giorgio Moroder had caught lightning in a bottle.

Chapter 24

AUTOAMERICAN

The record company wanted a new album in stores before Christmas. With "Call Me" still hanging around the top of the charts, the sessions for our next record, *Autoamerican*, were set to begin in the spring of 1980. We were told the new record was a top priority for the label, and no expense was to be spared. Notably, this was going to be the first time we recorded outside of New York City, with us heading to the West Coast to renew our working relationship with Mike Chapman. Mike was always encouraging us to come out and record in Los Angeles. Having dragged him away from the comfort of his Beverly Hills home for *Parallel Lines* and *Eat to the Beat* it looked like he was finally getting his wish. No small feat that Mike got us on his turf—Chris and Debbie were New York City royalty and weren't keen about leaving, especially for the length of time it would take to record a new album. I felt open to having a change of scenery and maybe a new adventure.

We flew into LAX and set to work at United Western in LA almost immediately. The studio, located near Gower Gulch on Sunset Boulevard, had been used by everyone from Frank Sinatra to the Beach Boys. Mike had been working there for a while, and he made us feel at home. The hours were usually noon until midnight. While we were there, the Bee Gees were holed up in the adjoining studio. I was relaxing in the lounge one day listening to Barry Gibb ordering food from Roscoe's House of Chicken and Waffles, which was nearby. I guess even a Bee Gee needed to know where to find good soul food in LA. Besides the proximity of Roscoe's, being in LA gave us access to the town's great session players. There's a cast of great artists who came by to lend a hand: jazz bassist Ron Carter is on the record, the great arranger Jimmy Haskell worked on Chris's instrumental track "Europa," and Tom Scott played the sax solo on "Rapture." Alex Acuña and Ollie Brown joined me on percussion for "The Tide Is High," making the song, and me, sound great.

The session players expanded our musical palette, but they were also out of necessity. We were recording but barely using Frank Infante, who had become an essential member since he'd joined the band. No real explanation was given to me, maybe because I was the one who'd brought him in. I had no idea as to why Frank had been sidelined, what the politics, motivation, or mood shift was about. Blondie fans still ask me what happened and I still don't really know what to say.

Frank's contributions to Blondie are indisputable—even Mike Chapman has gone on record saying that Frank was the best musician in Blondie. On "Autoamerican," even Debbie and Chris reversed course and included Frank on the sessions near the end of the recording schedule. Most of the band was absent when he did his guitar overdubs with Mike, but I stayed and watched him lay down a stellar solo on "Rapture." With Frank estranged, I was in a difficult position. He was my longtime friend. I missed hanging out with him and was sure it would be a backward step to not have his talent all over the new record. I had to choose between friendship and my Blondie career. I'd always known what the pitfalls of playing rock and roll could be, but I'd never thought that success would lead to dilemmas like this. Blondie was my life, and if Debbie and Chris had a vision for the band, I could fight, but they knew what they wanted. The problem though was Frank leaving wouldn't be as cut and dried as when Gary Valentine had left. That was mutual. Frank wanted to stay, and was contractually tied to us. So not only did siding with Debbie and Chris and their vision mean going against one of my best friends, it meant I had to partake in the legal mess that ensued.

Even with the studio drama, it felt good to be back in LA. At first, Chrysalis had us staying at the Oakwood Apartments in Hollywood Hills, near Warner Bros. studios. It was the place all the TV companies put up the actors and crew during pilot season every year, so everyone staying there was either in the business of making TV or movies or were on the periphery, hoping to catch a break. There were dozens of generic apartments over three floors and a few swimming pools scattered around the grounds, in case the actors got tired of rehearsing their lines inside. It was a bit far from the recording studio, and being LA, we were given our choice of cars to rent at this "car rentals to the stars" place on Sunset Boulevard across from Tower Records. Over the course of our stay, I kept switching cars: one week a Camaro, another week a Mercedes, on to a Cadillac. Just to keep things interesting.

Driving to a recording session and parking in the VIP parking lot instead of taking a Checker cab or catching the subway was cool. A couple of weeks into our Oakwood stay, there was a shooting at the apartment parking lot. I'd seen all kinds of crazy stuff go down in Lower Manhattan, and even though our band was streetwise, we were shaken and decided to relocate to the Chateau Marmont on Sunset Boulevard. The Velvet Underground had stayed there on their first trip to the West Coast, so we figured that was a better fit for us anyway.

Chateau Marmont is a place that's steeped in Hollywood history and notoriety. It had fallen from favor and was closer to the dark edges of Hollywood than it is today. Hookers still walked the street on that part of Sunset Boulevard. They used to line up in front of the hotel, scouting for passing trade. We stayed in the cottages, situated behind a gated entrance, with a small courtyard leading to the swimming pool, so it made for a more secluded, relaxed atmosphere when we weren't in the studio. Jimmy's cottage was the one John Belushi died of an overdose in, a few years later.

In our downtime from recording, we'd hang by the pool and hold court. David Lynch, the director, was staying there around that time, and we talked about maybe working on a project together. "Call Me" and *American Gigolo* made it obvious how much a hit song could bring attention to a newly released film. Working with Lynch didn't come to pass, but that's how most Hollywood projects seem to go, never getting beyond an initial pitch.

Parallel Lines might be the record that comes to mind when people think of Blondie, but *Autoamerican* is my favorite and the most ambitious. Just "Rapture" itself is a groundbreaking piece of music. We were taking the band to places no one else was going at the time. Hip hop was happening in the South Bronx but was still years away from breaking into the mainstream. Debbie and Chris were completely keyed into hip hop. Living in NYC, I was aware of the genre and the cultural significance, but it took their vision to see the potential to cross over with rock. I always kept an open mind to new ideas and was willing to adapt to whatever material we were experimenting with. I really got an understanding one night when I was at Hurrah—a rock and roll club on the Upper West Side—and the DJ played "Rapper's Delight" by the Sugarhill Gang. It brought the house down. At the time of release, some people struggled to get a handle on *Autoamerican* and how it sweeps through the musical genres, but I think it's our masterpiece. We covered so much ground beyond rock and roll and pop. I was growing as a player, venturing into jazz, rap, and reggae.

Blondie had gone from being considered the least likely of all the CBGB bands to make it to being the innovators, trying something new on every new record. We were part of that Beatles, Stones, Bowie tradition, where you never knew what to expect next. Those artists were always changing musically and broadening their horizons. This approach and eclecticism gave Blondie an anything-goes attitude. After *Autoamerican* was finished, I had a playback party for my close friends in my loft. When they heard Debbie's rap on "Rapture," they were all completely gobsmacked. No one knew what to make of it. It took a while, but eventually the world caught up with us.

Once we left LA, we got together for a couple of days to shoot "The Tide Is High" video, on West Broadway in the SoHo district of Manhattan. It shows Debbie trapped in a

Talking to Joel Siegel after a
soundcheck in Central Park, 1979

Trouser Press cover photo shoot at
SIR rehearsal studio, NYC, 1978

In a vintage hotel room with Frank

Success

With Frank on the set of Blondie's "Island of Lost Souls," filmed on the Isles of Scilly, 1982

Giving it my all

In the Eurythmics movie

Always in the moment

With girlfriend Kathy Valentine, 1986 (*above*); bands from the other side of the dream (*overleaf*)

Early days of
Chequered Past

Performing with Dramarama
at the KROQ Weenie Roast,
Irvine Meadows, 1993

Photos with my dear friend
Dawn at Malibu Inn (now called
Aviator Nation Dreamland)

Backstage before
a soundcheck

Warming up prior to a
London performance

My wife Ellen

A real honor to receive an
honorary doctorate

In my favourite seat

Reunited

My mate Glen Matlock
joins me in Australia, 2023

Full circle

Pollinator recording
sessions, 2016

Older and
a bit wiser

flooding apartment, trying to find her way back to the band. I guess it was art. I mean, we were in SoHo. We reconvened soon after to make the "Rapture" video. This time, it depicts Debbie marching through this urban landscape, past graffiti-sprayed walls, with each bandmember awkwardly taking a turn to dance with her. We had our friend Jean-Michel Basquiat, the artist, step in as the DJ when Grandmaster Flash didn't show for the shoot. In the video, I can be seen sporting a beard—a result of our extended time apart and out of the public eye.

When we originally submitted *Autoamerican* to our label Chrysalis, they were lukewarm. "Where's the hit?" they said. They couldn't have been more wrong. The singles from *Autoamerican*, both "The Tide Is High" and "Rapture," were met with worldwide acclaim, reaching number one in the US and in the UK, just like the trajectory of "Call Me."

After *Autoamerican* came out, Blondie dropped out of sight. The six of us didn't see one another for two years. Success had taken its toll in ways none of us could predict, but I had no idea that the momentum that had brought us to the top of the mountain, to our commercial peak, was over. We would never scale those heights again. It was, and remains to this day, a bitter pill to swallow.

Chapter 25

I NEED MORE

Without any Blondie activity, I was at loose ends. Instead of touring the world in support of *Autoamerican*, we were on a hiatus. Debbie was working with Chris, Nile Rodgers, and Bernard Edwards, from Chic, on a solo record. I headed over to England, where I ended up working with a new band, Eurythmics. Returning to New York, I checked in with our new management—more on that later—Shep Gordon, and he had nothing for Blondie in the pipeline. Out of the blue, I got a call from Jimmy Destri. He'd wrangled a solo deal for himself with Chrysalis and wanted me to play on the sessions. Jimmy had assembled an intriguing group of A-list musicians for the record, including Carlos Alomar, David Bowie's bandleader. Michael Kamen, the distinguished composer and one-time member of the New York Rock & Roll Ensemble, was brought on board to oversee the production. My immediate thought was, what could go possibly wrong? Well, everything.

Jimmy got a substantial budget to make his album with but it's likely that a lot of the funds were siphoned to Jimmy's "logistics coordinator," a guy whose chief role was to procure cocaine. During the sessions, Jimmy had some sort of nervous breakdown. I think it was probably drug-induced, so to keep things going Shep assigned a guy to keep Jimmy in line. Upon release, *Heart on a Wall* didn't crack the top 200 in *Billboard*, but on a positive note, the album has become a collector's item for hardcore Blondie fans. There are some good ideas in there despite being recorded in the midst of cocaine chaos.

Debbie's solo record *KooKoo* didn't fare so well either, surprisingly. The H.R. Giger cover image that had Debbie with needles sticking in her face led to promotional posters being banned in some territories. I couldn't help but think that with both albums falling short of expectations, Blondie could have chosen the best songs from each and added a few new cowrites with Nigel, and we'd have had the bones to a great follow-up to *Autoamerican*.

I got a call from Iggy Pop. He was in the city working with Rob Duprey, my friend from the Mumps, and was looking for a drummer for his upcoming tour. I said yes immediately. Hearing that Gary Valentine and Carlos Alomar would both be in the band was icing on the cake. Carlos and I'd become friendly on the Jimmy Destri record, so I knew the tour would be a blast. A few weeks later, I was in my loft on a nostalgia binge, watching a bootleg tape of every Rolling Stones appearance on *The Ed Sullivan Show*. As Mick Jagger swaggered and sang in black and white on my TV, there was a knock at the door. It was Iggy, wanting to go over a few details about the upcoming tour. He was all business: Jim Osterberg, rather than the streetwalking cheetah, Iggy Pop. Unfurling his scarf, he glanced at my TV set, and almost as an afterthought told me, oh yeah, the upcoming tour included two dates opening for the Stones at the Pontiac Silverdome. Like a series of connected dots, just as I heard that news, the Stones on my TV were interrupted by the sound of stones hitting my front window. I looked out to see Ronnie Toast yelling, "Clem, you motherfucker, open the door! I need some money!"

Usually when he yelled up like that, I'd run downstairs and hand him some food and drug money, but not today. If there was a bigger Iggy fan in New York City than Ronnie, I haven't met him. Years later, after losing both legs in a horrific subway accident, Ronnie was so dedicated an Iggy fan that he boarded a Greyhound bus on crutches to see Iggy play a New York show. I buzzed him up, enjoying the perfect picture of surprise on his face when he saw my guest. Immediately, Ronnie launched into a spot-on impersonation of Iggy, circa *The Idiot*. If he thought that would endear him to Iggy, he was wrong: Jim grabbed his coat and ran out the door, leaving behind his scarf. I still have the scarf.

The Iggy Pop Follow the Sun Tour began at the Bus Stop club in Michigan, followed by a show on Iggy's home turf, the Royal Oak Music Theatre, just outside Detroit city limits. There, we met Iggy's parents backstage—they were very proud and supportive of their boy. Iggy's dad, Mr. Osterberg, looked like a more evolved version of his son, especially when Iggy donned his reading glasses. Onstage, Iggy's brief to the band was simple: play as loud and as fast as possible. It opened the door to a no-rules needed, very creative atmosphere. Improvisation was the norm, and the looseness made those shows some of the most exciting sets I've ever played. After shipping out from Michigan, the tour swung south, taking in shows in Memphis, Atlanta, and a wild sold-out gig on a Mississippi riverboat in New Orleans on Halloween. In Texas, we played a memorable two-night stand at Austin's Club Foot.

Iggy introduced an unrecorded song he said he'd written with "Bill Shakespeare," called "The Winter of My Discontent." In the middle of the "to be or not to be" soliloquy part of the song, Iggy went off script and started saying, "There's a bomb, and we're all gonna die." From the riser, I thought he was talking about the big picture, like the state of the world. Turns out he was poetically warning the audience of a phoned-in bomb scare in the club. There was chaos as everyone ran out of the club, screaming and trampling over one another. Eventually, order was restored and the audience returned and we finished our show with an extra rush of adrenaline from our near-death experience.

Iggy's concert rider dictated that there be no food backstage, only alcohol and drugs. He could go days without eating. Then, on a rare day off, we'd go out to a band dinner, and he'd order three entrees at once for himself. I learned a lot from that tour, most importantly, to exercise and rest before the next round of hedonism. Iggy had his own routine, constantly stretching and doing jumping jacks and multiple sets of push-ups in whatever parking lot we were stopped at. When he retired to his hotel room, he'd go into sleep seclusion and wouldn't be seen again until showtime. Meanwhile, the rest of us would head off to soundcheck, while his tour manager, Henry McGroggan, began his ritual of laying out Iggy's stage wear: a miniskirt, garter belt, nylons, and motorcycle cap. It wasn't like Iggy was dressing in drag; it was meant to provoke a reaction.

After shows in Tempe and San Diego, we played the Hollywood Palladium. We'd been on the road for more than three weeks, so we were well primed. The show was one of the tour's highlights. Afterward, Iggy told us we were the best band he'd ever had and the gig was his best ever LA show. Following a few days of rest, we made our way to San Francisco for two shows. The first was on my twenty-sixth birthday, November 24. Allen Ginsberg came to the show, and he, Iggy, Gary, and I shared a joint and chanted "om" before we took to the stage. I was presented with a cake and a funny oversized birthday card signed by everyone on the tour. I have a neat Polaroid of the band, all smiles, gathered around me and the cake after the show. Markie Ianello, our one-man road crew, handed me a cassette of our performance, and all modesty aside, the band was incredible. Our

Best 26th birthday with Iggy

show at the Market Theater in San Francisco was filmed and commercially released a few years later and shows us in all our glory, gunning through most of our repertoire. I'm so happy to have this time and place in my life so well documented; the video is easily found on YouTube.

The next day, it was back to Detroit for our two shows with the Stones. As we were exiting the airport, Iggy unexpectedly ran into Stooges saxophonist Steve Mackay. The first words out of Steve's mouth when he spotted Iggy were, "Hey, man, I thought you were dead!," and they greeted each other like long-lost brothers. We drove directly to a Holiday Inn in Pontiac, on a service road in the middle of nowhere. After the previous four weeks of debauchery, I needed some heavy rest. I lay down on my hotel bed and wondered what it'd be like opening for the Stones. Essentially, this was Iggy's homecoming show, so I expected a warm welcome. I'd heard it was Keith Richards who got us on the shows to add some local flavor and figured Keith's blessing meant things would run smoothly. I was wrong. It didn't go smoothly, but it was incredible anyway.

Driving to the gig the next day, I was struck by the enormity of the Silverdome as it appeared on the horizon. It was the largest enclosed football stadium in the country, way bigger than any place I'd played before. After being swept from the parking lot into the belly of the stadium, I found myself kicking around backstage, anxiously awaiting our soundcheck. I remember half watching Bill Wyman and Charlie Watts playing ping-pong, but Iggy was a no-show. The band headed back to our dressing room where we were told Iggy had gone off to have a chat with Keith. By the time he returned, it would be showtime. No soundcheck. Finally,

Iggy showed his face, and we walked down the hall. The stage door opened, and I felt a gust of air and the roar of eighty thousand people. Promoter Bill Graham announced us, and as we walked out, I felt like a gladiator entering the Roman Colosseum. Given our lack of soundcheck, there were sound issues.

I was fostering a naive hope for a triumphant hometown hero's welcome, but we were met with jeers. Our time on the road had made us a tight unit, but maybe a little too loud and fast for a Midwest crowd—maybe they'd forgotten the rebellious aspect of the Stones. That night, Iggy was wearing a T-shirt and blue jeans instead of his usual miniskirt and garter belt, probably thinking a more conservative approach might help win over the crowd, but the next day, any ideas about playing it safe went out the window. There was some drama going on; word was he'd gone to the Stones' dressing room the night before, and Mick Jagger didn't come out to say hi. Iggy was pissed by the apparent snub. Consequently, he had a change of heart about his stage attire for the second show, coming out in a motorcycle jacket and a pair of opaque pantyhose. When hit with a megawatt spotlight onstage, he appeared naked from the waist down, which just riled the Stones fans.

As we began to play, objects started hurtling toward the stage. Mike Page, our bass player, got cut on his hand by a knife thrown from the crowd. I was hit with shattered glass from beer bottles crashing into the drums. My arms were bleeding, but we persevered. As we broke into "I Need More," Iggy was at the edge of the stage, provoking the crowd, in full *Metallic K.O.* mode. The song's lyrics call for more of life's indulgences, "more champagne ... more cocaine," and Iggy was wailing, "I need more than I ever did before" while challenging the crowd to throw more bottles, more knives, more shoes. The set ended in chaos, and we beat a hasty retreat offstage. While we nursed our wounds, Bill Graham had the crew collect all the stuff and returned to the stage holding all the shit that was thrown: twenty cigarette lighters, six sneakers, a dozen pairs of underwear, several bags of coins, and a bunch of knives.

With the Stones debacle over, the tour headed across the border to Canada for shows at the Music Hall in Toronto, and an apparently endless snowstorm. Canadian fans never let a little blizzard prevent them from rocking out, but the weather did hinder our travel and start times. On top of the weather, at our last show in Montreal, there was a lengthy delay in the delivery of the night's illicit supplies. We were all sitting around backstage, with no sense of urgency to get on stage. Iggy had a policy, "no blow, no show," and he was sticking to his guns. The venue was surrounded by huge snowdrifts, preventing most of the audience from arriving on time, but also, Iggy's drug connection. Finally, right before we were due to go on, there came a knock at the dressing room door and in walked Long John Baldry, the British blues singer. He'd relocated to Canada and had the goods. With that, it was showtime, and the end of one of the most exciting rock and roll adventures of a lifetime.

Chapter 26

THE HUNTER

Blondie began to fall apart in the summer of 1982. It happened in slow motion, and nobody except me seemed to see it coming. Or maybe, they all saw it, and I was the only one who gave a shit. It seems so obvious we were in trouble. Our final record, *The Hunter*, marked our demise. We were selling records by the ton, but we weren't exploiting our recording success by touring. As Frank said to me a few years later, it was like having a winning lottery ticket but not cashing it in. Jimmy, Chris, and Debbie were awash in songwriting royalties from the hit records, so maybe touring money seemed expendable. It wasn't like today, when a band has to tour to make money from tickets and merchandise. Back then, touring was expensive, often subsidized by the record company—another way to keep the band in debt. Blondie made most of our money from record sales.

Chris and Debbie could of course do whatever they wanted, and were involved in other pursuits and projects. They acquired the rights to film a remake of the Jean-Luc Godard movie *Alphaville* and spent a while trying to get that off the ground. Chris was caught up with his New York circle of artists doing the late-night *TV Party* on public access. I felt like the side stuff was taking precedence over Blondie and didn't understand why the band was the backburner project.

Our manager was now Shep Gordon, and he tried to keep Blondie on track but couldn't. Shep was a widely acclaimed businessman, with many facets—friends with the Dalai Lama, all kinds of crazy stuff, but once he hit a little opposition from Chris and Debbie, he followed the path of least resistance. Before going with Shep, the sharks had been circling. Once news broke that we were seeking new management, it had created a buzz in the industry. Everyone wanted a piece of Blondie. We talked with Sid Bernstein, the Manhattan promoter, famed for bringing the Beatles to the US. We held a meeting with Jake Riviera, the English impresario and manager of Elvis Costello and the Attractions. Bill Graham was touted as a potential replacement, so we met with Bill and his people in the boardroom of our accountants in New York. It was always difficult to get all six members of Blondie in the same place at the same time, even for someone as prestigious as Bill. I was the only band member to turn up for that one, so he was more civil with me than during our last encounter.

Shep's office was in the same suite as our business manager, Bert Padell, the so-called accountant to the stars. Whether by default, or as a foregone conclusion, Shep became Blondie's manager. During our meeting with Shep, he said, "You guys can go on the road for the next year and, by the end of that year, you'll all be millionaires. Or you can sit at home and watch TV. What do you want to do?" I remember Chris's answer clearly: "I want to sit at home and watch TV." He might have been kidding, but that wasn't the whole of it. Chris had developed a serious drug habit.

Blondie may have been sidelined, but the phone continued to ring off the hook. Someone somewhere was always looking to work with us, and whatever proposals they presented got shot down. I stayed busy in the interim—recording with Eurythmics, producing the Colors and the Speedies, two young New York power pop bands, touring with Iggy Pop, and more. Still, I was perplexed to see us turning down these amazing opportunities. We declined a big offer to headline Apple cofounder Steve Wozniak's first US festival alongside the Ramones, Talking Heads, the Cars, the B-52s, and the Police. We passed on an offer from Chrysler to cross-promote their new K-car with our *Autoamerican* album. It was 1980, and art and commerce weren't aligned the way they are today, so there were legitimate concerns of being accused of selling out. It seems quaint now, to have such integrity, but really, it was poor judgment. For many artists nowadays, it's a commonplace way of getting your music heard, and no one worries about being sellouts. "Heart of Glass" is currently the soundtrack of a Nissan ad, and it hasn't hurt our reputation one bit—if anything, it's enhanced it.

The worst thing was not touring. Momentum is meant to carry you upward, not to a plateau. To me, it felt like Blondie was giving up and had no purpose. I called management practically every day asking why we weren't touring. Looking back, I don't know why it didn't seem like I could just call Debbie and Chris to talk about it. Backstage one night at the Clash's debut at the Palladium, promoter Ron Delsener was tearing his hair out. He said we were "absolutely fucking crazy" to not capitalize on our success. Money is a factor, but it wasn't solely about that. I've underlined the point before now that success and money are two separate things. I wanted us to be successful, but more than that, I wanted to play. We were one of the biggest bands in the world, and I wanted to go out there and show people why. Wasn't this what we'd been working toward all along? I was banging my head against the proverbial wall and becoming increasingly frustrated about what was not happening.

It was against this unhappy backdrop that we began recording our sixth album, *The Hunter*. In early 1982, yet again, we dragged Mike Chapman from the warmth of Beverly Hills to the Hit Factory in midtown Manhattan. He arrived dramatically, in the middle of one of those snowstorms that happens once in a century. He was pissed with us from that moment onward. He'd been a hard taskmaster before, but now, with the band coming apart at the seams and him not wanting to be there, the atmosphere was adversarial at best. The Hit Factory was the studio where John Lennon and Yoko Ono had recorded their *Double Fantasy* album and the place they'd last been on the night John was killed. All the time we were recording, I couldn't help but think of John and his murder. In 1980, "The Tide Is High" took over the number one spot from John's swan song, "(Just Like) Starting Over," and now here we were in the same studio. Given how much I idolized the Beatles, it felt too dark. I wasn't haunted by John, but it shadowed the proceedings in sadness for me.

Drugs and drink were very much present at those sessions and, as was the case on *Autoamerican*, our guitarist Frank Infante was not. Frank went down swinging, of course, because that's his character. He exercised his contractual rights to make sure he was able to play on the record and appear on the album's ridiculous cover. The cover photograph was supposed to depict us as cats, and it's a painfully bad concept tied to a dreadful execution. I don't know who had the idea or who gave the artwork the OK, but it was as if we'd abandoned every bit of New York cool that was once our trademark. Just as he had with *Autoamerican*, Frank was forced to record his parts for the new album in isolation from the rest of the band. If the Frank situation wasn't bad enough, and I assure you it was, the sessions were strained and volatile. You put rock star and producer egos along with drug- and alcohol-enhanced erratic behaviors in a room with the pressure to deliver a hit record, things can get rough. When Jimmy hurled a priceless (and heavy) vintage Moog Vocoder at Mike Chapman, he gave up on us. I can't say I blamed him.

As for me, the guy who signed up in part for the camaraderie, I just wanted to get my drum tracks down and get out of there as soon as possible every day. The atmosphere was plain horrible. I kept my head down, tried to weather the storm, but whatever fellowship we had before was entirely gone. The exception was Nigel, who seemed to be the only other member not to lose himself to drugs or to fall out of favor. The curious thing was, to an outsider, everything probably appeared fine. We were still the toast of the city, but the band was just going through the motions.

Despite its troubled creation, we all thought *The Hunter* was a great record—as I recall, it was the only time we all felt that way about one of our albums. Everyone seemed certain it would be a success. Maybe because it was such a struggle to make, it led us to an exaggerated measure of confidence.

The reality was that in terms of sales, it was our biggest failure.

There are a lot of factors to consider with a new album. The first single can make a big difference in how a record is received. In the case of *The Hunter*, the wrong song was picked. Dave Stewart of Eurythmics had been my house guest before the album was released, and I played it for him one night. He and I agreed that "English Boys," with its melancholy mood, reminiscent of "Sunday Girl," should have been the first single. It's one of my favorite Blondie songs to this day. To my mind, we were making all the wrong moves, but I stayed optimistic. The album would soon be out, and surely followed by a summer tour. I had no idea how bad things were going to get.

Chapter 27

THE END

In 1982, Blondie traveled to the UK to start promoting *The Hunter* and to shoot the video for the album's lead-off single. "The Island of Lost Souls" once again saw us going against people's expectations of what we were, with another genre switch, this time to calypso. Creatively, even in turmoil we could still be musically ambitious. The video was a different story, driven more by hubris than art. We were due to fly out to the Isles of Scilly, off the southwest coast of England, to shoot the video. It was a curious location choice. Our director had palm trees flown in for the shoot, so immediately I thought it was dumb. Wouldn't it make more sense to just shoot the video where they already have palm trees? It was typical of the excess you were starting to see in pop videos. MTV had begun to pervade the culture, so every band was trying to outspend and out-stupid each other. We were no different. Frank was still in dispute with the band, but contractually, he had to be in the video, so he was flown in on his own helicopter to film his parts of the video, quarantined from the rest of the band. It was ridiculous.

The night before the shoot, I was in London, making the most of the city and getting into a heap of trouble. Chris had an exhibition of his photographs at an East London gallery, so I went along in solidarity. Afterward, we were taken out to dinner by some record company representatives. It was on the company's dime, so we were enjoying the night, having a few drinks, when one of the executives handed me a small bindle of coke for later. I shrugged, thanked the guy, put it in my pocket, and forgot about it. After dinner, I headed off to meet some friends at the Venue, a club across from Victoria Station. I was waiting outside when I saw a couple of beat cops on the road opposite me. I don't know if it was my motorcycle jacket or my Ray-Bans, but they stopped in their tracks when they saw me. Before I had a chance to react, they were on me. One of the officers put a hand in my pocket and pulled out the little package of coke. "What have we got here?" he said. I'm thinking, can cops just search you like that? Don't they have any due process? The officer asked for identification, so I pulled out my wallet. Because we'd just been handed our per diems for the trip—our daily expenses for food and coffee and what have you—I was carrying a lot of cash. Looking at it from the perspective of an English bobby, it was way more than you'd expect some young guy in a leather jacket to be carrying, unless he was up to no good. Cut to me being dragged off to the nearest police station and getting charged for possession. I explained to them who I was and where I was staying. As they closed the door to the holding cell, I heard them bragging to each other they were heading to the hotel to bust the rest of the band.

When you're arrested in Britain, you get to make a call, so I rang Bruce Patron, our tour manager. Bruce sent Big John, our minder, to the station to see what he could do. Big John was an ex-cop, but he couldn't pull any strings or get the charges dropped. According to British law, cocaine is a class A substance, and they don't take possession lightly. After getting out, John took me to one of those cab drivers' cafés over by Hyde Park, the only places open in the middle of the night—a place to warm up and to mull over my predicament. "You got lucky," he told me between slurps of tea. "If you'd had your passport, they'd have taken it and stopped you from leaving the country."

John and I had to drive through the night to get to Penzance and then charter a (third) helicopter to the Isles of Scilly. I'd been arrested and was making a dreadful video and my band was self-destructing, but the setting wasn't lost on me: it's beautiful with or without palm trees.

Eventually, I had to return for my trial at the Old Bailey. I didn't have much defense; they had me dead to rights. On advice from my barrister, I cited the usual music business–related pressures and the fact I had an upcoming tour of the UK. I made the appeal that my nonappearance would mean a lot of lost income and work for all the truck drivers, crew, and all manner of people tied up in a big venture like that. The case was argued back and forth, until, unbelievably, I was given a £50 fine; essentially, a slap on the wrist. Leaving court, there were a couple of reporters waiting to interrogate me. I told them I wasn't Clem Burke and hailed a cab. *New Musical Express* carried a small news story that week, but other than that, the news of my bust was effectively brushed under the carpet.

With the US tour approaching, we had to think about booking an opening act. No one seemed that engaged, but

Nigel and I had seen Duran Duran on the last date of their US club tour the previous fall. One thing led to another, and they were booked for our summer 1982 tour. Although he was still a member of Blondie on paper, I was told Frank wouldn't be coming along. In his place, we hired guitarist Eddie Martinez, based on a recommendation from Nile Rogers. Eddie went on to play guitar on Run DMC's "King of Rock." A week of production rehearsals was booked at the Palladium on Fourteenth Street, but we barely managed a few days of rehearsal. Chris seemed unwell and fatigued. Trying to salvage the situation, we asked Mike Chapman to fly in. He'd rallied us in dire situations in the studio many times. To make things worse, Jimmy was undependable—we never knew if he'd show up. Once again, my history of working with great musicians in my past came to the rescue. My former bandmate and old friend in Sweet Willie, Abel Domingues, stepped up ready to take over whenever necessary.

In terms of sales, *The Hunter* was underperforming. I figured I could write that off as an inevitable dip on the rock and roll rollercoaster and not worry too much about it. Every band has their peaks and valleys, right? I wasn't naive enough to believe every new album was going to succeed like *Parallel Lines* had.

When the Tracks Across America Tour got underway and I saw that we were playing to half-empty arenas, my concern increased. After three recent number one singles, it was assumed demand would be there, but in retrospect, we should have tested the waters in a few smaller venues. On top of everything else, Duran Duran started to break. Not just a little, but a lot. With the rise of MTV and the accompanying second British wave of British bands, our support act were becoming superstars. They were on every pop magazine cover and all over the radio everywhere you went. You can't begrudge another artist their hard-won success, and I was happy for them, but it was hard to watch their fortunes ascend just as ours were beginning to plummet.

The tour began on July 23 in Baton Rouge. Between the reports of poor ticket sales, Chris's health problems, and the band being under-rehearsed, I had a sense of impending doom. Most of the familiar faces, the people who knew us well from past tours, were absent. In place of our long-serving tour manager Bruce Patron, we had two new ones. They were a study in extreme opposites: one was a hyperactive hit-the-ground-running type, while the other was perpetually laid back. Usually, though, he was nodded out. The reason for the disparity was simple. The first's manic style was from cocaine. And the latter, on the other hand, was a heroin addict.

The tour was a catastrophe. In every new city we found a new way for things to go awry—it started to feel like we planned it that way. After soundcheck in Providence, Rhode Island, our road crew's bus was raided by the police. After the cops rolled up to find the crew enjoying a preshow joint, someone had to take the rap, so my drum tech was hauled off to jail. Something must've gotten lost in translation because the news reported that Blondie's drummer had been detained. A few days later, we played a hometown show across the river from New York at the Meadowlands Arena in New Jersey. All our families were present to share this great moment. I hired a limo to bring my dad and a few of his friends to the show. David Johansen opened the show, followed by Duran Duran, and you could feel the anticipation in the crowd, even backstage. By the time we took to the stage, the excitement generated by Duran Duran had left with them. Blondie was a complete anticlimax. Just to rub salt in the wound, during "Dreaming," the stage power cut out. I tried to keep the audience entertained and improvised a spontaneous drum solo. I don't know how well that went down, because even for me, the solo seemed to last an eternity. We never got the momentum back.

When the curtain came down, I just wanted to get out, but with my friends and family there, I had to show my face backstage. Probably the only highlight I can recall is bumping into Andy Warhol. We chatted awhile, and Andy took a photograph of me with my dad that I dearly wish I had. Ronnie Toast was among the well-wishers, lurching around, drunk and stoned out of his mind. He later told me he passed out and got himself locked in the arena overnight. I stayed as long as I could stand it, smiling and making nice until exiting discreetly and slipping away to my Manhattan hotel room. Although I had a place in the city, I didn't want to go home. My relationship with my long-term girlfriend, Diane, was a mess. She didn't come to the show, but she didn't miss much.

I had a day off to lick my wounds, then on we went to Merriweather Post Pavilion, outside Washington, DC. From there, we took a private jet to Toronto for a show at the Canadian National Exhibition, which was filmed for a video release. I'm pleased to have a document of one of our final shows, but in truth, when I watch the footage now, the main thing that strikes me is the number of Duran Duran T-shirts visible in the crowd. It's like it's over; even the crowd knows it, but we didn't get the memo. Following the show, we were running on fumes, real zombie energy, flying back to the States in the claustrophobic space of a Learjet. No one was talking much because what was there to say? I got the prime seat next to our nodded-out junkie tour manager. A few days earlier, in one of the more satisfying moments from the tour, I'd thrown a chair at him. The penultimate show was at Nassau Coliseum on Long Island. Landing at Teterboro Airport in New Jersey, we ran into the singer Paul Anka—the writer of "My Way," made famous by both Frank Sinatra and Sid Vicious. He was still working his ass off, making his way to Las Vegas and wishing us good luck as we passed through the terminal. Seeing him reminded me what a challenge it is to stay the course in show business.

Our final show was at John F. Kennedy Stadium in Philadelphia, in front of thirty thousand people on a bill with Elvis Costello, Genesis, and A Flock of Seagulls. The date was August 21, 1982, and it would be our last show for fifteen years. In retrospect, it was a most fitting gig to end a tour—and the band. Something was seriously wrong with Chris, but none of us were sure what it was. Throughout the tour, he hadn't been himself. He'd always shown up and done what was needed, but now it seemed like he didn't want to be there at all. I was even paranoid about AIDS; the epidemic had reached the East Coast by now. Blondie always had a strong connection with the gay community in the city, and suddenly, people we knew around New York were contracting HIV and developing AIDS. Our friends were literally there one day and gone the next. It was a terrifying, paranoid moment in the city.

By the time the tour landed in Philly, it seemed like no one wanted to be there anymore. We shared a dressing room with Elvis Costello and the Attractions. Normally, that would have been a riot. We'd always had a good relationship before now, but that day, maybe they picked up on the sour atmosphere around us, and the shared dressing room became just another miserable scene in an increasingly depressing movie. One bright spot for me was a brief conversation I had with Phil Collins. Phil said some nice things about my playing. I was a closet Genesis fan, especially the Peter Gabriel era when I saw a couple of shows, so the compliment meant a lot.

When it came to our set, our intro music began, and the call came for us to walk to the stage. Usually, a tour manager led us to the stage, but this time it was a stranger, which struck me as weird. Still, I settled in behind my drum kit as the show was about to begin. The first song was "Rapture," a full-on production complete with the five-piece horn section. The sound mix included a prerecorded handclap track that I played along to. Obviously, I needed to hear it to keep time, but the handclap wasn't coming through my monitors. All I could hear was the echo of the claps reverberating off the back wall of the stadium. I looked to my left and then to my right—where was my drum tech? Where were the rest of our crew?

When a drummer has a sound problem onstage, it's not an option to stop playing, maybe take a casual stroll over to the sound engineer and calmly explain what's wrong. It's the reason drummers and monitor engineers have been known to have some dramatic confrontations during shows. In the disastrous spirit of the tour, Ed, my regular monitor guy, had been injured in a pyrotechnics accident during one of the earlier shows, so today I was working with a replacement. I started screaming at Ed's stand-in to fix the problem. Jesus, I'm thinking, all you've gotta do is press a button or raise a fader, but the guy's just staring out into the crowd, completely oblivious. Unable to get my message across via words or hand signals, I got up from my kit, grabbed one of my two gongs, and threw it across the stage at the guy. If this sounds dramatic, I can only say it's hard to keep your cool when things are going wrong in front of a huge crowd.

So where was our crew? I later learned that they were in their trailer smoking a joint before the show started. You'd think they'd have learned their lesson from the drug bust in Providence, but no. Anyway, Elvis's crew sussed this out, got hold of the key to the trailer door, and locked them in from the outside. It was a funny stunt to them, but it wasn't so funny for me and the band. They just added a horrible ending to a not-so-great tour. There was more misery to follow.

The way things were scheduled, there would be short break after the US tour before flying to Japan, followed by a UK tour. The big climax was four shows at Wembley Arena, an honor reserved for the biggest acts in pop. I thought that during the break, we'd regroup and find whatever it was we'd lost. I went to Martha's Vineyard to clear my head a little. I was enjoying my time in one of my favorite places, feeling the weight of the past few months fall away, when Shep phoned. The call was brief, and painful. Because of poor ticket sales and Chris's serious illness, the rest of the tour was canceled. He didn't say the band was over, but he didn't have to. When I asked what the plan was to bring the band back from the brink, he admitted there wasn't one.

Hanging up, I realized that for the past months, I'd zoned out. I'd been hoping for the best, that things would somehow fix themselves, and my denial made the pain even more acute. I was in a full-blown state of shock. I genuinely don't remember much about the rest of 1982. I returned to Jersey to tell my dad that Blondie was done. I recall sitting in my car outside his house and just staring out the window, wondering what I was going to do, how I was going to break the news. Since the tour was kaput, I decided to try and spend more time at home with him. My relationship with Diane was a mess, so I'd moved into the house I'd bought for him a few years earlier. A nice place, in the nicest neighborhood of Bayonne, overlooking Newark Bay. It felt like I was in a bad movie. People were talking; the press was murmuring. There was a lot of speculation about our future. The consensus seemed to be that the band was over. For all intents and purposes, I suppose it was.

I rang in the New Year, out of my mind drunk, watching Duran Duran play the MTV New Year's Eve Rock N' Roll Ball. It was a tough pill to swallow. Watching our former opening act standing at the top of the pops underscored how fragile a thing success can be. If you don't nurture it, it's going to go away. The thing I didn't realize was that I was about to begin a new life. Life on the other side of the dream.

Chapter 28

WHO'S THAT GIRL?

At the start of 1981, I was in London for a visit. Blondie were on hiatus and hadn't made *The Hunter* yet. Following a brief tour of the UK with Michael Des Barres's band, I decided to hang around awhile. London was fast becoming a home away from home for me. I figured I'd be across the pond for a month, maybe six weeks tops, but I was having such a good time, I wound up staying for seven months. I found a beautiful penthouse on Curzon Street in the heart of Mayfair, not far from where Keith Moon had died. Around the corner in Burlington Arcade, just off Piccadilly, there was a great club with a vibe reminiscent of Club 82 called Planets, which became a regular haunt. The DJ was this androgynous ex–punk rocker and Bowie freak, a guy named Boy George. He was eighteen months away from finding global fame in Culture Club.

Aside from becoming one of the hottest underground clubs in London, Planets opened the door to another chapter in my life. I was in the VIP room, coincidentally *Autoamerican* was playing in the background, and I was approached by a striking short-haired blonde. She introduced herself as Annie in a strong, sweet Scottish accent. She was a singer, she said, and a big Blondie fan. She told me she'd recently split from a band called the Tourists and was in the process of making a record with the guitarist. Would I be interested in hearing some songs and maybe working with them? I said sure, and we agreed to meet for Sunday lunch at her flat in Crouch End, an arty hamlet in the northern reaches of London. That lunch marked the beginning of my ten-year working relationship with Eurythmics. It was as serendipitous as that.

Although they'd recently parted ways as lovers, Annie Lennox and Dave Stewart were very much partners in Eurythmics. In some ways, their creative dynamic reminded me of Debbie and Chris's in the early days, and it felt strange to be the third corner in yet another musical love triangle. At the time, Eurythmics was recording their debut album, *In the Garden*, with Conny Plank, the German producer and innovator, at his farmhouse studio on the outskirts of Cologne, Germany. I was flown over to play on half the tracks, which was a wonderful and enlightening experience. As soon as we met, Conny told me how much he rated "Heart of Glass" and that he immediately recognized the influence of Kraftwerk in our song. Conny had produced so many great records that defined the Krautrock genre, it felt like the highest of praise. Conny and his family were such welcoming, beautiful, artistic souls, and the atmosphere at the studio couldn't have been more conducive to creativity. At night, everyone gathered around the kitchen table for wonderful suppers prepared by Conny's wife, Christa. Their young son, Stephan (whose favorite word at the time was *Scheisse*, German for "shit"), usually joined us, as did Holger Czukay, of the German experimental band Can. Holger played the French horn solo when we appeared on the British TV show *The Old Grey Whistle Test*, promoting the album. That was the British public's first exposure to the group, and I feel privileged to have been a part of it.

Back in London, with the sessions for the album complete, I found myself gravitating to Annie and Dave. By night, I was a fixture in London's clubland or seeing bands around town, but my days were spent in the calmer atmosphere created by Annie and Dave. We'd become so close, our working relationship so intuitive, I was invited to join them permanently as a partner in the band. I had to decline. Blondie were merely on a break, and I had an obligation, but I also had no idea things would end as badly as they did. I figured we'd dust ourselves off after the break and come back stronger.

I think about that decision not to join Dave and Annie a lot. At the time, I remember Dave encouraging me to buy a flat in Crouch End, but I was living in a penthouse with a private elevator at the epicenter of New Romantic, post-punk swinging London, and Crouch End seemed a million miles away from the action. It felt like I wasn't ready to quit the city life just yet, but maybe I was tempted for a minute or two.

With the Eurythmics recording completed, my girlfriend, Diane, and I took off to Crete for a much-needed vacation. Diane had entrusted the keys to our loft to a friend to keep an eye on things till we got back. Be careful who you trust with your apartment keys—especially if all your buddies are rock musicians. After being abroad, Diane and I arrived home, tired and jet-lagged, wanting nothing more than a relaxing evening. As we climbed the stairs with our bags, I could hear the strains of David Bowie's "Heroes" playing loudly inside our apartment. Immediately, I felt myself tense up. I was in no mood for a welcome home party. I turned the key and opened the door to find Jimmy Destri and Billy Idol sprawled out on my couch drinking beers, with fat lines of coke on the coffee table in front of them. In our absence, Jimmy had convinced our friend to hand over the keys to him. I turned the music off and in no uncertain terms told them to split.

Dave Stewart and I stayed in touch, with promises to get together the next time I was in London. This coincided with the disastrous Blondie promo for *The Hunter*. I called Dave, and we met up for a drink. Although the Eurythmics' debut had been well received by the critics, it wasn't a commercial success. Dave explained that he and Annie were in the process of reassessing their creative situation and had set up their own studio in Crouch End, where they'd been recording on their own, using synthesizers and a recently purchased state-of-the-art analog drum machine. After their time in Germany, they felt inspired by Kraftwerk. It wasn't until the next year that I'd see the fruits of their labors and Eurythmics would go from critically successful to commercially massive.

Taking me up on a previous invitation to visit New York, Dave suggested he come over in June. I told him he was welcome to stay at the loft, and a few weeks later, in the middle of an early summer heatwave, he arrived. He'd visited New York before, but never during summer, and was unprepared for the oppressive temperatures and humidity. Dave and Annie had been gracious hosts in London, and I was anxious to reciprocate, so I offered to show him around. First stop on day one was the Whitney Museum and an exhibition of video work by the Fluxus artist Nam June Paik. The Whitney was on Seventy-Fifth Street and Madison Avenue on the Upper East Side. I thought it would make an interesting stroll from my place on East Twenty-First and Park—probably sixty-five blocks, a little more than three miles. Living in Manhattan, you get used to walking everywhere. The traffic is horrible, and the subways are crowded and dirty.

By the time we reached midtown, the temperature was still rising, and it was apparent Dave wasn't over his transatlantic flight. We stopped for a drink, but between jet lag and the heat, Dave seemed to be in an altered state of consciousness. That sounds bad, but it was the perfect state of mind for him to view the art. Basically, he was tripping. At the entrance stood a huge pyramid of consumer-grade TV monitors that used magnets and other devices to distort the images and an outsized aquarium filled with water and a TV showing footage of tropical fish. We entered a huge gallery with mattresses on the floor and a hundred TV screens attached to the ceiling and lay down and stared up at the images on the ceiling for maybe an hour. Dave welcomed the opportunity to rest.

Dave stayed with me for a week. Heat exhaustion and jet lag aside, I think he had a good time. We made plans to meet up again in September when I was due in the UK for a few days of rehearsals for the Blondie shows, leading up to our never-to-be four-night stand at Wembley. Of course, the British tour was canceled and the reunion with Dave postponed.

As 1983 began, I was still reeling from news of the canceled tour and what looked like the end of Blondie when Dave called me up. He and Annie had been hard at work in their little studio above a picture frame shop and just released an album, *Sweet Dreams (Are Made of This)*. Dave asked what was going on with Blondie. When I told him I had no clue, he invited me to join the small group they were putting together for promotion and a UK tour beginning in February. I was happy to forget about all the issues with Blondie. Two weeks later, I was in London for rehearsals. Dave had sent over a copy of the duo's album, and I already loved the new songs—as would millions of other people.

With Blondie inactive, there wasn't much for Shep Gordon to manage. He and I had a meeting at the Savoy Hotel while I was in town, and he told me he was done with the band. The drug problems were a major factor in his decision. I wasn't sad to see him go, but I hated that no one was doing anything to keep Blondie together. At least I got Shep to agree to stop taking a cut from our future income.

Fortunately, I had other things to focus on and was able to put Blondie in the rearview mirror and turn my attentions to Eurythmics. On Tuesday, February 15, our newly formed pop group piled into a Transit van and headed out on a tour that had been dubbed Folie à Deux—a French phrase to describe a delusion shared by two people in close association. It can start to feel like family pretty quickly when a band goes on tour in a van. You're either on the way up or on the way down, and Eurythmics were on the upside of that equation. I remember passing U2 in their van on their way out of Glasgow as we drove into the city. Passing other musicians on the same road, on the same journey, is one of the nicer little happenings when you're in those early days of building a band.

Our first stop was Hull, and we set off early to leave time to run the entire set at soundcheck. I felt relieved to be back in the UK and on the road again, although the circumstances were very different. Had the Blondie tour gone ahead, we'd have been playing to audiences of 12,500 a night, while the Hull club held fewer than 500 people. That situation changed soon enough.

Six weeks later, when we played the tour's final show at the Lyceum Theatre in London, the single "Sweet Dreams" was number two on the UK chart. I couldn't help but notice the echoes of my past. Being in a band, just as it was about to become one of the biggest acts on the planet, I felt like I'd been here before. I couldn't have been happier for Annie and Dave.

As the tour progressed, the mounting excitement around the album and the single was tangible. We did a punishing run of five shows in a row that brought us to a sold-out gig at the Sugarhouse, on the campus of Lancaster University, followed by a day off. There'd hardly been time to catch our breath since the beginning of this whirlwind of rehearsals and shows. With the initial success of the tour and positive chart positions, everyone was in a celebratory mood, so band and crew decamped to a pub. Some of our fellow drinkers had been at the show, and word about the gig spread fast among the good people of Lancaster. As one person after another came by to say how much they enjoyed the show, I realized just how successful Annie and Dave were set to become. We were enjoying the attention when we got the news we'd been booked to appear on *Top of the Pops*. That was all the evidence I needed to know that Eurythmics would become major stars and never look back.

We had to postpone a few shows to be at the BBC in London to tape the TV appearance, after which we turned back around and headed north to play in Newcastle. Our episode aired the evening we played there; by the time we went on, the audience was in a frenzy. The timing couldn't have been more perfect—we were headed to Glasgow, followed by a show in Annie's hometown in Aberdeen. We met Annie's parents that night. Although a little stoic and reserved, they couldn't have been prouder of their daughter's success. It was a tonic for me to be around such positivity and to share her joy. After all the disappointments of the last year, I was in a new group, with a single racing up the UK charts. Thinking back to their invitation to join them as a partner in Eurythmics and my decision to stick with Blondie, I realized I enjoyed being a sideman without the day-to-day hassles of being a partner in a business. I was a hired hand, happy to be on tour with this small tight unit of gifted musicians. Ego be damned.

I reunited with Dave and Annie on their fifth album, *Revenge*, in 1986. We recorded the album in Paris, where I reconnected with producer Michael Kamen, from Jimmy's disastrous 1981 sessions. Michael's string arrangement on the smash hit single from the album, *The Miracle of Love*, still takes my breath away. Following the album's release, we flew to Los Angeles and set to work rehearsing for the world tour in a vacant building on La Brea Avenue. It was a very convivial setup. People were constantly stopping by to hang out during rehearsals. I remember Jodie Foster came by one day around the time we filmed the promo video for the single "Missionary Man." The shoot was on the soundstage at A&M Studios, just a couple of blocks along La Brea. Since 1991, that place has been the home of the Jim Henson Company, but back then, it was still Herb Alpert and Jerry Moss's base of operations.

While we were working on the soundstage, Bob Geldof was recording a solo album, his first record since Live Aid, in a newly renovated recording studio in one of the buildings. They were giving the new studio a dry run to try and get the kinks out. Because Dave was involved on a few numbers, I was drafted in to play on a few tracks while the video crew was doing setups. I arrived to add the drum parts to a couple of songs, only to discover that there was an army of people in the studio watching the recording.

I think Geldof has everyone's number in his little black book, and probably half of them had turned out to show their support. A&M head Herb Alpert was in the control booth, along with Jimmy Iovine, the record's producer—and later the founder of Interscope Records and cofounder of Dr. Dre's Beats headphone empire—and half the great and the good of the recording industry of the time. Bono, the Edge, and Larry Mullen Jr. were there, too, along with Maria McKee, the singer-songwriter from the LA band Lone Justice, just hanging out and socializing. I was laying down a drum track to a prerecorded backing, and it was quite arduous, going back and forth, trying to get it just right. It was a complex passage, but I finally got it straight. Bono was singing on a live mic in the control room, so there was sound leakage everywhere because the studio was still incomplete, and half a dozen people were standing around talking. There was some added pressure, given the cast of characters who were listening back, but finally, I completed the track and was proud of my efforts. Then our director called me back to the soundstage to shoot more material for the video.

When I returned to the recording later, I found Larry Mullen at my drum kit, playing the track I already finished and assumed was in the can. Maybe they thought having the drummer from U2 was more of a draw than the guy who used to drum for Blondie, but I don't know. I remember being pissed, though, which was kind of funny. I started shouting, "What the fuck is going on?" I was half joking, but just for added spice, when Larry got to the part I'd spent so long working on, he asked me to show him how I did it, so that was like a handful of salt in the wound. I wish someone had captured my outburst on film, because I don't get mad too often, but there I was, flipping out in front of these legendary producers and a bunch of famous rock and rollers.

The Eurythmics tour that followed was incredible. The band was hot, and Dave and Annie were at their peak, so it was a very positive environment. I've so many beautiful memories of those times on the road, vivid reminders of how fulfilling this life can be. Playing Wembley Arena and looking across the stage to see George Harrison standing in the wings watching the show with Jeff Lynne and getting my photograph taken with him after the show. Before the fall of the Berlin Wall, we played at the Reichstag with Tina Turner and Joe Cocker as our opening act. The people on the eastern side of the wall, still under Soviet control, were coming out into the streets and cheering. One night in New York, I got off stage with Eurythmics and found my dad deep in conversation with Mick Jagger, like they were old friends. Another time, we found ourselves at the Checkerboard Lounge, Buddy Guy and L.C. Thurman's blues club in Chicago's South Side. It had a big sign outside bearing the legend "Home of the Blues." We asked if we could get up and play. It was a mostly Black Chicago crowd and a musically discerning one. They said yeah, okay, but you'd better be good. We had Joniece Jamison as a backing singer on that tour, along with the great harmonica player Jimmy Z, and the crowd went insane. It

was so gratifying and a good life lesson to know that even with all the highs and lows of Blondie, the other side of the dream had just as much to offer.

Eurythmics played a run of shows at Wembley Arena at the tail end of 1986, including a gala performance for the Prince's Trust charity, playing for ten thousand people and a whole bunch of VIPs and dignitaries, including Charles and Diana. Prior to the performance, there was a receiving line, so the band lined up and was presented to their Royal Highnesses. I was standing in the queue with Jimmy Z, looking back down the line as Charles and Diana shook hands with Dave and Annie and worked their way down, making royal small talk. Soon, we found ourselves being introduced to Princess Diana. We're telling her who we are, where we're from, and all the places we've been on the tour. She was about to move on, but then stopped to ask, "How do your wives or girl-friends feel about your traveling so much?" Without missing a beat, Jimmy replies, "My wife doesn't mind, but my girl-friend gets very upset." Diana's face flushed completely red with embarrassment.

The last show the *Revenge* band played was an anti-apartheid concert at Wembley Stadium for Nelson Mandela's seventieth birthday. As is usual at a festival, there's no sound-check, so you get maybe a few seconds to do a line check before you play. We played a warm-up show the previous night, but to all intents and purposes, we hadn't played together for months. I was doing a line check in front of a vast Mandela backdrop; the stage seemed as big as a football field. We were trying to dial in the drums in my monitors, so I wasn't paying attention to anything else. The monitor guy's telling me to hit the drum, hit the drum, and I'm doing just that. It's only then I realize Richard Gere is at the front of the

The luxury of being a "sideman"—with Annie on the
Eurythmics Revenge Tour

stage trying to announce the band. I can't hear the exact words, but I'm sure he was making a heartfelt speech about Mandela, and I'm just banging away at the drum kit. I wind up punctuating some remark Richard made and he looks one hundred feet across the stage and asks, "Is that for me?" It was simultaneously funny and embarrassing; eighty thousand people in the crowd and untold millions of people watching a live feed of the show across the world and I'm highlighting Richard Gere's speech like he's a Vaudeville comedian. Hopefully, I didn't undercut his message too much because it was a special day. We played a great show, and I was proud to be part of such a historic moment.

Chapter 29

CHEQUERED PAST

The roots of Chequered Past can be traced back to early 1981. Blondie wasn't on the road or in the studio. I wanted to play, so I traveled to the UK to work with Michael Des Barres, the singer from Nigel's old band, Silverhead. Michael was a well-spoken, highly educated Englishman, with maybe a couple of pints of aristocratic blood in his veins from a dozen generations back. He had a strong voice and wrote great songs, but maybe if I had one criticism, you couldn't vouch for his authenticity exactly. Because Michael was an actor, it sometimes seemed like he was just playing the role of a rock and roll frontman. The plan was to go out on a short tour in support of Michael's new album, on Mike Chapman's Dreamland label. Nigel and I helped Michael get a band together for the shows.

Michael was at a crossroads in his life. We all drank too much, but Michael was at the point where he needed to decide whether to carry on like that and die or quit forever and have some sort of life. As a unit, when we were good, it was great, but a lot of the time, things were chaotic. I have a hazy recollection of a show in Nottingham, after spending the entire day at the Trip to Jerusalem pub. We all got blasted and the gig wasn't one of our finest.

One good thing about this tour was getting to fulfill my boyhood dream of playing London's Marquee Club. I enjoyed the revered tradition of having drinks at the nearby pub the Ship before the gig. The Ship became an adjunct to the Marquee because prior to 1970, the Marquee had no license to sell spirits. Having a quick pint at the same pub bands like the Yardbirds and the Who would drink at before their Marquee gigs was part of the ritual. Overall, the tour with Michael was kind of a debacle, but I'll always cherish the memory of playing to a packed crowd at the Marquee.

Dreamland Records rented the band a nice four-bedroom flat in Pimlico, behind Victoria Station. Michael was coming to the end of a chapter in his life, and although I didn't realize it, so was I. After a time, Rory Johnson, Malcolm McLaren's US consiglieri from the Sex Pistols era, moved into the flat. Rory introduced us to Pistols' guitarist, Steve Jones, who was trying to get straight with this ginseng and curry cure he'd read about. Don't ask me how that was supposed to work, but I imagine if you're looking to clean up your act, there's more reliable methods. Steve developed a habit of leaving empty ginseng vials scattered around the flat, so you had to be sure not to walk around the place barefoot. Not everyone got that memo because one morning, I heard a nasty crunching sound after our unfortunate housekeeper was on her knees cleaning and came down hard on one of Steve's glass vials. We were all slightly out of control, in our own way, with these histories we were trying to live up to, or to live down. Michael was always joking we should form a band, call ourselves Chequered Past—because we all had one.

The tour came to an unexpected halt one morning when the housekeeper came into the living room and informed me that "Mr. Michael" was gone. Hungover, I followed her to Michael's bedroom and surveyed the empty room. He'd left all his possessions behind, and his clothes were hanging neatly in the wardrobe. It looked like Michael had left in a hurry. His solo career wasn't taking off, and he needed to go somewhere and reassess his life: the deal he had with Mike Chapman had felt like his last chance.

The next time I saw Michael was in 1982 when he showed up at my loft in New York. Michael was in a far better head-space this time around. He'd gotten sober and was keen to start working again. As we were catching up, he reminded me of the Chequered Past idea we'd had on our ill-fated tour. We all started hanging around together again, along with Frank Infante, and realized we had the nucleus of a band. Steve Jones, who was living in NYC as an illegal alien at the time, rounded out the lineup. His post-Pistols band, the Professionals, had been derailed in November 1981 by a car accident in Minneapolis. Three of his bandmates were injured and flown back to England to recuperate. Steve, who wasn't involved in the incident, had other plans. I guess the ginseng and curry thing hadn't worked out, because he'd since embarked on a life as a full-blown heroin addict on the streets of New York. Occasionally, he'd stop by my loft and tell me he was up for doing the gig for a few dollars quick cash, and so he filled out the band lineup, if only to keep up the payments to his dealers.

Chequered Past made our live debut at the new Peppermint Lounge on lower Fifth Avenue on September 26, 1982. Frank

Roccio, the club owner, offered us a Sunday slot and we sold it out. The band was intended as a strictly for-fun, one-off set of covers. For me, it was a way to lift the gloom after a miserable summer. Blondie's fate appeared to be out of my hands; certainly we were in limbo, so the Chequered Past show was an opportunity to maintain my profile on the New York scene.

It was a memorable night. The first song in our set was a cover of the Go-Go's hit "Vacation," written by Kathy Valentine. The crowd had no idea what to make of a former Sex Pistol playing an American pop song. We threw in a few Pistols and Blondie numbers for good measure, alongside the show's highlight, "Suspicious Minds," which Steve sang in his best Vegas impression of the King. After the show, we were greeted backstage by some friends from Blondie's publicity team. Everyone was encouraging me to strike while the iron was hot and make Chequered Past permanent. Go out on tour. All that stuff. I had to wonder, if they were so enthusiastic about Chequered Past, did they know something about Blondie's future I didn't?

I don't know that the iron was still hot, but in mid-1983, Nigel, Steve, and I flew to Los Angeles to reconvene the band. Over the past months, I'd been on the road with Eurythmics and coming to terms with Blondie being finished and figured maybe after all we should make a go of Chequered Past. Steve wanted to get away from the drug scene, so he tagged along for the ride. He assured us he'd kicked his habit, so our prospects looked bright. Frank was touring with Divinyls and Iggy Pop, so we enlisted guitarist Tony Sales, our old friend from the Iggy tour, to join the group in his place. It was a completely clean slate for all of us. We figured we'd work the LA club circuit and find a record company to sign us.

Naturally, there were a couple of red flags along the way. I think we were a little naive taking Steve at his word about his recovery because on our flight to LA, literally as we began our descent, he admitted he'd need a fix immediately upon touchdown. Pardon the cheap shot, but Steve was jonesing. Nigel suggested we contact Danny Sugerman, the Doors' biographer and manager. Danny was a writer, and knew the ins and outs of band management, but more crucially, he was a junkie. A phone call and a connection later, Steve's immediate problem was solved. Not the most auspicious start.

Michael Des Barres was the first person I knew to get sober and has (on his own account) remained sober since 1981. With his example, Steve got into recovery and managed to try to stay sober—or, at least, off heroin—while we were putting the band together. Steve cleaned up his act and moved in with me and Nigel at Nigel's place in Studio City.

We approached Danny Goldberg, an old contact from Nigel and Michael's Silverhead days, about managing Chequered Past. He agreed and booked us a few club shows. One of the first was a high-profile gig at the Roxy on the Sunset Strip. The club has a low stage, and in the middle of the set, what we assumed was an overzealous fan jumped onstage holding some papers in his hand. It wasn't fan mail. Mr. Udo, Blondie's Japanese promoter, had sent a guy with writs of summons, served to Nigel and me, over the cancellation of last year's tour.

My and Nigel's legal worries aside, we continued to rehearse and work on new material. Steve moved out of Nigel's place and in with Michael, and they began writing songs for the Chequered Past album. It was good for Steve. When we started out, the rest of us were friends and he was something of an outsider, but he was looking to find a little direction in his life and happy for us to lead the way. And musically, we all clicked. We sounded great together and the live shows were always a treat. Our time coincided with the beginnings of the "hair band" phenomenon in California, so every show we were playing to members of Poison or Guns N' Roses. At first glance, we were probably strange bedfellows, but we were playing rock and roll, same as those guys.

One of our favorite venues was the Music Machine, a club on Pico Boulevard in West LA. We played there constantly and treated it as an informal HQ. It was hard work, followed by plenty of after-hours drinking and partying. A few Go-Go's turned up to see us play one night, and that was the start of my relationship with their bass player, Kathy Valentine. At the time, the Go-Go's were a huge deal, and I was a fan. Kathy was so great to be around. Always writing songs, always singing, always motivated to keep pushing herself and her career. She got on well with everyone in the band and, essentially, she became one of the guys.

Kathy and I became a seemingly perfect LA rock and roll couple and stayed that way for years. We had some great times. She had an apartment at the Shoreham Towers in West Hollywood, overlooking the Spago restaurant parking lot. I recall one year looking out from her balcony and seeing Swifty Lazar's Oscar night party getting underway, so we crept in the backdoor and spent the night partying with Hollywood stars, movers and shakers. She was with me in the studio when Chequered Past recorded our album, and I was at her side when the Go-Go's eventually imploded.

Ultimately, Kathy and I parted at the end of 1989 when she got sober and saw the need for us to go our separate ways. It wasn't something I easily got over, but for a while, all was good in LA for me, the band, and my new relationship.

Eventually, Chequered Past was offered a record deal by Gary Gersh, A&R for EMI America. I distinctly remember his pitch to the band: how honored and proud he'd be to have us on his label, that he wasn't concerned about achieving immediate success. He was happy to sign us to a multiple album deal and see how things developed. He said everything an artist wants to hear from a record company. We had the perfect situation: high-powered management, a record company that believed in us, sold-out gigs all over the West Coast, and access to EMI's studio on Sunset Boulevard.

Somehow, we blew it. To helm the album, we settled on Michael James Jackson, fresh off producing *Lick It Up* for KISS. He wasn't my choice, and he and I butted heads at times. I felt he didn't connect with the band's punk rock roots. We all envisioned the band as this rock and roll force of nature, but he tried to rein us in, to control how we played. Those were my feelings at the time, although the record has held up better than I remembered. British rock magazine *Kerrang!* placed the album at number three in their 1984 chart, behind *Purple Rain* and Van Halen's *1984*, at number one.

Somehow, we managed to get through a photo session for the album cover, despite Tony having a seizure in the makeup chair. The distraction of piles of cocaine didn't help; it was the 80s after all. When Tony came to, we just kept going like nothing had happened. The album cover features us—including the conveniently revived Tony—on stage at Perkins Palace in Pasadena in all our rock and roll splendor, surrounded by various ephemera. I'm holding a copy of Friedrich Nietzsche's *Beyond Good and Evil*. I don't know why. Maybe I was just passing through a period of existential ennui.

When the album was released in 1984, our management changed hands, with the affable Bill Siddons taking the reins, and we took to the road, opening for the hair metal band Ratt, with fill-in gigs on off days at various rock dives. We were booked to play a couple of nights opening for Duran Duran in San Diego but missed our stage time the first night after spending most of the day trying to track down Steve Jones after he'd gone AWOL. The EMI America roster at the time included Steven Van Zandt from the E Street Band, who was on a nationwide tour with his band the Disciples of Soul, and he invited us to be the opening act. It seemed like an incredible opportunity. The tour was initially booked into large venues, but weak ticket sales meant a bunch of shows were hastily moved to clubs. It must have been tough for Steven, who was accustomed to selling out huge arenas with Bruce Springsteen. He was carrying the expense of a full concert production and a six-piece band. Steven's drummer was one of my biggest influences, Dino Danelli of the Young Rascals. Whatever was going on with ticket sales, I loved watching Dino play every night.

It seemed like the agent who booked the shows hadn't looked at a map; we often had to drive through the night to reach the next town in time. The last week of the tour was a little easier: After a show in Denver, we flew back to LA for a break before our hometown show at the Hollywood Palladium. I think we were well placed to build on the momentum of that first year, but it wasn't to be. After the tour, Michael, who was clean, came back to find Steve in the middle of a drug binge at his house. Once again, I found myself in a band where a key member couldn't keep it together. We tried to start fresh with Laurence Juber—formerly a member of Wings. Laurence was an incredible guitarist, but he was the antithesis of Steve in every way. The new lineup played a showcase for a few record execs, but it was clear the magic had left the room. One of the A&R guys, Paul Atkinson, the former Zombies guitarist, told me afterward he'd never seen a showcase where the band broke up in front of his eyes. Shortly thereafter, Michael got a call from Andy and John from Duran Duran and he left to work with their side project, the Power Station. Suddenly, I was back to square one, and Michael was performing at Live Aid with the Power Station.

I needed to blow away the Los Angeles cobwebs, so after a trip back East to visit my dad, I flew to Austin to meet up with Kathy and her mom. Just a few months earlier, it seemed Kathy's career with the Go-Go's was only going to go up and up. They'd had a bunch of hit records and were well positioned to really make an impact. She'd just bought a house in West Hollywood, and life was looking good. Mike Chapman had been hired to work his magic on their next album, and then out of nowhere, her bandmates, Belinda Carlisle and Charlotte Caffey, decided they didn't want to be in the band anymore and turned Kathy's life upside down. The band was over.

We were out at dinner at Spago in Beverly Hills the night after it went down. I was on the phone to her management, frantic. How could you let this happen? It was like history repeating itself. Mike, who hadn't heard the news, came over to our table. He started telling Kathy how excited he was to get started on the new record and Kathy's just broken up, crying at the table. Having been through a similar trauma, it was especially painful for me to see her suffer like that. It took a long time to heal the wounds. Over the years, the Go-Go's reunited a few times. I even got to play with them at their arena homecoming show in 2022, but a lot of water had to pass under the bridge before that happened.

With the Chequered Past and the Go-Go's unraveling, Kathy and I decided to take off for a vacation in Jamaica, staying at a private resort in Negril, not far from the famous Rick's Cafe on the cliffs. Although private, the accommodations were basic, but you don't need amenities in paradise. We stayed in a clifftop hut overlooking our own private lagoon. There was no TV, no air conditioning, and no distractions—just beautiful sunrises and sunsets. I brought a tape deck and radio, so we could listen to the rebel music broadcasts on the local radio station at night. Add to that some glorious mixtapes we bought along with fresh juice and ganja from a vendor's shack. One luxury we allowed ourselves was a cook, who'd bring us a breakfast of fruit and porridge each morning accompanied with a pot of strong Blue Mountain coffee. After breakfast, we'd smoke a joint and snorkel for a few hours, the colors of the tropical fish and plants vividly illuminated by the Jamaican sun shining through the water. Our cook would return to fetch the breakfast dishes and list off our options for dinner. I couldn't have been happier. In the afternoon, we'd leave the compound and get lost awhile, talking over the chaotic past months, helping one another move on. We befriended a local kid who became our guide. Kathy and I were both keen to hear live music, and he brought us to clubs deep in the bush. We were completely off the grid, so I had no clue manager Bill Siddons had been frantically trying to reach me. He'd received a fax from Pete Townshend's office enquiring about my availability.

Kathy was understanding and said of course I had to go, so I dropped everything. I booked flights back to the States, and following a brief layover in New Jersey to visit my dad and to pick up some warmer clothes, I boarded an overnight flight to London. All the way across the Atlantic, eight hours straight, my mind was buzzing. Pete Townshend of the Who was trying to track me down. I could scarcely conceal my delight.

Chapter 30

PETE TOWNSHEND

My love of the Who began back in 1965, when I was still in elementary school. Once a week, I traveled by bus with my mom to Sickles Music Store in Jersey City for drum lessons. I was eleven years old. Most of each lesson was spent with a Mel Bay instruction book, but for the last ten minutes I'd get to sit at the drum kit and play along with a record I'd brought from home. Usually, it might be a new Beatles or Four Seasons 45 blasting out of a tiny record player, competing with the volume of the drums.

One time, I came to the lesson with a new album I'd picked up at Wolfson's record store in Bayonne. That record was *My Generation*, the first LP by the Who, and it was a revelation. I first read about the Who in *Rave*, the English fan magazine. I first heard the Who when the US TV show *Shindig!* showed some film from the Richmond Jazz and Blues Festival during a segment, "Shindig Goes to London." Just seeing them, even in that grainy black-and-white footage, I knew I had to find out everything about this band.

Knowing it was something not everyone was turned on to, it was as if I'd stumbled on this great secret.

Playing along to the Who in my drum lesson immediately felt different. I don't think my drum teacher had heard anything like it, but I guess nobody had heard that drum sound before. Keith Moon's seismic, almost chaotic drums were as far away from Top 40 radio as you could get. Hearing him play with such abandon gave me a whole new perspective on rock and roll drumming. There was never another player like him.

From that point onward, the music of the Who was always the gold standard for me. It was their attitude, their songs, that defined what it meant to be in a rock and roll band. And it was Pete Townshend who wrote those songs. Although we'd briefly met once, I could hardly say I knew Pete. Our brief encounter happened around the swimming pool of the Knightsbridge Holiday Inn at a party celebrating drummer Kenney Jones joining the Who, so who knew if Pete even remembered the party, let alone me saying hi?

I arrived in London, armed with an approved work visa, and was met by Billy Nicholls, a good friend of Townshend's. Nicholls's "lost" 1966 album *Would You Believe* is a psychedelic masterpiece to rival the Beach Boys' *Pet Sounds* album, so it was very cool to meet him. Billy immediately made me feel welcome. He was very affable and helped keep my tired eyes open on the short drive from Heathrow to Richmond, briefing me on what was going on in the world of Pete Townshend. Apparently, just prior to the album getting underway, Pete had checked himself into rehab and was now starting anew.

Billy brought me to the Petersham Hotel, an elegant Victorian four-star hotel on Richmond Hill with breathtaking views of the Thames and Petersham Meadows. Directly behind the hotel stands a Georgian mansion known as the Wick, once owned by Ronnie Wood. Former Faces/Small Faces Ronnie Lane owned the cottage in the house's back garden. I'd only just landed, I hadn't even met Pete, but already I was knee-deep in history.

I woke up way too early, jet-lagged the next morning and went for a jog in Richmond Park. I always have a pair of running shoes with me. I started exercising in the early 1980s during the extended downtime from Blondie, if only to have a reason to get out of bed in the mornings. My girlfriend hooked me up with a personal trainer at the New York Sports Training Institute over on East Forty-Ninth Street and since then, I've kept an exercise regimen. I believe it is my responsibility to feel healthy and be positive. One of my favorite things to do if I'm in a new city is to run until I lose my bearings and then try to figure out how to find my way back. I mean, for a drummer, cardio is important anyway, but if you can find a new place you haven't seen before, all the better. With that in mind, I deliberately got myself lost in Richmond Park. I expected to be alone, but through the early morning fog, I saw a herd of deer. It's such a magical place. You're right on the edge of the city but caught up in this lush ancient countryside.

Back at the hotel, I found bassist Phil Chen in the breakfast room. Phil and I'd worked together on a session a few years before and became fast friends. After some tea, we made our way to Pete's Boathouse studio in Twickenham, where we were greeted by Pete's longtime personal assistant, Nicola

Joss. Nicola ushered me into Pete's office, where I found him sitting behind a desk in front of a giant poster of Meher Baba, the Sufi mystic. Pete was a devotee of Meher Baba and had penned the song "Baba O'Riley" in tribute to his spiritual teacher. We said hi and he asked me to take a seat and we made small talk while I cast an eye around the office. It seemed a very professional operation, and Pete looked every inch the executive. Pete sometimes has a reputation for being an intense character, but he was welcoming and keen to talk about his ambitions for the album he was working on, *White City: A Novel*.

He explained he had all these songs ready to go and how keen he was for us to start work. After some well-documented hedonistic years, Pete was trying to stay on the straight and narrow. He didn't seem to mind what the rest of us got up to in our downtime between sessions, but he was going to stay clean. He mentioned John "Rabbit" Bundrick would be on hand to play keyboards. I was only aware of Rabbit from his work on the Wailers' *Catch a Fire* album. I always assumed he was a Jamaican Rasta, so it came as a surprise later when I was introduced to this tall white Texan. From the start, I got a taste of Pete's humor when he told me "Rabbit's only on the sessions because he owes me some money."

We set to work almost immediately. My sense of anticipation was high, but I was a little apprehensive going into the studio and meeting Pete's producer, Chris Thomas, along with his brilliant engineer Bill Price. Chris is a great producer with a real pedigree for working with musicians. You need look no further than to his work with Roxy Music and their drummer, Paul Thompson, a player I've long admired. I felt for the longest time that Blondie carried a Roxy influence and imagined Chris would have made a great producer for Blondie. As well as having a natural rapport with musicians in general, Chris has a real knack for arrangements. He has a keen ear and an ability to take a song apart and put it back together again and make all those elements gel in a way they hadn't before. In my experience, that's the definition of good music production. He was an all-around nice guy with a terrific, easy-going temperament. That spilled over into the atmosphere in the studio, making the recording process a real pleasure.

I wasn't sent any demos of the songs beforehand and had no idea what to expect, but I felt ready for the challenge. Initially, I was expecting to let my inner Keith Moon come to the fore, but the sessions were a little more controlled, more song oriented. It was a surprise to learn the sessions were being documented on videotape. At the time, it was unheard of to have a full film crew in the studio while you worked, so I was a little on edge at first. I'd gotten used to making videos with Blondie all this time, but not so much while rehearsing new material. A lot of the footage has found its way online, and there's some great stuff out there.

Given that Pete was cleaning up his act, studio hours were distinctly straight: noon through to 6 p.m., leaving a lot of time for mischief. It being November and Beaujolais Nouveau season, every night was seen through a red wine haze. I'm no wine snob, but for my money, drinking Beaujolais Nouveau is an overrated experience. It's a terrible wine, fermented from all the leftover grapes from the previous season, but somehow it became our default drink for the duration of our stay. Rabbit, Phil, and I spent way too much time propping up the bar, laughing and sharing our old road stories. In the hotel restaurant, there was a piano on a rostrum and Rabbit got up and played one night when we were all a little pissed. As he played, the piano shifted and moved, eventually sliding off the side of the stage, almost in slow motion. Somehow, we weren't asked to leave. I guess even the stateliest hotels in London have come to expect a certain amount of abandon when they have rock musicians as paying guests.

During my two weeks in the studio there was a lot of jamming on rough ideas and sketches of arrangements as we assembled the bits and pieces of songs in Pete's head. Townshend is an interesting character, a gifted and purposeful artist. Maybe because he spends so long on the writing process, once he has the idea in place, he can be quite single-minded. That said, he was open to ideas, and it was cool to bounce some around with him. I think it was the first time he'd picked up a guitar in a while, and it was a thrill to be in the studio helping him commit his vision to tape. It goes without saying that he's extremely driven and has a razor-sharp intelligence, but I was surprised at the more human side of the guy. He was getting a kick out of the camaraderie in the studio. It was a happy time, with no discord or ego. Often when Pete and I spoke, I'd get to hear him reminiscing about his friend Keith. I could tell that he'd lost a brother, and it still hurt him to the core.

Besides Keith Moon, whom, of course, I never tired of hearing about, Pete was talkative about other topics. We shared a love of Springsteen—he was proud that he'd played "Born to Run" with Bruce onstage. I was kind of soaking up everything Pete I could: listening to him send his assistant off to pick up a suit from South Molton Street, okaying the use of "See Me, Feel Me" for an Australian shampoo commercial. After school, Pete's teenage daughter, Emma, used to come by and hang out, with Justine, one of her school friends, in tow. They were great kids. I remember during a break from recording, they made a beeline for me and my kit, so I took a bit of time to show them a few things on the drums. The camera crew were on hand to capture everything and unbeknownst to me, everyone was watching the footage in the control room and getting a kick seeing the guy from Blondie nursing a Beaujolais hangover while patiently giving a drum lesson to a pair of teenagers. It would be funny to see that footage after all these years, especially as Emma's friend Justine was Justine Frischmann, later the frontwoman of 1990s rock band Elastica.

One night after the sessions, Pete took me to one side and offered me his tickets to the premiere of Paul McCartney's new movie, *Give My Regards to Broad Street*, in Leicester Square. He explained he had other plans, so I went in his place, with Phil Chen as my plus-one. I'll be honest, it was a real thrill, but only up to a point. We arrived unfashionably early and made our way to our seats in the auditorium and waited while the seats around us gradually began to fill out. Slowly, it dawned on us we were in the seats allocated to McCartney's closest friends and associates. Pete and Paul go way back, and we had Pete's tickets, so we were breathing the same air as Paul's VIP friends and family, feeling like imposters on the scene and half expecting to be asked to move along. We were caught between Bill Wyman on one side and Denny Laine from Wings on the other side of the stalls.

Then the lights were dimmed, and Paul and Linda entered to a round of applause and took up their seats directly behind us. There we were, surrounded by some of my absolute heroes. The only thing was, and I'm sure Paul will forgive me for saying it, *Give My Regards to Broad Street* is not a good film. I think it was a labor of love for Paul, but after maybe twenty minutes, it became clear this wasn't going to be *A Hard Day's Night*. As the film wore on, I turned to Phil in the darkness, and he made a face. I gave him a shrug, like what can you do? We wanted to leave so bad, but we were hemmed in on all sides by all these rock and roll luminaries, with Paul beaming proudly behind us. We had no choice but to stay in our seats and endure the movie. Probably, if we'd been out of McCartney's line of sight, we'd have snuck out early. After the curtain came down, Phil and I ducked out of the theater and walked into Chinatown for a couple bowls of noodles. Regrettably, the next day in the studio, I found out everyone in the VIP section was invited back to Paul and Linda's house for a premier party. If I'm going to put a positive spin on missing that, at least we didn't have to look a Beatle in the eye and tell him his movie sucked. And the Chinese food was good, as I recall.

That brief spell in Richmond was such a special time; I suppose I knew on some level that it couldn't last. After a couple of weeks of sessions, I arrived one morning and was ushered straight into a "meeting" with Alan Rogan, Pete's guitar tech. Turns out Alan was the first stop on the way to the exit door. Nicola came in to take me to see Pete. Just like when I arrived, he was sitting at the desk under the wall hanging of Meher Baba. I could feel it in my gut, unwelcome news was coming. Sure enough, while I tried to look professional and pleasant, Pete told me he was going to pull the plug on the recordings. He wanted to reassess the project. Sorry. Thanks for coming. The other side of the dream had its lows too.

Chapter 31

BOB DYLAN

I was staying at the Lodge, Nick Lowe's giant house in Chiswick. Nick and his wife, Carlene Carter, were in the middle of a divorce, and because neither of them wanted to be around, I was offered the use of the place while I was in town. That part of West London is one of my favorite places in the world. It's set apart from the rest of the city and there's a lot of green space. Grand Victorian houses, set back from the street, with neat lawns and tidy gardens. The urban sprawl of Hammersmith is only a couple of miles down the road, dirty and vibrant if you know where to look.

At the time, I was working with my friend Dave Stewart from Eurythmics. Aside from his duties with the band, Dave was now one of the UK's most sought-after record producers-for-hire. Producers need musicians, so Dave asked me to be one of the studio's on-call house band members whenever I was in town. I didn't set out to be a gun-for-hire, but I enjoyed doing it. There's no politics. No one is behaving like a diva. You just turn up and play.

Every morning, I caught the N20 bus across London to Archway Station, before walking up Crouch Hill to the studio. It was like a daily commute but without the drudgery of a desk job at the end of the ride. Since I boarded the bus at the start of its route, I was usually guaranteed a prime front seat at the top of the bus to watch the London cityscape unfold in front of me as the bus heaved through the London traffic. Sure, it's an hour's journey, but the view is wonderful, and the time flies by.

Crouch End was a curious place in those days, like a village tucked away among the North London suburbs. Similar to Chiswick, it's only a step and a jump away from the craziness of the city. To the north is Muswell Hill, the birthplace of the Kinks, and in the other direction is the heart of Finsbury Park and the 24/7 hubbub of London's Irish community. At the top of Crouch Hill, there's no tube, no train stations. The place is a little like Dave. He can be in the room with you, but his head is in the clouds—clouds of dreams and schemes. He's a one-man font of creativity and ideas, operating slightly outside of the norm. Dave's imagination seems to be always on the go, running wild and free. England in the 1980s was still something of a dark place, but Dave was always upbeat and positive.

Dave and Annie found a grand deconsecrated church in 1984, at the beginning of their Eurythmics empire, renting and outfitting a huge room as a studio. It was known, of course, as the Church Studio. As their success grew in the 1980s, they bought the building outright and began renovations. The Church Studio would go on to become one of the world's premier recording studios, famed for its acoustics and atmosphere. Everyone from U2 to Adele has recorded there, but in 1986, it was still a work in progress.

As I arrived the first time, the building echoed with the sound of the Eurythmics' crew and friends, shifting equipment and preparing the room for a session. Dave had asked me to play on a record he was making with the singer Kiki Dee. I was looking up and around at the high, cavernous ceilings thinking, wow, the acoustics here are going to be incredible. Even in its unfinished state, I could tell it was going to be a great space to work and record. Friends of Dave and Annie were setting up a recording session in little side rooms, and Dave's engineers were untangling a spaghetti trail of cables; it felt like a real creative hub. While we caught up and introductions were made, Dave asked if I was available in November to work a couple of sessions with a famous American singer. I told him sure, why not, and we set to work on Kiki's session.

I'd invited my girlfriend, Kathy Valentine, to come along. Kathy was still going through a tough time with the Go-Go's breakup, and I was doing my best to support her. I figured she needed a way to move on, just as I had, and wanted to plant the idea that there was the possibility of a career outside the band. I asked Dave if we could demo a few of Kathy's songs. Dave gave her a room and the use of an engineer. I was very protective of her, and it felt good to be able to contribute to rebuilding her confidence. After the sessions were over, I flew back to the US to visit my dad and take care of some business. It was a short trip because I had to be back in London to record with Dave and this famous American singer.

It was November when I returned, the renovations were still underway—we'd be recording in the midst of a building site, basically. The weather had turned wintery, the Church was cold and drafty, but there was nothing downcast or chilly in the atmosphere. Giant portable heaters were being set up on the studio floor, and the whole place was a buzz of activity in anticipation of the mystery star's arrival. Dave and I were joined by bassist John McKenzie and keyboard player Pat Seymour. Pat and I would later tour as part of the Eurythmics *Revenge* band.

As we set up, the mood was talkative and upbeat. When the door swung open, everybody stopped to look over. It was just a guy in a green anorak with the hood pulled down over his head. He had a female companion at his side. The door closed behind him, and the guy lowered his hood to say hello. I think anyone would have recognized the voice. The guy in the anorak was Bob Dylan. The woman at his side was Carole Childs, a record executive and Dylan's close friend. It was so cold in the studio I could see his breath when he spoke. "Hello" might have been the only thing he said that whole day.

I worked on some tracks for a few days with Bob and the band Dave put together for him. It's something Dylan is known for: assembling a bunch of musicians and getting into a studio to see what comes out. I guess being Dylan, he doesn't have a record company breathing down his neck telling him they need a new record by a certain time. They've learned over the years to trust the process and to let him follow his muse. No one can argue that his method hasn't worked out quite well.

During the recording there wasn't much verbal communication; everything was done via the music. Bob starts playing and you follow his lead. Mostly it was instrumental stuff. Bob would signal the changes, and we'd move up and down through the gears. Between takes, Bob would pull the anorak tight around himself, fold his arms, and doze awhile on the sofa. I don't know that spending time with the guy reveals that much because he has a suit of armor he wears against the world, but one night, we went out for some Indian food, and we broke the ice. In the back seat of the car, I was sitting with Bob on one side and Dave on the other. Up until then, Bob and I hadn't spoken much. You know, he's Dylan and he's an enigma. As the car pulled away from the curb, Bob turned to me and said, "So, what happened to Blondie?"

I gave him a one-word answer, the one I give to everyone: "Drugs." Bob just nodded his understanding. Over dinner that night, he and I got to talking. He's a contradiction in terms. He's easy to get along with, but he's also so self-aware, it's like he realizes every word he utters is going to be analyzed from now until the end of time. It can seem intimidating, but even with iconic figures, your heroes, there's common ground to be found. All the old-school guys started out as big fans of music, and a lot of the time they're into talking about the music that inspired them. With Bob, he was more than happy talking about Woody Guthrie or the old blues singers he loved. I sat back in my chair and listened intently while Bob told me about when he was a kid and had gone to see Buddy Holly play just a few days before the plane crash that killed him.

After that first conversational breakthrough night, whenever we took time off recording, Bob would put on his green anorak and pull the hood over his face and we'd head to the Harringay Arms, a smoky working-class pub next door to the studio. He and I would grab a table and have a pint and chat for a while. Much of the time, Bob's disguise worked, and the day drinkers didn't realize he was in their midst. He didn't have an entourage, and I got the idea he liked being able to move around freely. Sometimes, though, it was amusing to see it slowly dawn on some guy standing at the bar or at a nearby table, taking a sip of beer and watching them narrow their gaze or do a doubletake, like, what the fuck? Is it him? No one bothered us, which was great, but over the few weeks we were working together, word eventually got out that Bob was in Crouch End, so fans and reporters started showing up outside the studio, hoping to catch a glimpse.

Arriving at the studio one morning, there was a crew waiting on the street for Bob's first British TV interview in years. While the crew got set up, Bob, still in his green anorak, switched clothes with Dave, putting on his fringed "Let It

Getting along with Bob

Rock" leather jacket. He went from anonymous to Bob Dylan in moments. In addition to the brief interview, the crew recorded the band playing an improvised performance of one of the instrumental tracks—a Booker T. & the M.G.'s type of groove—we were working on, basically flying by the seat of our pants, following Bob's lead. Bob's first appearance on British TV in forever, and he doesn't sing a note. He follows his own path, always.

After the TV crew disappeared, it felt like the spell had been broken, and the recordings came to an end. A little like it had been with Townshend, just one day it's all happening, the next day it's over. To my knowledge, not much from those sessions came to light, other than "Under Your Spell" on the album *Knocked Out Loaded*. I can't imagine how much music is in Bob's personal archives. Because the music had started to gel, I hoped someday Bob would write lyrics to accompany the instrumentals we were working on, and it would end up being *Blonde on Blonde*, Part Two, or something.

I did get to work with Bob again. He and Dave were shooting a video for "When the Night Comes Falling" in Los Angeles. In terms of a storyboard, I don't know what the idea was, but we were all on a school bus driving around Hollywood with Bob and a bunch of Dave's musician friends. At one point, we stopped on Hollywood Boulevard. Bob and I were standing around under a theater marquee in front of the ticket booth, just small talking, and I looked across the street and caught sight of a couple of my LA friends. They'd stopped in their tracks and were staring back across the street at me hanging out with Bob in broad daylight on a Tuesday afternoon. The shoot carried on in that vein for a while, and finally we pulled up at the top of Highland and Franklin

Avenues and shot the performance stuff on stage at a church hall. You know, I've had worse days.

Dave had a house in Encino with a recording studio out back, where the Traveling Wilburys—the supergroup featuring Bob, George Harrison, Jeff Lynne, Tom Petty, and Roy Orbison—recorded their first LP. It's a minor claim to fame, I'll grant you, but I gifted Dave a huge gong as a housewarming gift and a set of drums for the recording studio. You can see those drums in one of the Wilburys' videos. While they were working on the first album, Dave threw a party, a party that only someone like Dave could throw. In addition to Dylan, Tom Petty was there, Malcolm McLaren, guys from the Stray Cats, George Harrison. As the party spilled out of the house and onto the tennis court, someone produced a couple of guitars and Bob and Tom broke into a version of "Them Old Cottonfields Back Home" and it turned into a drunken sing-along. Later, I was standing around talking with Kathy, and Bob came over to say hi. I introduced the pair, and Bob nodded in recognition. Kathy probably thought he had no clue who the Go-Go's were, but without missing a beat, Bob said, "So, Kathy, what do you think about the Bangles taking the space your band once had?" Maybe in his mind he thought they were stealing their thunder, and he related it to the Dylan/Donovan rivalry portrayed in the film *Don't Look Back*. You think he's not paying attention, but he's all over every tiny detail. His antenna is always up.

The last time I saw Bob in person, outside of attending his shows, which I do every time I can, I got a call saying he was switching out drummers and would I audition. It hadn't panned out that first time my name was in the mix, so I dropped everything, and we met up at a rehearsal studio above a car dealership in Uptown Manhattan. Bob was in a relaxed mood, and we got to talking about music. I guess one of us must have brought up the U2 record *Rattle and Hum*, which had recently been released. I asked what he thought about it. The press was throwing all this "U2 getting back to their roots and recording at Sun studios" stuff out there. Bob just laughed. "Going back to their roots?" he said. "U2's roots were Celtic, last time I checked."

We played awhile and went back to talking. Bob was very cool, but it was obvious he wanted something simpler than my style, and he started talking about some of the old jazz drummers. Guys like Philly Joe Jones and Elvin Jones. That bop style of playing isn't exactly my forte, but I admire their playing. Bob eventually hired a great New Orleans player, who was probably a better fit. I later bumped into Jay Dee Daugherty, Patti Smith's drummer, whom I replaced in the Mumps. "I heard you tried out for Bob too," he laughed. Apparently, he auditioned right after me but had to readjust the kit—I play with a pretty simple setup, nothing too elaborate. He was adding these extra drums and cymbals, and Bob was scratching his head. Finally, he asked, "Are you gonna hit ALL of those things?"

Chapter 32

ELVIS RAMONE HAS LEFT THE BUILDING

The Ramones were Joey Ramone on vocals, Dee Dee Ramone on guitar, Johnny Ramone on bass, and Tommy Ramone on drums. The Ramones were all from Queens, New York. While they shared the same appropriated name, the Ramones was never a happy family. There's a moment in the 2004 Ramones documentary *End of the Century* that illustrates this point perfectly. The interviewer asks Johnny if Tommy was important to the sound of the band. Johnny doesn't even take a beat before saying no. They might not have been real brothers, but it was the type of diss a brother might say about a sibling. Bear in mind that, besides drumming on all those great records, Tommy essentially put the band together and wrote and produced some of their legendary records—so it struck me as a ridiculous thing for Johnny to say. But that was the Ramones. They were the greatest, but they were entirely dysfunctional.

If you saw the movie *Help!*, you came away with this idea that the Beatles all lived together in the same house, like a family doing everything together and living together in peace and harmony. We grew up with those bands, and we all bought into that mythology. The Beatles' movies and the Monkees' TV show are works of fiction. They're neat stories, but they're not a true picture of life in a band. There's a spectrum of behavior, with the "best of friends" bands at one end and at the other, well, you'll find our New York friends, the Ramones. Four guys from Forest Hills who got off on the Stooges and the girl groups of the 1960s.

One of my first Blondie gigs we opened for the Ramones over on the East Side. Tommy and Ramones' tour manager Monte Melnick had a place called Performance Studios on East Twentieth Street, just off Madison Square. Over the years, I've seen a few disputes break out between band members on stage, but the Ramones took infighting to a whole new level the night we opened. Everyone was so high-strung, they'd finish a song, then break into a two-, three-, or four-way argument over some minor dispute, and then at the height of the tantrum, DeeDee would shout "1-2-3-4" into the mic, and they'd launch into the next song. In 1975, all the talk was about how the Ramones were THE band on the scene. Everyone was convinced they were the guys who were going to make it out of CBGB and take it to the mainstream. For me and a lot of my friends, they were our generation's Beatles.

Debbie and Chris were already friends with the band, but that show was the start of my acquaintance, and later friendship, with various members of the Ramones—as well as with Arturo Vega, the Ramones' artistic director. I can't ever think about the original four Ramones without Arturo Vega coming to mind. If you think you don't know his name, you know his work. Arturo designed the Ramones' iconic

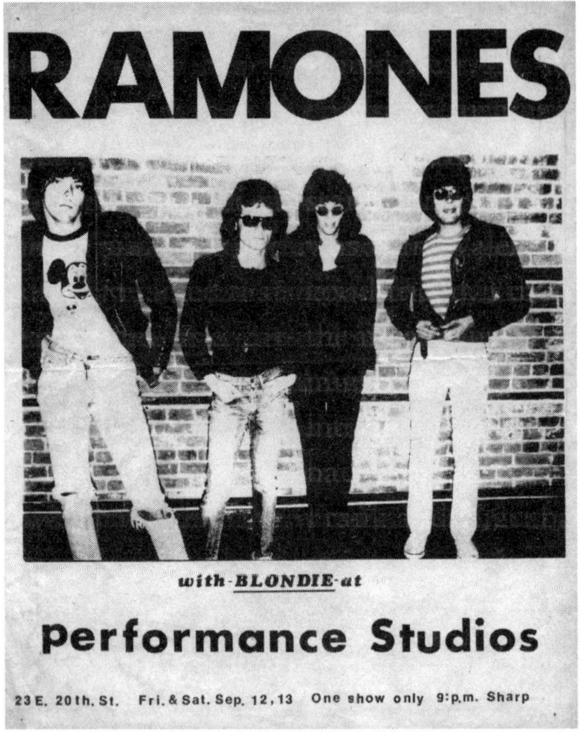

presidential seal logo you see on T-shirts everywhere, having cribbed the idea from the logo of this gay club on the West Side called the Eagle. Vega had gravitated to Lower Manhattan from Mexico in the early 1970s, where he had a grand, 2,500-square-foot loft overlooking East Second Avenue and Bowery—later known as Joey Ramone Place. Blondie used to rehearse in Arturo's loft, and we all got to see the Ramones' dysfunction at close quarters. Joey lived in the back, behind a huge Ramones banner, while DeeDee had a mattress he angrily dragged around from floor to floor when Arturo threw his home open to the entire CBGB crowd. Those nights were crazy. You'd be enjoying a drink with a few friends, when out of nowhere, Legs McNeil would come tumbling down the stairs from the second floor and land in a drunken heap at your feet, before dusting himself down and walking off like nothing happened.

Over the years, I was asked a few times to join the Ramones, but the timing was always off. The first time was in 1977. The Ramones were on tour with Talking Heads, and Blondie was on tour with Television. On a day off, we were in the same town, and I was at their gig when Tommy told me he was leaving the band and would I consider taking his place. Blondie was starting to take off, so I had to pass. I was asked again when Tommy's replacement got out of hand with his drinking and was shown the door. Once again, I had to decline, for Blondie commitments. That led to Richie Ramone joining the band. Richie stayed until 1987, but when he asked about getting a small cut of the merchandising royalties, he was out on his ass. Following his departure, and the subse-

"Fifth Ramone" Arturo Vega

quent Ramones drummer crisis, I guess it was inevitable I'd get the call again, and that's what happened. Manager Gary Kurfirst was working with both Eurythmics and the Ramones, and he approached me as the Eurythmics *Revenge* Tour was winding down. The band was so intent on making it happen, they announced my joining before I'd even agreed. I know because I read it in *Rolling Stone*.

I wasn't ready to become a fully-fledged Ramone, so I said I'd take the gig on a trial basis. I knew they were in a bind, and they were friends, so I agreed to help out for a while. Apparently, things in the Ramones' world moved as fast as their music. Johnny's mantra was always "What's the hold-up?" Case in point: I agreed on a Monday, and the first show was scheduled for Friday. The same week. When it

Here today, gone tomorrow

came to me getting my Ramones name, I think they presumed I'd be Clemmy Ramone, but I suggested Elvis Ramone. I knew the Ramones—Johnny in particular—were big Presley fans. Plus, I'd just come off the Eurythmics tour and my hair was styled differently, slicked back, more retro than mod, so I looked the part.

"When do we rehearse?" I asked Johnny. It seemed a reasonable question.

"No rehearsal," Johnny told me. He wasn't into band practice. The idea was that I just turn up and play, prepared for whatever was to come. I like to work and most of my bands think I overwork in the rehearsal room, but I want things to sound the best they can. Even knowing all the discord between them, this seemed like a willfully self-

sabotaging approach. I pulled my Ramones records off the shelf and spent a couple of days playing along to them in my basement. It was no substitute for an actual rehearsal, but I gave it my best shot. I must have seen the Ramones a hundred times, but that didn't prepare me in the way I would have liked. Still, I figured, this is their band and their show. So, that's how I started my—short-lived—career as Elvis Ramone. Trial by fire.

They were a paradoxical group of people, and I guess the public never knew what to make of them. They were smart guys, but they deliberately played it dumb. It was almost conceptual what they were doing, like being a Ramone was a sort of art project to them. Compared with other bands, I found life with the Ramones curiously regimented. Johnny made the rules, and everyone else followed them. A tour bus was seen as an unwanted expense, so they arrived everywhere in an Econoline van, like they were still a teenage rock and roll band just starting out. Every band member had a spot set aside for them in the van. Monte Melnick always sat in the driver seat, with Johnny Ramone riding "shotgun," with the radio tuned to that night's baseball game. DeeDee's spot was in the back row, isolated from whatever was going on up front, patiently rolling a joint for the journey. When I played with them, I was allocated a spot in the first row of seats, in front of Joey's. "That's the drummer's seat," Monte leaned back and told me as I climbed in the back. Maybe it was a weird compulsive disorder they all shared, but you had your spot, and there was to be no switching seats under any circumstances.

Once I saw them play a big show in Detroit on the Escape from New York Tour, alongside Debbie's solo act and the

Tom Tom Club. Seeing that same battered van parked up beside the huge tour buses in the parking lot outside the venue, I had to laugh. Right to the end, they chose to never travel on a tour bus.

The atmosphere between them was frosty as hell. This was shortly after Johnny had stolen Joey's girlfriend, Linda, so those guys weren't speaking to one another at all. Because of the passive-aggressive, silent acrimony between Joey and Johnny, I took it upon myself to act as a buffer. Before and after the shows, I'd endeavor to break the tension. Since the CBGB days, Joey and I had always gotten along well; we always found time to hang out and grab a drink. He had his little idiosyncrasies. His obsessive-compulsive character has been well documented over the years, so he was always a little unusual. He and I would discuss the stock market, and Johnny and I would talk about the things I knew interested him. Mostly that meant talking about baseball. The New York scene might have been artsy, but Johnny was strictly blue collar, all the way down the line. I always thought that whenever he picked up a guitar, he might just as well be picking up a jackhammer. Like playing the guitar and being a Ramone was no different to him than if he had a job on a construction site.

My first show in my Elvis Ramone persona was at the City Gardens in Trenton, New Jersey. The place was completely packed, and the audience was wild. The next night, we played this place called Lupo's Heartbreak Hotel, in Providence, Rhode Island, and that show was similarly crazy. Given the lack of preparation, they were great shows. Just on a physical level, they were the hardest gigs I ever played. We had a couple of glitches, but you can find those shows online and the band sounds great. Johnny disliked any changes to the status quo, but Joey was more open. He and I had a couple of conversations about making some changes to accommodate my playing style, to maybe make things a little more improvisational, and we talked about writing some songs together. Before he was thrust into the limelight as the band's singer, Joey had started out as a drummer. He was a big fan of Keith Moon and the Who, so we had that in common.

After the second show, a rehearsal was called, and I showed up at the rehearsal space in Midtown Manhattan. As I walked in the door, Monte Melnick took me to one side. "The rehearsal's canceled," he said, and handed me a fistful of cash. Apparently, Tommy's replacement had got himself straight and wanted to come back. I said that was great news. I'd only agreed to join the band on a trial basis, so I wasn't surprised or disappointed.

Sometimes, it's hard to believe the original Ramones lineup, and Arturo, have all gone now. From my brief time working with them and seeing how they went about things, maybe it was to be expected. They were unlike any band before or since, and I'm proud of my time with them. We came up together from the same CBGB scene and made our marks in bands, playing our music our way, something not every musician gets to do. And I got to be Elvis Ramone until Elvis left the building.

Chapter 33

REUNION

Blondie never officially split up. There was no statement in the press. We didn't get the catharsis of a farewell tour and album to mark the occasion. There was no closure, and it was a lot for me to process, but Blondie or no, I was convinced I wanted to carry on making music. For the next fifteen years, that's what I did. My friends always had an inkling that Blondie would get back together someday, but I didn't see it in the cards. It felt to me like we'd had our shot.

In 1996, I was at a very personal low point. My father died and I was grieving. It was a complete surprise when Debbie, Chris, and Jimmy turned up for Dad's funeral. I'd never have expected them to be there consoling me at the graveside. But there they were, and they were a great comfort to me. I never had any siblings, so to see there was still love between us meant a lot. It made me remember some of the times Chris and Debbie came over to my dad's place in Bayonne. My dad driving us around town so Chris could check out a new amp. It gave me solace to know, despite everything, we still had this connection. In the months prior, there'd been conversations about doing something. We hadn't agreed to anything, but I know my dad was happy we were talking about Blondie again. He knew better than anyone how bad I'd taken it when we broke up. There was something nice about the full circle aspect of our reconnection happening at his funeral.

Prior to this, in the mid-1990s, I was spending a lot of time in the Midwest playing with the Detroit band the Romantics. The band had this bar where they used to hang out, and one night a woman approached me and said her friend wanted to buy me a drink. I went over and met her friend. We had a drink, got to talking, and clicked right away. Long story short, she and I got caught up in a relationship. She was working as a record plugger, working for Giant Records. After she wound up getting a promotion and moving to Illinois, she and I lived together in Chicago for a time. I guess I was all in with this woman, like this was the person I was going to spend my life with, but it didn't pan out. She was away promoting this band Big Head Todd and the Monsters, who were opening for Hootie and the Blowfish, when she called me to say we were done. She'd hooked up with Hootie's drummer and wanted me to move out in a week. I didn't see it coming at all. Emotionally speaking, I switched to auto-pilot. I packed up my life into a couple of suitcases and before the week was out, I was back on the West Coast.

That Hootie and the Blowfish record was inescapable at the time. It sold something like a zillion copies, so every store, every coffeehouse or bar was playing that album on repeat. It was a daily, sometimes hourly, reminder of my broken heart. Literally, the minute I arrived back at my LA place, my neighbors were having a cookout in the yard, and they played that whole album from start to finish. Maybe I wouldn't have minded so much if the record that soundtracked my heartache hadn't totally sucked.

I was still reeling when an old friend of mine, the Plimsouls' guitarist Eddie Munoz, got in touch. Eddie and I had been good friends since spending time on the Blondie and Rockpile tour when he was working as a guitar tech. He explained that the Plimsouls planned to tour and record again and asked if I'd be interested in joining them. Bands re-forming without their original drummer and me getting a call has become a recurring theme. By the time I hung up, I had a new gig and another band to add to my resumé. Along with bands like the Knack, the Plimsouls were big on the California power pop scene—scoring a modest hit with "A Million Miles Away" before disbanding in 1983.

Immediately, there was a buzz around LA that the band was back together, and we set to work making the record that came to be known as *Kool Trash*. We were playing a lot of shows around LA, and there was a US tour planned to coincide with the album release. Somehow, I was tracked down at the studio while we were working on *Kool Trash*. I got a call from New York. It was Jimmy. "Are you sitting down?" he said. "Chris wants to re-form Blondie." I took a seat and listened. Jimmy said the reunion would be the original four members: Debbie, Chris, me, and Jimmy. "Frank and Nigel?" I asked. "Nope," Jimmy told me, and then explained how we got here.

The story was, Chris had taken out an ad in the *Village Voice* trying to sell off his gold and platinum records. One of the people who responded to the ad expressed shock and suggested that rather than sell off all his gold and platinum discs, re-forming the band might be a better way to make some extra money. He knew someone who might be interested in helping. Which is how Harry Sandler came into our lives.

Harry was a sweet guy, with a reputation in management circles as someone who puts the artist first. Harry happened to be in LA at the time, staying at the Sunset Marquis. Since I was in town, Harry called me, and we arranged a breakfast meeting at the hotel's poolside restaurant. Harry struck me as warm and affable, and we began a casual discussion of the prospects for a Blondie reunion. As we talked, I glanced to my left and saw Bruce Springsteen and his wife, Patti Scialfa, at a nearby table. Bruce looked our way, nodded in recognition, and then got up and headed toward us. I'd met Bruce before, but I hardly expected him to jump out of his seat to come over to say hello. He didn't. Instead, he greeted Harry like a long-lost brother.

After Bruce returned to his table, I raised a few concerns about Frank and Nigel not being involved. Harry, who was already acting like the deal was done, said everything would come out in the wash. As I made to leave, he suggested we meet up in New York with Debbie, Chris, Jimmy, and Allen Kovac. Kovac was the boss, but Harry would be our designated point man. A few weeks later, having finished recording with the Plimsouls, I flew to New York for the meeting with my three partners in Blondie. Over the years, we'd all bumped into each other socially, but this was to be the first time the four of us were together in one room since 1982.

We had this body of work from our time together that would tie us to one another for the rest of our lives, but other than via the attorneys and accountants who handled our interests in Blondie, we were practically strangers now, so it was a weird feeling. I was ushered into a small conference room and was greeted by Debbie, Chris, and Jimmy. Everyone looked good, considering the time that had gone by. The one person I didn't recognize was a small, somewhat sheepish man in an expensive suit. That was Allen Kovac. I asked where Harry was, and Allen motioned to a speakerphone and explained Harry would be conferencing in. I'm thinking, why did I fly all this way at my own expense when I could be sitting in Harry's LA office? We thought Harry was a great guy, and he'd done all the legwork to set this up, but suddenly this was starting to feel like we were being manipulated.

The meeting started off with Allen telling Chris that most people in the music business thought he was dead. Allen was all business, the absolute antithesis of Harry. He didn't pull any punches, basically laying out this plan for us to record two new songs for a Blondie greatest hits package he had in mind, followed by a promotional tour. I began shaking my head, and Allen asked me what was wrong. I said we weren't really into that, that we wanted to create new music. It was a relief to hear my bandmates voice their agreement, but Allen disagreed. It wouldn't be the last time he and I didn't see eye to eye.

After our initial meeting, the four of us got together to play some music. We booked a basement rehearsal studio on Ludlow Street on the Lower East Side. Chris and Jimmy were brimming with ideas. I was still concerned about the Frank and Nigel situation, but once we started, I think we recognized that the chemistry was still there. I sensed Debbie wasn't as keen as Chris to take things forward. This was the first time since I'd known them that they weren't a couple, but they still had an unshakeable bond. I knew the band would always be secondary to her concern for Chris's welfare.

After returning home, Chris called to tell me he'd had a change of heart. I was relieved, thinking he'd reconsidered his stance on Frank and Nigel. I was wrong. What he wanted was Gary Valentine back in the band. Although Gary was a good friend, I didn't think it was a good idea. Gary had left the music business. I was still holding on to the faint hope I might convince my partners to allow Frank and Nigel back into the band. I don't know if it was wishful thinking, but I had the idea that once the four of us had reunited, we'd bring Frank and Nigel back into the fold amicably, and we'd revert to our classic lineup.

Before too long, Frank and Nigel got wind of the Blondie reboot and called me. It was left to me to tell them they were both out. I hated being pitted against my friends. They responded by taking all of us to court. I couldn't do much else but give them my blessing. Again, I was caught between warring camps. The trial went ahead some months later in New York. Before the judge heard the case, there was a round of depositions. Getting coached by our team of attorneys, then being deposed, while at the same time hoping Nigel and Frank would prevail, it felt like I was in a real emotional bind.

Throughout the process, I was convinced Frank and Nigel would win. I was wrong. On the day of the trial, the entire Eastern Seaboard was hit by a hurricane, and we arrived at the courthouse amid swirling, biblical winds and driving rain. Save for ours, all the courts in New York were closed. We took the stand in turn and gave evidence. The first thing that worked against them was the Blondie website. It was early days of the internet, but Blondie had an online presence, and the judge looked us up, only to tell the plaintiffs that they were not anywhere to be seen on it. Of course they weren't—it had just been set up by our managers.

Their lawyers then subpoenaed Mike Chapman as a star witness to attest to their importance to Blondie, but because of the hurricane, he hadn't made it to the city and wasn't in court. Their side asked for a continuance into the next day so that Mike could appear, but the judge said he didn't care who was coming to testify, he'd already made up his mind.

Stepping outside, the rain pelted down on us. We went out for drinks with our legal team to celebrate. I was only drinking to drown my sorrows. It didn't feel like we'd won anything.

All the while, I was dealing with the ongoing bizarre situation of Chris getting Gary back in the band. Eventually, Gary relented and arrived in November 1996 to work on new Blondie tracks. It took a while to pull together, but we went into a studio with Nick Rhodes and Warren Cuccurullo from Duran Duran to record two songs they'd written: "Pop Trash Movie" and the title track for an upcoming film, *Studio 54*. "Pop Trash Movie" was meant to be for the greatest hits package that Allen was trying to push through. The combination didn't seem to have chemistry. The sessions became laborious, and *Studio 54* never saw the light of day.

We made another attempt at recording with Gary in January, but that went nowhere. Gary returned to London at the end of January; the band was inactive until he returned to the US in May, and we began rehearsals for a few live shows. Our first in more than fifteen years. I was apprehensive about performing without a second guitar player and thought we didn't have the necessary ingredients to pull off a great live show. To replace Nigel, we brought in Leigh Foxx, who'd served time with Debbie and Chris on some of Debbie's solo records. The four of us discussed it, and he made the most sense. Leigh is a great player and a good guy. After a week of on-again-off-again rehearsals, we did a warm-up show for an invited audience at a Manhattan studio before heading to Robert F. Kennedy Memorial Stadium to play a radio festival with Beck, the Cranberries, and Bjork in front of eighty thousand people. We went down okay, but something was lacking. Another radio festival followed the next day at Riverside Park in Massachusetts with Moby and Echo and the Bunnymen, followed by a third date in Dallas on June 6. For the time being, that was that. And after all the efforts and promises to bring Gary back, he went home expecting to return to record a new Blondie album—but instead he never played with us again.

Chapter 34

NO EXIT

After we'd settled the ugly business side of things, I went out to dinner in LA with Chris and Jimmy and the agent, Shelley Lazar—daughter of the legendary Swifty Lazar. We kicked a few ideas back and forth across the table for a couple of hours.

The issue with Blondie was getting things done. I wasn't sure this was going to lead anywhere, but I wanted to hear them out. It was strange to see everyone so motivated. Suddenly, time was of the essence, and we had to strike now if we were going to make any headway. I wondered if part of the motivation was Chris's issues with the IRS, but whatever the impetus, I thought we had unfinished business. I felt in my prime, and that life was going good, but if Allen Kovac could push the band into a greatest hits record and a money-grab tour, maybe it could go further. I wanted to write new songs, get a new record deal, and make an album. It seemed like a miracle when that became the plan. Anyone can get back together for money, I figured, but we could buck that trend and get back together for love *and* money. I'm sure if we'd followed Allen's short-term vision, we wouldn't still be together today. As artists, making new music was key to Blondie continuing as a band.

Once the idea of the quick cash grab abated, we started talking about who might be a good fit as a producer. I suggested we bring Craig Leon back into the fold. I'd been working with him on a few different records over the years, including one at Abbey Road with Mark Owen from Take That called *Green Man*, and another with Marillion lead singer Steve Hogarth called *Ice Cream Genius*. Craig was from our early days and had done "X Offender" with us. I reached out, and he came straight out to New York. Just days later, we convened at Chris's place in Tribeca to start work. Craig brought along his RADAR digital recorder, which was a relatively new bit of tech—like a precursor to Pro Tools— and we decamped to Chris's basement to record a few demos. Craig was great, and his affinity with new technology was a godsend. Recording to tape can be an arduous process some-times, but with the digital recorder, we were able to capture whatever we played, and Craig could make edits on the fly.

When we were happy with the demos, we moved the oper-ation across to Electric Lady Studios on West Eighth Street in the Village. Electric Lady is a special studio, built by Jimi Hendrix in 1968. I'd produced a record there a few years before, and I knew the place inside out. In terms of location, it couldn't be more perfect for us. It felt right to be in that part of Manhattan again, like we were heading back to our roots, back in the studio with Craig, like old times. West Eighth Street held a special place in the band's history. It was the main drag between the East and West Village, and the area was alive with activity.

To expand on the original core lineup, we already had Leigh Foxx on bass, but we brought in another native New Yorker, Paul Carbonara, on guitar. Paul was a friend of a friend of Debbie's. There was a conscious decision to make the new album a group effort, so it really felt like we were a band again. The process was democratic, with all the members participating in every aspect. I came up with the album title. It seemed like we'd come to accept we needed each other, and there was no escaping the fact that we were Blondie—hence *No Exit*. There was no animosity and we enjoyed each other's company. I felt like my voice was being heard more than it had in the past. People looked to me for my take on whatever we did. There was some disagreement about the switch from analogue to digital recording, but ultimately, we stuck with Craig and the new technology. Even though we were working in the digital realm for the first time, we recorded the basic tracks spontaneously. Aside from some guitar overdubs from Chris, the nucleus of the band—guitar, bass, keyboards, and drums—was all captured live. Everyone was pulling in the same direction.

There was no master plan or theme for *No Exit*. The songs could come from anywhere and were chosen on merit. I had always added a lot in terms of arrangements, but I had some cowriting credits on *No Exit*, which felt like a great new direction. I don't write many songs in the way a definitive songwriter does. I can collaborate to the extent that my input is a big part of the result, by being in the room, bouncing ideas, banging out rough ideas on an acoustic guitar, contributing titles, beats, stylistic approaches. Debbie had been working with the band the Jazz Passengers, so I worked with guitarist Denny Freeman and his then girlfriend, also my ex,

Kathy Valentine, on a jazz-inflected song, Debbie wrote the lyrics and title: "Boom Boom in the Zoom Zoom Room." There was another song, "Divine," which I wrote with Kathy. It may have gotten lost in translation; originally, we'd intended it as an homage to the actor of the same name, whom I knew slightly from the early days in New York.

No Exit kept all the Blondie hallmarks of eclecticism that always set us apart from other bands. The finished record contained stylistic elements of pop, reggae, hip hop, and even country music, but it still sounded like only we could have made it. In the earlier sessions with Gary, Debbie added vocals to a demo of "Amor Fati." It was Gary's finest song to date, and I fought to get a version included on the album, but without success. As a nod to our past, we returned to one of our early covers, the Shangri-Las' song "Out in the Streets," which we'd recorded when we were first looking for a record deal.

We put our heads down to work but had no real idea what the reaction was going to be. It couldn't have been more different from the albums where it was taken for granted that we'd have an audience and hit songs. By making a record, Blondie had another chance at success, but who knew where it might lead? There was a collective sigh of relief when the reception was as much as we dared to hope for.

Jimmy Destri had written us a pure pop hit with the song "Maria," which was clearly the leadoff single. In February 1999, within a couple of weeks of release, it hit number one in the UK. It was our sixth chart topper in the UK, exactly twenty years after "Heart of Glass" occupied the top slot. We had a track record of going left of center whenever we released a new record, and that holds true with *No Exit* as a whole, but "Maria" connected because it was the record many fans would have hoped for. A "classic Blondie" song. We sounded like we'd just picked up from where we left off.

It's a great song and always a set highlight, but the real masterstroke was taking the band on a tour of the UK a few months prior to the album's release. That really set the stage. We played the old hits, of course, but also previewed songs from *No Exit*. Tommy Hilfiger outfitted us with a great tour wardrobe based on a Las Vegas Rat Pack look. Blondie was back, not as a nostalgia band but as a creatively active entity.

It felt like a vindication of the band, and this was a good time in all our lives. It was almost therapeutic knowing people still valued us and our music and feeling that what we had was worth saving. The album did great business. We got in just under the wire before the record industry went through some big changes that signaled the end of the way thousands of bands had been able to find success or survive in the music business. None of it was lost on me; I was grateful to be feeling the respect and acclaim—more so this second time around than I ever had. I wasn't a kid anymore; I'd just started dating my soon-to-be wife, Ellen, and it was cool to have someone to share in my success.

In the fifteen years before *No Exit*, I'd been working constantly. I never stopped playing and had built an impressive rock and roll resumé. I was more confident as a musician and as a human being, but it still felt that I'd come back from the rock and roll wilderness. This wasn't the case with all of us. Jimmy had stepped away from the business entirely after the band's demise to deal with his addiction issues and start a family. Same with Chris. Debbie had an ongoing career— she released solo records, acted in movies, and did a lot of interesting stuff, but it wasn't on the same scale as Blondie.

Over the years, the royalties from Blondie would ebb and flow, but it was always enough for me to get by and to live the life I wanted. We didn't tour at all between 1980 and 1982, when we were one of the biggest bands in the world, so it felt like I'd earned the right to finally start making some real money for a change. The only disappointment was, and it still bothered me, I didn't have my two friends, Frank and Nigel, along for the ride.

Chapter 35

THE SINATRA PARTY

It was never intentional, and just seemed to happen this way, but I could go on record here and happily say that my success is intertwined with an abundance of iconic, amazing women.

There's Debbie Harry, obviously, and the incredible Annie Lennox. I worked on an Elvis tribute with rock and roll pioneer Wanda Jackson, and have toured with her as well. I've played in bands with members of the Go-Go's and female indie artists from New York to London. But one of my favorite female collaborators was born just one town over from me in Jersey City, and she grew up to be showbiz royalty. I'm talking about my friend Nancy Sinatra.

I first met Nancy shortly after Blondie reunited in the late 1990s. We were set to play an album launch show for *No Exit*, at the El Rey Theatre in Los Angeles, but the show coincided with the premiere of the movie *200 Cigarettes*. Usually, the opening of a Casey Affleck movie doesn't cause too many ripples in the Blondie pool, but the film's soundtrack featured one of our songs—"Rapture"—so we were invited to the LA premiere. We walked the red carpet with the stars of the movie, posing for photos, and went in one theater door and left through another into a waiting car so we could get to our El Rey concert. Nancy was at the show that night, and we were introduced. She couldn't have been nicer. I felt as though we'd known each other for years.

Sometime later, I got a call from Nancy's longtime musical director, Don Randi. Don was part of Phil Spector's Wrecking Crew, and he played piano on the Crystals record *He's a Rebel* and the Beach Boys masterpiece, *Pet Sounds*. I'd known Don for a while from hanging out at his club, the Baked Potato, in Studio City, and we'd become friends. He asked if I was available for some upcoming sessions for Nancy's next record, *California Girl*. I was a long-standing fan of her work, so it was an easy decision. To my ears, "These Boots Are Made for Walking" is basically a punk rock song, and Nancy's classic *Nancy & Lee* LP of duets with Lee Hazlewood has long been a favorite of mine. I always felt a kinship with her because of our shared North Jersey background.

As the title suggests, it was a California concept album— with the theme of California running through all the tracks on the record. It was an honor to play with Don, and I learned a lot from him. Although I couldn't sight-read Nancy's charts, Don said I had "elephant ears," meaning I could pick up the arrangement of a song quickly. I figured that was high praise, coming from a guy like Don. Hal Blaine, the Wrecking Crew drummer and one of my heroes, had worked with Nancy for a long time, and she'd kept all his drum charts, all of them bearing his "Hal Blaine Strikes Again" rubber stamp. Hal is acknowledged as the most successful session drummer of all time, and here I was, taking his place.

Through working with Nancy and Don, I eventually came to know Hal and got to play at his eightieth birthday party, with both Hal and Nancy in attendance, and played the Ronettes' "Be My Baby," which has Hal's immortal drum intro. I was nervous as I sat behind the drums until I looked over at Hal and he gave me a thumbs-up. After being accepted into the fold, I was sad to be out of town for his ninetieth birthday. He passed away soon after. I spoke at the dedication ceremony for Hal's star on Main Street in Palm Springs, with Charlie Watts and Jim Keltner in attendance. After the unveiling, I joined Don and a group of musicians, with Nancy spontaneously joining us to sing "Boots." All in all, a fitting tribute to Hal—one of the greatest players there ever was.

Once Nancy's *California Girl* album was finished, I was invited to be in her touring band. Let me tell you right now, there's no better feeling than arriving at a hotel and announcing to reception "I'm with the Sinatra party." The Sinatra name still carries a lot of weight. Just based on name recognition alone, Nancy could have booked and sold out any theater she liked all over the country, but we were playing intimate club shows along the Jersey Shore. One was in Hoboken at Maxwell's, in the back room of a bar, but we put on a show as if we were playing to two thousand people. Only a couple hundred people saw us, but because it was essentially her hometown gig, it was a magical night.

Working with Nancy brought me a lot of unforgettable experiences. In Frank's hometown of Hoboken, we were stopping traffic across the city, and the mayor gave us his chambers in City Hall for a dressing room. Our group was swept from one fancy restaurant to the next, day after day.

We had a corporate event in Istanbul booked to play to two hundred guests at a VIP dinner. Gentlemen in turbans and tuxedos, shaking their booties, accompanied by extraordinarily beautiful women—probably the finest money could buy. The Zildjian cymbal company was founded in Istanbul, and they provided the most exquisite cymbals I'd ever heard. After the gig, we retired to luxury accommodations at the Four Seasons Hotel for dinner and drinks. In time-honored Sinatra fashion, we were treated like visiting dignitaries by the hotel's staff.

Nancy herself treated everyone she met with kindness and generosity and kept her feet squarely on the ground. She enjoyed hanging with the band, and it was amazing to ask her about everything from Elvis to the Wrecking Crew to recording with the genius Lee Hazlewood. The things she's done, the people she ran with, the eras she was in the middle of—there's no one like Nancy. On the last night in Istanbul, Nancy found out one of her guitarists had been rolled by some locals the previous night and lost all his money. On hearing this, she quietly tapped me under the table and handed me a wad of cash to pass down the table to him. When I turned back to her, she said, "Like my dad used to say: Show me something I can't fix."

Nancy was invited to perform at a festival in Vienna in 2002. The promoter had booked an arena and filled the bill with Presley-associated acts. It was a once-in-a-lifetime bill featuring most of Elvis's TCB Vegas band, with Ronnie Tutt on drums and James Burton on guitar. Elvis's backing singers, the Sweet Inspirations, were there too, alongside Elvis's original drummer, D.J. Fontana. Having the opportunity to rub shoulders with those musicians was an unbelievable experience. For the finale of the show, they had Ronnie, D.J., and me all drumming together.

Another memorable show was in Budapest. It was set up by a trucking mogul at this vast new warehouse. The guy was a huge Sinatra fan, so he invited both Nancy and Frank Sinatra Jr.'s big band to play. The show was invite-only and attended by the cream of Hungarian society. When we landed at the airport, we were met by a fleet of limousines and a police escort to our hotel, like we were American royalty—which, I guess, the Sinatra family is. The following night, the entire entourage was invited to dinner on a private boat along the Danube River. I was sitting with my wife, Ellen, Nancy, Frank Jr., and his wife and enjoying the entertainment—an authentic Romani Gypsy band.

In contrast with Nancy, Frank Jr. was a lot less personable. He was a complicated guy, with a curious style. He would only communicate via Nancy and was constantly whispering in her ear, asking questions about who was who and who said what. He'd had a strange life. I remember it was big news in the 1960s when Frank Jr. was kidnapped and held for ransom. Maybe it was understandable he was so guarded around people. Frank wasn't a fan of rock and roll, and when we were introduced during rehearsals, he said to me, "Hi, I'm Frank. Why does it have to be so fucking loud?" The show itself was as unusual as all the gigs I'd come to expect from being part of the Sinatra party. The Hungarian president delivered a speech, Nancy played with her rock and roll band, and then Frank Jr. performed with his big band.

Over the years, band members came and went, but I worked a lot with Nancy. In the summer of 2004, we were invited to play Little Steven's Underground Garage Festival.

It wasn't Woodstock exactly, but it provided me with some of my happiest memories as both a musician and a music fan. Iggy Pop and the reunited Stooges were headlining, alongside the Strokes. The third headliner was a new version of the New York Dolls, with only David Johansen and Sylvain Sylvain remaining from the classic lineup. It was a prestigious bill, a real labor of love for Steven Van Zandt, just littered with garage rock legends from the previous forty years. He'd booked Bo Diddley, the Pretty Things, the Creation, the Chocolate Watchband, the Chesterfield Kings, the Electric Prunes, the Fleshtones, as well as the Romantics, my old friends from Michigan.

The day before the festival, I was in New York City with Nancy and the band to rehearse at one of my old stomping grounds, Studio Instrument Rentals. Our friend, the ever-reliable Little Steven, arrived with a full horn section in tow—a bunch of these legendary players who'd served time with Springsteen and the Asbury Jukes. When we arrived, the place was buzzing with activity. Steven's wife, Maureen, lent a hand, running through the choreography for Nancy's set with a troupe of dancers on the soundstage, while Steven rehearsed the horn section and acted as musical director. Everyone was going all out to ensure her set would be exactly how she'd want it to be, even though it was only scheduled to be a short segment of the show. It was a testament to the high regard in which we all hold Nancy.

After rehearsal, I was at the hotel reflecting on the great day when Nancy called and said we were all going to dinner at Patsy's restaurant on West Fifty-Sixth Street. Patsy's is a legendary Italian restaurant and an old haunt of Nancy's dad's back in the day. To be a part of the Sinatra party at

Patsy's restaurant was unreal—the place is untouched by the past fifty years of history. The walls are lined with black-and-white photographs of every famous or infamous Italian American you can think of. If those walls could talk, they'd never shut up; they'd have a thousand stories to tell. With an actual Sinatra being in the house, the staff acted as though it were a presidential visit. The chefs came out from the kitchen in their stained whites to greet her, and the wait staff hung on Nancy's every word. Patsy's has become a favorite restaurant of mine, and I always enjoy bringing my friends along. Obviously, I make a point to drop Nancy's name as I take my seat or book the table. Just the mention of her name and suddenly you're Henry Hill walking into the Copacabana in *Goodfellas*, and everyone is falling over backward to make sure you're happy.

The day of the festival, storm clouds were gathering over New York. The event was taking place on Randall's Island, across the Fifty-Ninth Street Bridge in New York City, which also happened to be in the direct path of a colossal storm that was supposed to hit land later that day. Even so, upward of ten thousand garage rock fans braved the conditions, making their way to the island. We spent the morning holed up in our hotel, waiting for the inevitable cancellation. It was touch and go for a while, but the organizers decided to press ahead. Bands had come from all over the world, so Steven was mindful that canceling would cause major problems and disappointment for the thousands of fans already on site. The only concession made was that everyone had to cut short their set to avoid the storm wrecking the festival for everyone.

When we finally got to the island, the skies above our heads were black and the wind was picking up. I had a creeping sense of foreboding, but I shouldn't have worried. It felt like Mother Nature saw all the effort, time, money, passion, and talent that had collected in one place, and it proved to be a remarkable day. The cast of the TV show *The Sopranos* were acting as masters of ceremonies—of course, Stevie played Silvio on the show—so the backstage area was a sea of friends and happy, familiar faces. Bruce Springsteen was in attendance, having arrived on the island on his boat. He watched practically every act from the wings. There was a revolving stage, so while one act was playing, the next act was being set up backstage. Something went wrong with the mechanism, so as each band concluded their performance, the road crew had to manually push the stage into place for the next artist. When we finally hit the stage, Nancy and the band put on a great performance. I couldn't resist looking to the side of the stage and seeing all these garage rock guys getting a real kick out of our set, seeing an icon like Nancy fronting a raucous rock and roll band.

The Asbury Jukes' horn section joined us, along with a set of go-go dancers, and then before I knew it, the revolving stage was being pushed and pulled to make room for whoever was following us. The band took a bow with Nancy, and everyone but me hightailed it back to Manhattan. I was having way too good a time to even consider leaving. I was glued to the side of the stage, hanging out with Springsteen, watching at close quarters all these incredible bands I'd loved all my life. Literally, with every band, Bruce and I were gushing about how great they were and what a great day we were having. One of my friends approached us and asked to take a picture of the two of us, but I told him no. I didn't want to detract from the moment, but I regret it now because who doesn't want their picture taken with the Boss? I did get a great photo of me talking with former Beatles' drummer Pete Best, thanks to Bob Gruen.

Iggy and the Stooges played the last set, closing the festival just as the storm was right on top of us. Everyone was hanging around the trailers backstage as if nothing were happening. I was chatting with Sylvain from the Dolls and a friend of mine from Detroit, Wendy Case, whose band the Paybacks had played a dynamite set earlier in the day. I realized I had no way to get off the island and out of the path of the storm. Wendy was stranded like me, but very drunk. I guided her out to the parking lot and flagged down a ride for the pair of us. Turns out it was a friend of mine, Kitty Kowalski, who offered us a ride back to Manhattan in her van. We climbed in alongside a bunch of other people, all desperate to get out of the way of the oncoming storm. Being an international audience, everyone in the back of the van was speaking half a dozen different languages. Back in the city, I went to the festival after-party at Handsome Dick Manitoba's bar on First Avenue. It ended a little frantically but still was one of the greatest days of my life.

Nancy decided she was going to embark on a tour of Europe in spring of 2005 with a show in Paris at Le Grand Rex, leading into a run of dates at the great classical concert halls of Europe and a bunch of cool festival appearances in the summer. I was happy to be in the Sinatra party again, this bubble of positivity. We had great support on that tour from the English singer Richard Hawley and his band. Richard played with us a few times; it was always magical. At the time, Nancy was promoting an album of songs by contemporary artists like Jarvis Cocker, Morrissey, and Bono and the Edge from U2. In the UK, we played Shepherd's Bush Empire, for a great turnout. We opened every night with a stripped-down acoustic version of "Bang Bang," which had recently been used in the soundtrack to Quentin Tarantino's *Kill Bill: Volume 1*. A highlight for me was getting to play on the old Nancy number "Drummer Man." It's a tune about a broke drummer who doesn't even have enough money to buy a can of beans. Getting to interpret Hal Blaine's drum part and to share the spotlight with Nancy for that song night after night—in fact, being a member of the Sinatra party and having all those experiences was a complete honor.

Chapter 36

PHIL SPECTOR

I first came into Harvey Phillip Spector's orbit in February 1977, during Blondie's extended run at the Whisky. One night between sets, when we'd really started to gain some traction, there was a knock at our dressing room door. A couple of guys standing in the doorway introduced themselves as Dan and David Kessel—sons of the legendary jazz guitarist Barney Kessel. They were associates of Phil—in fact, they used the Spector association as their calling card. Dan and David went on to produce a song we recorded with Rodney Bingenheimer at Phil Spector's Gold Star Studios under the moniker Rodney & the Brunettes—a cover of the 60s hit "Little GTO," from Blondie's live set. The whole recording has since passed into infamy. Rodney was set to record the vocal, but since he wasn't a singer, Debbie laid down a scratch vocal for him before he went into the booth. Dan and David released the demo with Debbie's guide vocal on their own label under the name New York Blondes. This wasn't authorized by us and we had to ask that the record be withdrawn or else we'd take legal action, although we did score a single of the week review in one of the UK music papers. Personally, I didn't mind too much.

A couple of nights later, I opened the dressing room door to find a very heavy, dangerous-looking guy dressed in black. "My boss wants to meet you," he said, and stepped aside. Behind him was a much smaller man, also dressed in black, wearing sunglasses and a long cape with a Blondie "In the Flesh" badge pinned to his lapel. It was Phil Spector, and he breezed past me, making a beeline for Debbie, calling her "my little chickadee," doing his best W.C. Fields. Over the next twenty minutes, he pitched the idea of him producing our next record, and a photographer appeared out of nowhere and we did an impromptu photo session.

A few days later, our then manager Peter Leeds told us we'd been invited to Phil's place for drinks. We piled into our station wagon and drove to his place in the Hollywood Hills. Phil came to the door with a bottle of wine in one hand and a pistol in the other. It was a curious way to greet your guests, but as everyone would come to know, very much in keeping with the man's reputation. Over the course of a tense evening, Phil proudly played us his latest production, the Leonard Cohen album *Death of a Ladies' Man*, at an insane volume. The record, which went on to be a commercial bomb, was Phil's last production, until he got his claws into the Ramones for the album *End of the Century*. Fortunately, Blondie never worked with Phil Spector, but it wasn't my last encounter with him.

After playing in Istanbul with Nancy Sinatra, I was headed back to Los Angeles with the band, while Nancy was scheduled to stay in London. Our flight was canceled, and our tour manager let Nancy know. Always generous and caring,

Nancy invited us to join her at her hotel for the night. We retrieved our luggage and headed to the upscale Athenaeum Hotel opposite Green Park. At the entrance, I said the magic words "We're with the Sinatra party" to the snooty doorman, and he welcomed us in. Nancy was in the lobby to greet us and mentioned she had a friend staying at the hotel. I put two and two together and realized she meant Phil—I knew Nancy had been casually seeing Phil over the last few months. According to her, they were just friends. Spector was in London producing the band Starsailor at Abbey Road, but his erratic behavior had just led to him being dismissed from the project. Nancy said Phil had invited her entire entourage to dinner, only he didn't want to leave the hotel. He'd booked the top floor for himself and was happy staying put.

Thirty minutes later, in the hotel restaurant, we were all seated at a huge banquet table, waiting for Phil to show up. When he arrived, he appeared to be in a jovial mood. Although Nancy had mentioned that Phil had stopped drinking, something had elevated his mood, because he was insanely upbeat. Phil pulled up a seat at the head of the table and began holding court, reeling off one story after another. I had to bite my tongue when he began gloating about a lawsuit against his ex-wife, Ronnie, and the other two Ronettes over record royalties. He referred to his lawyers as "the three wise men" and was positively gleeful as he recounted winning the case. Phil then proudly told a story about Stevie Wonder being sued for copyright infringement for "I Just Called to Say I Love You." Phil sent Stevie to a studio downtown that made old-fashioned record acetates—the template that records are pressed from—and advised

Stevie to just have one made and to postdate it for evidence in court.

By that point, I guess, Phil thought he'd ingratiated himself with the band enough, because what came next was pure farce. To the surprise of everyone, not least Nancy, he dropped to one knee and asked for her hand in marriage. The moment was met with deathly silence, followed by a few nervous snickers. Nancy made light of the offer, laughing it off as not being serious, and no more was said about it. For Nancy's sake, we all bit our tongues. We thanked Mr. Spector for dinner and said goodnight, but really, everyone thought he was a jerk.

Spector hosted an annual party at the Montrose Bowl in LA. It's a unique 1950s-style place featured in many movies. It's not far from Phil's mansion in Alhambra. Phil bought the house—known as the Pyrenees Castle—for the bargain price of $1.1 million in 1998. It looks down on a predominantly Mexican working-class suburb and probably made Phil feel like some feudal lord with his serfs. The last of those Spector parties was in the summer of 2002. I went, along with the rest of her band, but Nancy couldn't attend. The retro atmosphere was a lot of fun, as Phil's Wall of Sound greatest hits blared nonstop over the bowling alley's PA—in mono of course. My friends and acquaintances were having a good time, drinking fountain Cokes, eating popcorn, and bowling. There was no sign of Phil, but given his prior behavior, maybe that wasn't a bad thing. As I was leaving, I ran into my journalist friend Bill Holdship. We got to talking about not seeing Phil at the party when we noticed a white Rolls-Royce parked across the street with its back window rolled down. It was Phil, observing the goings-on at his party from a safe distance.

Bill waved to Phil, who got out of the car. Bill asked Phil if he could take a photograph and handed me his camera. I took a quick snap of Bill with Phil, almost smiling, the white Rolls gleaming in the background.

The next time I saw that white Rolls, it was blocking a half dozen cars in the parking lot of a nondescript building on a back street in the San Fernando Valley. I wouldn't have minded, but it made me late for a rehearsal with Nancy. When I finally got to the studio, Don Randi, Nancy, and half her band were present. As was Phil, sitting on a funky beat-up couch across from a huge ballet mirror. Only a few days earlier, Nancy had confided to me that Phil was drinking again. She'd been forced to throw him out of her Beverly Hills home after she refused him a drink and he became belligerent. I had the impression she was through hanging out with Phil, but he hadn't got the message. Yet here he was, one of the greatest music producers, an uninvited guest at an intimate band rehearsal.

If he had an opinion about what we were doing, he didn't share it. Don tried to ease the tension in the room by engaging Phil in small talk, but Phil was preoccupied with staring at himself in the huge mirror, occasionally adjusting his wig. Meanwhile, we rehearsed a song called "Flowers" from Nancy's album *Woman*. The lyrics seemed to be directed at Phil. "While you've been learning to love, I've been learning to hate" and "Take your silly little flowers and go to hell." Phil, being a narcissist, probably didn't pick up on the subtext, but soon after we finished, he said his goodbyes and left the building. Nancy was leaving for Nashville the next day to see her old friend and collaborator Lee Hazlewood and to do some recording, so we agreed to resume rehearsals when Nancy got back. The following night, after midnight, I stopped in a coffee shop for a bite to eat. I was sitting at the counter when there was a breaking news alert on the TV: Blonde woman shot dead at record producer's mansion. Police on site arrest Phil Spector.

If I didn't know that Nancy had flown that very day to Nashville, I would've been concerned for her safety. I later learned that other people who knew Nancy had that same thought. Even Nancy's mother called to check up on her when she heard the news. As devastating as the situation was to Nancy and everyone else who knew Phil, I don't think anyone was surprised. There were so many red flags and too many stories about Phil pulling guns on people. We saw it ourselves in 1977, and Dee Dee Ramone experienced it a few years after that. It took two trials and several years of back and forth, but ultimately, Phil was convicted in the murder of actress Lana Clarkson and spent the rest of his life in prison.

I did see Phil one more time after the murder. A month before his trial was to begin, still out on bail, he attended a surprise birthday party for Don Randi at the Sportsmen's Lodge Hotel in Studio City. My wife, Ellen, and I were seated directly across from Phil, flanked by two bodyguards. A microphone was passed around the ballroom, and guests offered words of praise in Don's honor. After I made a short salutation, I passed the mic over to Phil, who declared that he never wanted to live in a world without his friend Don Randi. And he didn't: Phil is gone, and Don is still with us. Hal Blaine was also there that night, and I'll give him the final word on Phil. Hal's daughter, Michelle, who'd been Phil's longtime assistant, had recently lost an ugly and expensive financial battle with him. On his way out, Hal quietly told me, "If I had a gun, I would've shot him right there and then."

Chapter 37

THE HALL OF SHAME

In December 2005, I was in London with Blondie for a sold-out show at London's Shepherd's Bush Empire, the climax of a UK tour that began in mid-November. I'm on record as loving the UK, but being there over the holidays always feels particularly special. Since our comeback, we'd established a happy ritual of touring in the weeks leading up to Christmas, and it was something I looked forward to every year. It became a popular tradition with our fans, since it made us part of their Christmas festivities; I heard of people buying tickets for friends and family as an early gift. This time is also fun because of all the great record company holiday parties. Whoever says there's no such thing as a free lunch is wrong; getting wined and dined on someone else's dime is a blast. Another great annual event I looked forward to was the *NME* party, attended by the current crop of happening bands. A free bar and a bunch of musicians is my kind of party.

While we were in London, we were booked at our usual digs, the exquisite Royal Garden Hotel, bordered by Hyde

Park on one side and Kensington Palace Gardens on the other—some of the most expensive real estate in the world. We've been staying there since the 1970s.

The day of the Shepherd's Bush show, my wife and I stopped at an internet café. Before we carried the world in our pockets, internet cafés used to be the place to go for a slow online scroll through the news. The news I had in mind was the next year's Rock & Roll Hall of Fame inductees, due to be announced that day. The rules for nomination for the Hall of Fame are very particular. It must be twenty-five years since the release of your debut album for you to even be considered. I won't say I was anxiously waiting because, in all honesty, I wasn't expecting Blondie to get in. Our first album came out thirty years ago, so we'd been passed over five times already. But when I clicked on the Hall of Fame website and checked the screen, I had to blink twice, then a third time for luck. Despite my pessimism, Blondie had been voted in on our first nomination.

The relative silence of the café was broken by the whooping and hollering of two loud Americans going absolutely bonkers over the news. I couldn't wait to get to the soundcheck and tell everyone. I figured my partners might be more blasé, but for me, this was one of the things I signed up for. At the venue, I rushed in like a proud father handing out cigars in a hospital waiting room. I made my announcement onstage to the assembled band and crew, to cheers and applause. As the crew dispersed, Debbie quietly took me to one side. I could feel the smile start to fall from my face. I'd expected her and Chris to be kind of New York aloof, too cool for school about the whole thing, you know, we'll attend, but we'll do it ironically maybe. Instead, Debbie told me point blank she wanted nothing to do with the ex-members of Blondie. I was shaken. "Can't we even get a picture together?" She made it crystal clear. There'd be no photo op. No onstage appearance. No just-for-old-time's-sake reunion performance for us and our fans. I looked over to Chris, but he merely echoed Debbie's sentiment.

Here I was, swinging wildly from elated to disappointment. It's not that I didn't understand; lawsuits don't usually leave you feeling generous about the people involved. But I'd thought to myself maybe for this one event, we'd put the past aside. As usual, playing that night's show, I was able to forget about it all and be immersed in music. Maybe I could just enjoy the honor for myself and look forward to the ceremony in March.

I hadn't cut Frank and Nigel out of my life. Soon, I'd be getting calls from them, maybe Gary too, about joining us. What the hell was I going to tell them? As the news made it to the wider world, other phone calls and emails started coming through. Everyone wanted to know if we'd reunite the classic lineup. I raised the subject with our management and was assured that everything was under control, not to worry, they were coordinating with the show's producers. Frank and Nigel both called to get my take on what I thought was going to go down on the night. "The reunion," I told them. "Well, it doesn't look good."

The ceremony took place on March 13 at the Waldorf Astoria in New York. The Hall of Fame really took care of us. Ellen and I were flown first class from our home in Los Angeles a few days before the ceremony. At the hotel, we were met at the VIP hotel reception area, given our room keys, escorted into a private elevator, and taken up to a beautiful suite. Everything was great for a while, but the night of our induction, I was on edge. I'd also gotten bad news, that an ex-girlfriend's dad had died suddenly of a heart attack. We hadn't been together for over a decade, but I had always liked him a lot.

The Hall of Fame held the event in the hotel's Grand Ballroom—I'd been there once before, as a teenager in 1973, to see the New York Dolls. That was the night Ronnie Toast, Gary Valentine, and I went together, dressed as droogs from the movie *A Clockwork Orange*. So much history, every-where. The Dolls crowd that night had been so wild, the hotel management permanently banned rock and roll from the ballroom, so it was ironic to be there waiting to be inducted into the Rock & Roll Hall of Fame.

I sat with my wife Ellen, Debbie, Debbie's sister Martha, Chris, Jimmy, and Jimmy's wife, Roberta. Across the ball-room at a separate table sat Frank, Nigel, and Gary. Frank was with his mom, and she was beaming with pride. I was so happy for all of us, despite it being so awkward.

At least, we were all in the same building, even if we were worlds apart. By contrast, the Sex Pistols were also being inducted that same night but decided not to attend at all. Johnny Rotten sent the Hall a ranting fax complaining about having to purchase tickets for the guests he wanted to bring. I still can't work out if that's in the spirit of punk rock or just John being a contrarian. Whatever was going on in John's head, he missed a memorable night. Memorable, but not good.

As our big moment arrived, Debbie, Chris, Jimmy, and I were led through the ballroom's kitchen to a staging area and told to hang tight. We were briefed by our management and given a speaking order, with me going first. That was the first I heard that the others wouldn't be appearing at all, seconds away from going on stage. From the wings, we watched a compilation video of our career on a TV monitor, but at this point it was a hard thing to celebrate. Nigel said later that watching the footage was like being at his own funeral. When the video finished, Shirley Manson of Garbage came on stage and made a speech. She did a great job, and I appreciated her taking the time to do it. She was completely the right fit: a strong female singer in a rock band. Her kind words made me forget the drama for a second—it's always special getting accolades from your peers.

The inevitable moment came, and we were announced. Holding a pair of drumsticks, I led the charge from the wings onto the stage. I could see Frank, Nigel, and Gary getting up from their seats and making a beeline for the stage to join us. I nervously collected my thoughts, stepped to the microphone, and shouted out a resounding "Hello, Cleveland!" in homage to Spinal Tap. The New York audience didn't seem to get the joke, but I was told by friends who were watching a live feed at the home of the Rock & Roll Hall in Cleveland that my comment received a roaring response. Given the drumsticks I was holding, I probably didn't need to announce that I'm the drummer, but I did, before thanking my parents and wife for their support. Meanwhile, the atmosphere was growing frostier by the second. I expressed my gratitude to CBGB owner Hilly Kristal, and namechecked my heroes: Earl Palmer, Hal Blaine, and Keith Moon. In closing, I thanked John, Paul, George, and Ringo for showing me the way. With my heart pounding, I stepped aside to let the others speak.

Chris and Jimmy both thanked Richard Gottehrer as well as Terry Ellis and Chris Wright from Chrysalis before handing the podium over to Debbie. She spoke in generalities but gave a shoutout to our Manic Panic pals Tish and Snooky, who sang backup in the first incarnation of Blondie. After the brief speeches, Debbie, Chris, and I headed over to join the members of our touring band for the performance segment. As I sat behind the drums and put my ear monitors in place, I looked over at Frank, Nigel, and Gary standing at the rostrum. They were saying something, but the feed wasn't being sent to my monitors. It felt surreal, like watching a silent movie take place in real time. As Frank spoke at the dais, he made a remark, like, can't we get up and play, just this once? Please, Debbie? Pretty please? Debbie left her spot with the band and went over to confront him, and they had a brief back and forth. Debbie saying, nope. Not tonight.

I took the monitors out of my ears, but I was so far back on the drum riser I couldn't hear what was being said, so I only got the story after the fact. Nigel and Frank felt they'd been written out of Blondie's history and were making that point. Fair enough, I thought, let them speak. Still, the optics were so bad. I'd expected bad, but not this bad. Then Gary pointed out it was a song he wrote with Debbie that landed our first record deal. The chaos finally ended, but we'd aired our dirty laundry in front of everyone on a night that was supposed to be about celebration. We played a few songs with the current Blondie lineup, but my heart wasn't in it. What should have been one of the best nights of my career turned into a nightmare.

My only hope was that the fracas might be edited out for the HBO broadcast, but it wasn't. HBO made a lot of money from pay-per-view boxing back in the day, so they weren't going to cut away from a New York street fight when it was handed to them on a platter like that. It was the dawn of reality TV, so our public embarrassment was video gold to them. When the show aired, the closing shot of our segment was a close-up of fellow inductee Herb Alpert with a disgusted look on his face, shrugging his shoulders with his hands out, palms up. Like, that's showbiz.

After the induction and performance, the three of us went to the press room. I still didn't know exactly what had been said, which put me in an awkward spot as I was bombarded with questions. Trying to be diplomatic, I had to grin and bear it all, saying, "There really are no rules in rock and roll and that's what makes it what it is. Freedom of expression. Everyone has the right to say and do as they please."

When the whole night was over, I went back to my room to change and meet up with two friends from high school who'd been waiting for me all night in the hotel bar. I wasn't exactly in a celebratory headspace. They had no way of knowing what had happened, and I was in no mood to relive it. While I had a few drinks at the bar with my friends, my wife, Ellen, went party hopping. After a while, I said good-night and went up to the suite. Ellen got back from the aftershow parties, and told me how proud she was of me. As I lay in bed, I assessed the day's events and decided that, aside from the deaths of my parents, this had been the most miserable day of my life.

A satellite press junket had been scheduled for the next day. In the days before laptops and apps like Zoom, you'd go to a radio studio and connect to various media outlets around the globe. I wasn't looking forward to having to explain the night's calamity to the journalists of the world. Also, we were supposed to announce a Blondie "farewell" tour. That was an idea dreamed up by Allen Kovac to garner publicity on the back of our induction. No one believes that whole "We're never going to tour again" line anymore. The morning's headlines were predictable: "Blondie Feud at Hall of Fame Induction," "Atomic Fallout as Blondie Feud Erupts Again," "Rock & Roll Hall of Fame Has Bad Blood," "Blondie Snubs Ex-Bandmembers." The *New York Post* summed it up best with the headline "Rock and Roll Hall of Shame." Our induction has been called one of the most awkward moments in Hall of Fame history *and* one of its most controversial and dramatic occurrences. All I can say is, I wish things didn't happen that way and my apologies to Gary, Frank, and Nigel, who were such a big part of our success. Their contributions should never have been overlooked. They deserved better. Let's be honest, Blondie deserved better.

Chapter 38

LAMF, EMPTY HEARTS

The Empty Hearts is one of those projects of mine that's tinged with regret. I appreciate that in most respects I've led a charmed life, but even so, it's often the one that got away that'll haunt you. That's the case with the Empty Hearts. They're my one that got away. It's especially gnawing, because when we came together, we were full of optimism about what we might achieve. The Empty Hearts were four guys attempting to reignite the fire they felt when rock and roll first entered their lives. Yeah, it was all very romantic. Seeking their neglected muse, reminiscing about that first guitar and the smell of its case, the first band, that first drum set. We were going to refill our empty hearts with the magic of rock and roll.

The band consisted of me, Andy Babiuk from the garage band the Chesterfield Kings on bass, the Cars' guitarist Elliot Easton, and Wally Palmar of the Romantics, on vocals and guitar. We were united in our goal to establish a working band, one that would be recognized. Not just for our past achievements, but for the great new music

314

we would write and play together. The idea was to bring the music forward into the twenty-first century while staying true to—and building on—our roots. It was probably the most excited I'd felt about a project since Chequered Past. We signed up because we loved playing. A bunch of battle-hardened musicians with chops to spare, but with the passion of a gang of teenagers. What could possibly go wrong?

The idea started to coalesce when I was working with the Romantics. I took their latest album to the launch of Steven Van Zandt's Underground Garage radio station. The entire cast of *The Sopranos* turned out for the party at the Hard Rock Cafe on Fifty-Seventh Street in New York. That's where I ran into Andy, the youngest of our group, who became the Empty Hearts' bass player. Andy was the DJ that night, and he was spinning all these classic garage records: the Seeds, the Chocolate Watchband, the Standells, and the Blues Magoos, and British records by the Yardbirds, the Kinks, and the Creation. It was a checklist of all our influences in the Empty Hearts.

I knew it wouldn't be easy to get a group off the ground: notoriety can only get you so far. I was prepared to do the work, and once we had assembled the band, I assumed everyone else was as well. For a while, the Empty Hearts was the perfect endeavor for all of us. We were only together a few short years, but in that time, we went through a bunch of managers, two record labels, and one global pandemic. I invested a lot of time and energy in the band, not as a Blondie exit strategy but as a platform in the music business. All I wanted to do was get in a van and travel up and down both coasts playing every dive rock bar that would take us. From my perspective, we had a great lineup and it really felt like the band had a bright future.

I do think we all started out with that same attitude. None of us wanted to wait around for success to find us again; we were going to get out there and take it for ourselves. None of us were under any illusions we were going to be a multiplatinum-selling band, but at the same time, we'd all had ambitions for us to be a real working group. We shared all the songwriting and the expenses of being in a band, trying to take it up to the next level. We made a great rock and roll album with Ed Stasium, who was the perfect producer for a band like ours, having worked with bands like the Ramones, the Smithereens, and Living Colour. With our collective influences and musicianship, we had a handle on everything from retro psychedelia to bluesy harmonica-driven stomps to high-energy power pop. I thought we'd be recognized as this great new motherfucking rock and roll band.

Unfortunately, the project was fraught with issues right out of the gate. Our first manager, a great guy named John Ferriter, who was really well connected, also had a band, the Tearaways. They were going to open for the Empty Hearts in the UK and needed a drummer. When I offered myself to do it, the band objected at the idea of me doing double duty. I didn't see what the issue was; maybe playing with both bands wouldn't make for the most relaxing of tours, but I was confident I could pull it off. I'd done something similar a few years back, touring with my friends Glen Matlock from the Pistols and Hugh Cornwell from the Stranglers on their doubleheader tour of the US.

A band is a delicate ecosystem: it needs to be nurtured; you need to know how to compromise. That element of give and take should be set in stone, but if you gather a few musicians in a room for a long enough time, especially older ones, the individual eccentricities, shall we say, are going to rise to the surface. There were rumblings that John was taking advantage of my good nature, and before I knew it, the rest of the band decided they wanted to fire John. When it came to the vote—because the Empty Hearts was a democracy right from the off—it was three votes against one and I lost. John was shown the door, and then I think we all lost.

It seemed like every move we made was cursed in some way. After the Paris terror attack at the Bataclan, we had to cancel a bunch of gigs and a scheduled tour of the UK because Elliot was convinced it was no longer safe for visiting Americans. Our first LP was released on a subsidiary of Universal. We agreed to license the record to them for $20,000, with $10,000 up front and the rest to be paid after we completed a certain number of shows to promote the record. Our new manager signed the deal and we played all the promotional shows but didn't receive the other $10,000 because four of the shows we played were in Japan, not North America. Apparently, the manager hadn't read the fine print of the contract. In the grand scheme of things, $10,000 isn't a ton of money, but we were funding this band out of our own pockets, so the money would've gone a long way to paying for recording the LP.

The last blow happened during the COVID-19 pandemic lockdown when Elliot decided he wanted out. I appreciate everyone experienced the pandemic differently, and we all carry our own baggage from that time, but I thought we'd managed to make the enforced downtime work for us. We talked, recorded videos, and even cowrote a couple of new songs over the phone with Steven Van Zandt. The second album had just been recorded, and once restrictions were lifted, we had ambitious plans to tour behind the record. It was a deep disappointment because musically we were a great band, with so much potential.

It's a genuine regret from my career—and I don't have that many—because I really should be talking about how well we clicked and the real chemistry we had among us whenever we walked into a studio or stepped onto a stage. The band seemed easy, like a slam dunk, but instead became very arduous. It's been hard to accept. I understand now why people opt to go solo when given the opportunity. Unfortunately, as a drummer, I'm at a disadvantage there. Out of necessity, I'm a collaborator. I can't pick up an acoustic guitar and do it that way. I can't tour the world and play ninety-minute drum solos all night. Being a drummer means I'm always looking for these collectives of people so I can keep my creative processes going. So, yeah, the Empty Hearts is the one that got away when it should have been the one to stay.

Amid all the Empty Hearts ups and downs, my friend Jesse Malin called to see if I was interested in playing a few shows in tribute to *L.A.M.F.*, Johnny Thunders and the Heartbreakers' 1977 album. For the uninitiated, L.A.M.F. stands for Like a Mother Fucker. Billie Joe Armstrong of Green Day was on board to take Johnny's place, alongside Walter Lure, the last surviving Heartbreaker. Tommy Stinson, originally of the Replacements and more recently of Guns N' Roses, had signed on to play bass. All they needed was a drummer. In theory, it seemed an exciting prospect. Walter was a friend, Billie Joe is one of the biggest stars in the world, and after a long battle with alcoholism, Tommy was sober.

You already know how I feel about the Dolls, so it won't be a shock when I tell you I said yes immediately.

Eventually, the plan changed, because that's rock and roll life, to some extent. Schedules conflict, plans shift. When it came time to get together, Billie Joe dropped out and another friend, Wayne Kramer from the legendary MC5, stepped up to take his place. Wayne was a great guitarist, but maybe not the first person who comes to mind for Johnny Thunders' role in this tribute. Still, Wayne had history with Thunders in a band called Gang War, so maybe it would work. I spent a few weeks in my home studio preparing for the shows, learning the parts created by the Dolls and Heartbreakers drummer Jerry Nolan—who was a god to me. I'm glad I put the time in because it turned out we didn't play together until the day of our first show.

I have a strong work ethic and figured the others would bring their A game to rehearsals, but not this time. After an initial run-through, things unraveled, fast. It's frustrating because I hit the stage that night at the Bowery Electric—a block north from the site of CBGB—with high hopes. The place was sold out and I was back on home turf, but the night was chaos and never seemed to lock in. Walter knew those songs like the back of his hand, and had probably seen worse in his time with the Heartbreakers. He just shrugged and carried on, but I just knew we weren't doing justice to the greatness of the band. There's a live album and DVD from that night, maybe one day I'll watch and see it differently.

A year or so later, we tried again. Walter and I roped in my friend, Sex Pistol and wonderful human being Glen Matlock, on bass, and singer-guitarist Mike Ness from Social Distortion. I like to think we redeemed ourselves that second time around. Walter, who passed from cancer in 2020, was a joy to play music with, and I'll hold the memories of our forty-plus-year friendship in my heart forever. R.I.P. L.A.M.F.

Chapter 39

POLLINATOR

No one could say Blondie was just a nostalgia act. The tours in support of new releases were always proof that we didn't play it safe and only trot out the hits. We could easily do a set of nothing but back-to-back hits, but it would go against the creative spirit that's always been at our core. One thing I can say is making records kept our profile up as a band determined to keep making new music.

Both *Panic of Girls* (2011) and *Ghosts of Download* (2014) were done more on computer and I felt like the band chemistry was missing. I had plenty to keep busy with, but in the back of my mind had really been hoping Blondie would make a record like we used to, with everyone in the studio playing together. When the songs that would make *Pollinator* started to materialize, they had the same diverse elements central to *Parallel Lines* and *Autoamerican*, and I knew I could bring what I do best to this record. Things moved very slowly, but over a couple of years, it really began to take shape. I thought tapping current stars like Sia and Charli XCX to contribute was smart, like a tribute to Debbie's influence. Songs from friends like Johnny Marr and Nick Valensi from the Strokes reflected yet another generation that had grown up with Blondie. The outside writers gave the band some new objectivity about the recording, and we've always had a knack for taking other people's material and making it our own. Our catalog has quite a few cover songs that have been hits: "Hanging on the Telephone" (the Nerves); "Denis" (Randy & the Rainbows); and "The Tide Is High" (the Paragons). It was a natural process.

More friends, old and new, tied it all together, with Joan Jett singing a duet with Debbie on a punk song inspired by the Ramones and Laurie Anderson playing violin on a song that was a Blondie homage to the Velvet Underground. Shepard Fairey created great eye-catching cover art. But even with all this energy and collaborating, the main influence overseeing *Pollinator* was David Bowie—not literally, but in spirit. We recorded at the Magic Shop, where he had been in seclusion for the last couple of years, recording. The Magic Shop was friendly, not your corporate type of studio. And knowing he'd been working there had an effect. We started working around Christmas 2015, and you could *feel* him in the rooms. There were reminders of him around the studio, like a champagne bottle he'd signed "David's birthday 2015."

A few weeks later, during our Christmas break, Bowie died, and when we got back into the studio it was different, but very inspiring. An engineer who had been there the whole time told us about what David had been going through, with his chemo and everything. It kind of informs a lot of the songs on *Pollinator*. We used a new producer, John Congleton, and the whole vibe just worked. *Pollinator* is very much an album, in our best tradition. The songs were there, intact, before the studio tricks. We spent a hell of a lot of time sequencing it. For me, the album is very reminiscent of *Parallel Lines* in a lot of ways—all the different types of tunes but with a cohesive Blondie sound at the same time. It was gratifying to get a very positive public and critical reception. The only sad part is we were the last band to make a full record at the Magic Shop. So many bands recorded there, like the Ramones, Sonic Youth, Lou Reed, and, of course, Bowie's last album, *Blackstar*.

Chapter 40

THE CURSE AND BLESSING OF BLONDIE

The problems in Blondieworld ran concurrent with our rise, an accompaniment to our good fortune. There were always camps within the band, pushing and pulling in different directions, but that seems to be part of the deal, in all bands. It's rare for a band to get a shot at greatness, but it's more rare for everyone in a band to have the same mindset. When I first auditioned and joined Blondie, I expected to be a member of a band, an equal part of a whole. I think one of the more difficult things I had to accept is that Blondie was never a democracy. Debbie and Chris always saw it as their band and their vision, and that sort of set up a division that affected me. Everyone else is free and welcome to contribute, but ultimately, it's not their show. I dealt with it by keeping my head down. I wanted to play. I wanted to keep growing. Often the situation left me wondering how our early days of camaraderie changed so much—was it success?

Most of the decisions I fight against come back to bite us on the ass. I've paid outrageous amounts of money to fix messes I wanted no part of. Everyone is always fine with us being equals when there's a lawsuit to pay for. Disentangling yourself from a deal and the subsequent rounds of lawsuits and litigation is never cheap. It's only good business for the lawyers. Peter Leeds's dismissal left me in a $250,000 hole. To put that in context, I had about $10,000 in the bank at the time. Aside from the financial aspect, it was a terrible drain on my mental constitution. I want to play drums, not spend half my downtime in boardrooms bickering over percentage points. So often, poor business judgment meant every cent the band made was offset against something else, if not legal matters, then the cost of recording or making videos. This started with paying back the debts of getting out of the Private Stock deal. When we were selling millions of records, nobody in the band was making millions.

When Blondie became a business, the relationships shifted, the kind of development you can only see with the benefit of hindsight. At the start of the band, Jimmy Destri and I were tight friends and hung out all the time. As he got more into drugs, we drifted apart. Then our relationship soured over some business dealings. The one that stings most goes back to early days when Blondie started to take off. My attorney negotiated a deal with my bandmates and partners to allocate a percent of the band's songwriting income to me. Not only in recognition of my musical contributions to the songs but also because we were building the band with an "all for one, one for all" foundation. Or so I thought. The splits still weren't equitable in terms of digging me out of legal messes, but I was happy to feel appreciated and compensated for taking hits that I didn't agree with.

But after the sales of *Parallel Lines*, when Jimmy turned around and argued against me getting my share, it didn't feel so friendly. It felt like my ally and bandmate was cutting me out. I'd made good money from the record sales and reasoned that band harmony was more important, so I acquiesced. But it's been hard to forgive and forget. In a band, these slights from way back have a way of sticking around, even decades later.

Blondie had everything I could wish for in a band. When Chris and Debbie were ready to give it another shot, without the drugs and excesses of another time, I was elated. Eventually, in that incarnation, Jimmy ended up not being a touring member. That left me, Chris and Debbie to carry on. You'd think that would make things harder for me, being the one-third that tends to disagree with the other two-thirds, but it's been a good dynamic—more like the very earliest days back in that Bowery loft when we really were "all for one and one for all."

I think we needed someone, a balance of power as it were, to protect us from ourselves. A strong manager might have been able to present solutions that would allow us to keep what we'd worked so hard for. Taking a break between projects, going on hiatus. I don't want to live in frustration about what might have been, but the 1980s were custom-made for Blondie. If we'd carried on, got through the problems, and continued making great records, MTV would have eaten it up. Debbie was, and still is, a one-of-a-kind star with more charisma and appeal than any of the superstars of that era. We would have been hard to beat.

We remain friends and we care deeply about each other, but the illusion of what I thought it would be versus the reality made me somewhat more cynical about what has always been the best thing in my life: rock and roll, playing in a band, creating music for the ages. I wanted to be successful, like the Beatles and the musicians I admired as a kid. To me, success meant freedom. Blondie made every dream I had come true, and even the other side of the dream, for all its ups and downs, was a result of the name and reputation that Blondie gave me as a drummer. These days, bands who had one hit forty years ago can tour and play to audiences—an indication of the impact that music can have on a generation and an entire era. Multiply that by the twenty-odd international hits Blondie had and the fact that we were the prototype for countless bands to follow—completely unique and original—and you have an idea of our influence on popular music.

The blessing of Blondie is not only that I was there for all of it but that I got to be there and made a difference by being there.

The only problem was I didn't see it ever coming to an end.

Chapter 41

MEET THE BEATLES— CHARLIE'S GOOD TONIGHT

We're all fans. Every musician, songwriter, and bandmember was, and is, inspired and in awe of another musician or song-writer. One of the great thrills of living this life has been that I got to meet a whole bunch of my heroes along the way. And maybe some of yours too. My story is highlighted by a series of vignettes of my encounters with the greats.

During our 1978 trip to England, we had to pick up our manager Peter Leeds on the way to the gig. He was staying at a far more luxurious hotel across town, the Montcalm in Marble Arch. Besides the costs, the hotel probably didn't want a bunch of rock and rollers spoiling their genteel vibe. I was waiting in the van, gazing at the lobby door, getting colder and more restless to get going. Finally, the doors open; there's no sign of Peter—instead, Paul and Linda McCartney come strolling out. I'm now staring at a Beatle and his wife standing on the curb waiting for their driver to pull up. Some of us were intentionally unimpressed—no way Chris was going to get out of the van to pay homage. I had no such issue and leapt out with Frank to run across the street to meet my first Beatle, even if it was just a hi.

It was more than "hi." I was trying to get as much info across as I could in the minute we had. "We're Blondie, we're touring the UK, we got a record out, maybe you heard it?" Paul was courteous and mannered, in that English way. Maybe a little bemused, like, who are these guys? He looked me up and down, checking out my black suit and skinny tie—probably wondering why I was dressed like a 1965-era Beatle. Blondie wasn't well known, and he obviously didn't know anything about us. After his car arrived and he politely waved goodbye, Frank and I climbed back into the van. I figured Paul would forget this moment as soon as it was over. He's Paul McCartney.

He must get a hundred people a day coming up to him and telling him their life stories. Maybe down the road, he'd know about us, when *Parallel Lines* was a hit. He owned Buddy Holly's publishing, and so he would have made a few bucks out of our cover version of "I'm Gonna Love You Too," but who knows? Both he and Linda were lovely, so that was my main takeaway.

I didn't meet John, but I saw him in the flesh, at least. In 1972, around the time of "Some Time in New York City," John, Yoko, and Elephant's Memory played a charity event for Willowbrook House at Madison Square Garden. I took a bus into the city to catch the matinee and was completely transfixed. John was so associated with the city in the 1970s, living in the West Village, living the life of a regular New Yorker. It seemed likely I'd cross paths with him, and if he hadn't been taken from us, I probably would have. John,

Yoko, and Blondie touched upon the same circles: Warhol and the Factory people and photographer Bob Gruen, who was friends with all of us and took some classic photos of John. It seems like John would've ventured down to CBGB one night, but I never got to meet him. But—he was aware of Blondie, which is enough to sort of blow my mind. There's a cool postcard John sent Ringo (featured in Ringo's book *Postcards from the Boys*) telling him, "Blondie's Heart of Glass is the type of stuff y'all should do—great + simple." I also saw a quote from Sean Lennon in *Rolling Stone* that said John had our version of "The Tide Is High" on his jukebox and played it constantly. That's too incredible for me to contemplate.

After working with Dylan the first time, I got a call from Bob's manager, Elliot Roberts, telling me I'd been recommended for an upcoming South American tour. "Bob knows you," he said. "There are no rehearsals, no audition. Just get to as many shows as you can between now and when we want to start. You'll pick it up." That's why I was at Dylan's Radio City concert in New York a week later with an AAA (access all areas) pass, watching the show from the wings and keeping a close eye on the drummer. Dylan at Radio City is a hot ticket, so everyone was there. When I looked to my left, I saw George Harrison and we nodded hello.

I'd met George and his wife, Olivia, over dinner one night at Dave Stewart's house. I remember that night so vividly. Dave and I were standing at the window like we were kids, watching as a taxi pulled up and one of the Beatles and his wife got out and rang the front doorbell. After Dylan finished his set, George came over, hugged me, and said, "I remember you, we had dinner at Dave's house." As people started to gather around him, George placed a hand on my shoulder and announced, "Clem and I are going to see Bob." Walking to the dressing room, George told me he'd been inspired by a drum part I'd played at the Eurythmics show at Wembley, and that he used a similar drum pattern on his single "Got My Mind Set on You." This shows how gracious and kind George was, going out of his way to make a connection with me. Publicist Elliot Mintz, formerly John and Yoko's spokesperson, stood guard at Bob's dressing room door. Seeing George, his face lit up. George smiled, nodded, and said, "Clem's with me," and then we were alone with Bob in his dressing room. He offered us a seat, and that's how I found myself on a sofa with a Beatle on one side and Bob Dylan on the other, a bottle of Jim Beam on the table in front of us. It was casual and relaxed, just sharing a drink and idle talk. When someone mentioned the Stray Cats were playing across town, I made a call to see about going, but it was too late. Elliot came in to let Bob know there were some more guests to meet, and then the dressing room filled up with the next round of folks: Lou Reed, Peter Gabriel, and New York photographer Kate Simon. I'd had a shot of bourbon but was mainly high on getting to hang out in such illustrious company.

Being a drummer, you'd think I'd have met Ringo a bunch of times. I'm good friends with his son, Zak Starkey, but I didn't meet Ringo for the longest time. Then in 2014, I got a call from the designer John Varvatos. John told me Ringo was the face of his autumn campaign and wanted me to participate in a day of filming at a beautiful Hollywood Hills house. Ringo's drum kit was set up by the pool: the idea was that a bunch of drummers and famous fans would show up at this house while Ringo played. Among those present were Steven Tyler, Tré Cool from Green Day, Jim Keltner, actor Jeremy Piven, and talk show host Jimmy Kimmel. It was a relaxed, good time hanging out and celebrating Ringo. Ringo brought his own bartender—no alcohol but serving fresh juices and drinks. All the drummers would sit at the kit and play Ringo's signature drum licks. I remember playing some Ringo solo stuff from "Carry That Weight." Chad Smith from the Red Hot Chili Peppers took a turn to play the opening of "Tomorrow Never Knows," doing a sixteenth note thing with two hands. Across the pool, Ringo's shaking his head. He gets up and takes over. "This is how it's played," he says. "One hand." And we're all watching Ringo's demonstration like excited kids. That was a cool day.

I became friends with Alan Rogan when I worked with Pete Townshend. Besides his long-running relationship with Pete, to get an idea of how good he was, his clients also included Eric Clapton, Joe Walsh, George Harrison, and Tom Petty. Alan was good humored and smart and treated everyone like they were on an equal footing with his illustrious bosses. Alan was in New York City with the Rolling Stones, who were recording their *Dirty Work* album at RPM Studios, located at 12 East Twelfth Street. In a lucky coincidence, my old friend Abel Domingues (also the guitarist in my high school band Sweet Willie) was the night manager at RPM. One of his duties during the Stones sessions was to keep a full bottle of Rebel Yell whiskey on hand for Keith every night.

Abel also took care of Keith's request to have draperies installed in the studio's east-facing windows so the band wouldn't have to face the glare of sunrise after finishing an

A great day

all-night session. I got a message to Alan via Abel to say I was back in town with Kathy Valentine and wanted to say hello, and he invited us to come by one of the sessions.

A few days later, Kathy and I met up with singer-songwriter Holly Beth Vincent for drinks. We both knew Holly from Los Angeles, before she moved to England and found success as Holly and the Italians with her fab song "Tell That Girl to Shut Up." I called Abel, who got the okay from Alan, and we headed over around midnight.

The reception and lounge were up a flight of stairs. The first sighting was Mick Jagger with Bobby Womack and one of Bobby's cousins. The control room door opened, and Ron Wood appeared, holding what looked like an ounce of marijuana in his two hands, followed by Keith, swaggering and swigging bourbon from the bottle. As a joint was passed around, Mick stood up and motioned Kathy to take his chair.

She did and was surprised when he sat on her lap as she passed him the joint. Alan popped out of the control room looking for Keith. Keith and Ronnie had gotten bored watching producer Steve Lillywhite work with Jimmy Page recording a guitar solo for "One Hit (To the Body)." When Kathy asked if she could go watch for a bit, Keith said, "Why not, we're all in the same union." The Stones RPM guests were joined late in the night by Santana drummer Michael Shrieve. (In the Woodstock film, Michael plays a fantastic drum solo in "Soul Sacrifice"—a favorite number that Abel and I played with Sweet Willie.) We stayed for hours; it was almost 4 a.m. when Alan stuck his head out of the studio door and said the session was winding down. We went off into the night.

In 2019, I went to see the Stones in Seattle. I was at the soundcheck, watching Charlie Watts from the side of the stage. He invited me to join him backstage in his dressing room, where we talked and listened to Duke Ellington records. It was interesting to see his dressing room. Just like I do in mine, he'd surrounded himself with little mementos, reminders of what it is you do and why you do it. There was a coffee table book on jazz drummers, and we leafed through the pages while Charlie talked about the rare drum kits he had in his collection. Michael Shrieve came in, and then Seattle's go-to expert on vintage drums, Donn Bennett, arrives.

Charlie and I got to reminiscing about one of our mutual heroes, Earl Palmer, the New Orleans drummer who played on all the Little Richard and Fats Domino records and, along with Hal Blaine, had been a big influence on both Charlie

My friend and hero, the great Earl Palmer

and me. I reminded Charlie about one night at Chadney's, the Burbank restaurant and lounge where Earl used to play. Great jazz musicians, young and old, would line up to play with him. Once I was there with Ellen in the cocktail lounge watching Earl play when Jim Keltner and Charlie came in. They were given a front-and-center seat, but because they're drummers, they want a seat at the side. It's a good way to spot a drummer in the audience of a show. If you're out front, you can't see what the drummer is doing; you want to see their technique, so your ideal position is from the back or to the side. When I brought it up, Charlie smiled at the memory.

Charlie's PA came in and said it was time for the VIP meet and greet, where people had paid large sums to get a photograph with the band or to meet Mick Jagger before the show. Charlie says to me, "Stay here. I'll be right back." The PA

Hanging out with Hal

nixed that, shaking her head, so we got up to leave. In the hall, I walked right into Keith coming out of his dressing room, Chuck Berry blaring from a speaker in his room. I'd met Keith before, so I said hi, but he just sort of growled at me. Donn and I exited as the paid VIPs walked in, and just as we left the backstage area, Donn says, "I guess you've known Charlie a long time? The way you guys were talking, it seemed like you were old friends." I said I'd never met him before.

When Charlie died, I thought about what Donn said a lot. I'd known the guy in person for maybe ninety minutes, but it felt like I'd lost a dear friend. That's what being a fan is, I guess. You're friends, from afar.

I was table hopping, catching up with friends, at a Grammy Awards party in the 2000s, and I spied Paul McCartney at a nearby table, chatting with Dhani Harrison and Jakob

Friends from afar

Dylan. I bided my time, waiting for the right moment to say hi. Finally, I make my approach and was about to say something just as Paul looks up. "Hi Paul, I'm Clem." I have a whole speech ready to go, but Paul interrupts me and makes my night.

"Oh yeah, Clem," he says. "I remember you from outside the Montcalm."

Epilogue

BOTH SIDES OF THE DREAM

Part of me will always be that kid in the back of my dad's car, tapping out a beat on the back seat to songs on the radio, but what I've learned is that I can't rely on other people to make the things I want to happen. Waiting for people to come around to take advantage of an opportunity is a waste of time. I want to tour, to get out in front of an audience and perform and see people having the time of their lives. I don't want to be sitting in limbo waiting for a decision to be made on my behalf.

I'm proud of everything we accomplished: Blondie blew up into the stratosphere but then, just as quickly, burned out. We came back, but in the meantime, I had to recalibrate and define the life I wanted to lead. As it turns out, it was the same thing I always wanted. Playing music is everything, and I want to be out there every night. Living the dream and the other side of the dream simultaneously.

I always have more than enough projects to keep busy with, in and out of Blondie. In the years since *No Exit*, we've toured and made a lot of new music—in fact five studio albums. One important thing we never lost was the motivation to work together creatively. I'm proud that every show features new Blondie music.

I was asked to sign up for a tour with some old friends, and a couple of new ones, to tour Europe as part of a live tribute to the classic Iggy Pop *Lust for Life* album. The band was me, my friend Glen Matlock (now Blondie's bass player), David Bowie collaborator Kevin Armstrong, Luis Correia, and Florence Sabeva, alongside writer and presenter Katie Puckrik on vocals. I had an opening, so I said, sure why not? Katie's a force of nature, perfectly suited to bringing those songs to the stage. I put her up there in the same bracket as Debbie and Annie and the other strong female artists I've had the good fortune to work with. Really, she's that good. We rattled around the UK for a while, packing out these clubs and going down a storm, just music fans playing to fans.

Arriving in London, there's no downtime. I have interviews to complete for the documentary *Blondie in Britain* for a prestigious "Blondie Night" on the BBC.

Next up, a little catch-up and work with some good friends in London: Debbie and Andy Harris. We began our working relationship in an unexpected way, when I sat in with their very successful Blondie tribute band, Bootleg Blondie. I had so much fun drumming with them on occasional sets that we ended up doing a tour together, including a show at Shepherd's Bush Empire, where I've also played with non-bootleg actual Blondie. When I got to the soundcheck, I saw that Debbie and Andy had a huge banner made as a backdrop, bearing the legend "Clem Burke and Bootleg Blondie." I assure you, that wasn't my idea, but nonetheless, I was touched. The time we've spent together over the years has made them two of my closest friends. We've also been hard at work composing and assembling a full-on rock opera, *The Big Smoke*. It's a dream project of ours. If we're not in a room together, we're on the phone or online, coming up with storylines and songs. It's a remarkable achievement, with over forty-eight original songs recorded and the entire book completed.

After working with Debbie and Andy, I head back to Los Angeles for a time. I'm playing a couple shows with Blondie at Coachella, with a show at the Greek Theatre in between, and then flying back across the Atlantic for more Blondie shows in Europe. We appear at several outdoor festivals around the castles of the UK and Ireland, headlining slots at the Isle of Wight Festival, the main stage at Glastonbury, watched by tens of thousands in person and millions at home on the BBC. Then it's off to the Dog Day Afternoon open air show at Crystal Palace with Iggy Pop, Blondie, and Generation Sex—featuring my old friend, Steve Jones, who is now off the ginseng and curry. Pause for breath. Hang out a few days. See some shows. Phone ringing. Emails pinging. More *Lust for Life* shows going in the diary a few months down the line. Bigger and better venues this time, up and down the UK for a couple of weeks. Oh yeah, and work on this book awhile. Couple more shows in the US with Blondie and wind down a bit.

Except I don't wind down; I'm back across the Atlantic again. Hooking up with the Split Squad, a bunch of friends I have a band with—we're self-professed purveyors of the finest "garage-power-punk-pop-classic-big-dumb rock around." I've been in the Split Squad off and on since 2011, and it's like the days of my teen band Total Environment transposed to the here and now. It's fun, but also, like when I was thirteen, deadly serious. We have two albums out, and everywhere we play, we're preaching the garage rock gospel. If my brain were wired differently, I'd realize I should be on a beach somewhere, but instead, I'm having the time of my life with my buddies while we're crammed in the back of a tiny van, up and down the backroads of the UK, pulling up at a community center somewhere, and wondering, is this Monday, because I've got no idea? Spilling out of the back of the van and onto the stage and 1-2-3-4.

The Split Squad is Eddie Munoz, my pal from the Plimsouls, and he's introducing us showband style; the Fleshtones' Keith Streng; Josh Kantor, the actual, honest-to-goodness Boston Red Sox organist extraordinaire from Fenway Park; and Michael Giblin, the glue that holds the whole enterprise together. Our leader, Mike, introduces me, "And in the Engine Room. From New York. The best drummer in the country right now ... damn ... the best drummer on the continent ... any continent ... Clem Burke!" ... And all the forty- and fifty-year-old faces in the crowd, they're sixteen again as we plow into "Green Onions" or the Small Faces' "Sorry She's Mine." An hour later, we retire to the bar, drinking red wine from plastic stems before falling into the back of the van, and it's on to the next show.

Back in LA, just long enough to crash and get past the jet lag before I'm back overseas: Ladies and gentlemen, the Tearaways! Back on tour again—different van, different band, same intensity. A slew of pub and club shows in England. Then it's off to Brighton with Debbie and Andy to see my friend and fellow Anglophile, *Saturday Night Live* alum Fred Armisen's one-man show and back for two gigs at

London's legendary 100 Club on Oxford Street. Catch a flight back to LA for Christmas and work on an AI Dead Boys project. Can we breathe now? Nope, because we're back in Europe for more *Lust for Life* shows. A sold-out tour. Looking out the tour bus windows and seeing the towns and cities of England and Scotland hone into view, just like forty years ago and that first tour with Blondie. Every show is a smash. Lines of eager music lovers hanging around afterward for the meet and greet after the show, getting up close and personal with fans, which is something I love. We sign albums, pose for a hundred selfies, hear about that time they met you forty years ago, because that's fandom. It's an undiminishing love of music, from both sides.

Occasionally, there's a spot of Clem Burke–mania, amid all these spinning plates: daytime radio interviews, local newspapers cornering me for a quick chat in the hotel lobby. There's Zoom meetings by the dozen, telling the story of Blondie for the hundredth time that week, meetings with publishers, literary agents, Blondie management calls, keeping an eye on business. Then it's home to LA to start production work on the Blondie Australian tour. Three weeks retracing our steps from that first world tour, only now it's massive, because whatever way you look at it, Blondie is classic, it's timeless. Okay. Now I can breathe.

The success of Blondie means I can play all the time and have it not be about how much money I'll make, but how much fun can we have? I'm not an elitist, I can have fun playing a festival, an arena, a theater, a club, or set up on the floor in the corner of a pub. I never wanted to have to go to work, and it's turned out well for me because I've been playing for more than fifty years now, and I can say I haven't worked a day in my life. I guess that's why they call it playing. But if I were holding down a regular job, I'd still be playing the clubs every night. That's who I am. If I'm lucky enough to be on tour, I always want it to sell out, but whether it's a hundred or twenty thousand people, there's no drug that can replicate the feeling of having played a great gig.

I'm not getting any younger, and I see myself cutting back at some point. Maybe. I guess we'll see. I've been saying it since the 1970s … I'll give it another eighteen months and see how it goes.

Afterword

CLEM BURKE
1954–2025

"He who has a why to live can
bear almost any how"
Friedrich Nietzsche

I was driving with Clem to his second chemo, a brutal protocol that called for half a day in the chair, followed by a take-home pump strapped to his torso that administered drugs for another 48 hours. We pulled into the parking lot, and he turned to me. "Clem Burke is dead," he said. "I'll never be that guy again." My heart shattered. Inwardly. Outwardly, I said: "No, Clem Burke is eternal, forever."

After 40 years of love and friendship, I was familiar with all of Clem's looks and facial expressions. The one I got at that moment was the little boy with the solid brown eyes of a puppy. Not frightened or helpless, not a glimpse into the innocent child: it was the skeptical look a kid gives you when you're telling them that the broccoli on their plate is really yummy.

One that says: Yeah, right. Sure.

Clem was intensely private about his disease. He didn't want pity or help. He certainly didn't want to be seen as a sick man. He didn't want to be a spokesperson for cancer or to be known as a brave "warrior" battling a terrible illness. Clem was a rock and roll drummer, a rock and roll star. To anyone with any knowledge of pop culture and rock and roll, there was only one Clem, and that was Clem Burke: a force, a personality, an image. He was proud, passionate, hard-working, full of vitality and health. He was a survivor.

The news that he had cancer was staggering, bewildering. But no one was more surprised than Clem. "Fuck," he'd say, so many times. "How did this happen?"

He faced the shocking news of his diagnosis the same way he dealt with other trauma in his life: by playing drums. Clem knew his illness was a serious matter of life and death and yet continued to show up for tours and gigs, whether they were festivals and concerts with Blondie, a run of club gigs up the California coast, or a sold-out series of halls with an all-star band in England.

His reasoning was entirely intact with his nature, a primal response to a reality he didn't want. And besides, he still felt okay most of the time, he could perform at peak level. In his drumming, Clem left all earthly problems behind. He entered a transcendent space that integrated his consciousness so completely with music and rhythm that any sense of self—with all attendant suffering, desire, needs, and worries—was either forgotten or beaten into non-existence by his signature blend of precise abandonment. Watch any performance and you witness his submersion into the great bliss that came from losing himself in time. When he was absorbed in the absolute presence of the music, the place where thought and emotions were suspended, he wasn't a sick man. He was Clem Burke.

And so, from January 2024 until his last live performance at the end of June 2024, Clem did what he loved more than anything. This was what being alive meant. While he admitted readily to the very few who knew about his diagnosis that he was "in denial," no one could argue that this choice also took immense courage and was a final testament to the passion and dedication he had for music, for playing drums. He stopped only when he no choice left, when he couldn't keep going.

We had the best talks of our life during his treatment. We talked about everything: music, movies, this book, other books, the coming election, LA, London, our history, his childhood, our parents, his marriage, my daughter, hotels, producers, TV shows, playing gigs. There were many good days, especially after he moved to a doctor who favored quality of life over typical scorched-earth cellular annihilation.

Good days, feeling good—these were the goals. Focusing on his business affairs, the company of a few close friends, his wife, trips to the beach, and working to finish this book broke the limbo. It was a pervasive neither-here-nor-thereness; all too often a monotonous cycle of repetition marked mainly by the sin of omission—the absence of the one thing that gave Clem Burke the "why" and the "how" of his life. Without the physicality of drumming and performing, the preparation for the next tour or gig, the learning of songs, the planning of drum kits and stage clothes, the packing of bags—without these essentials of his life, without his job, his career, his passion—Clem met an existential crisis that weighed much heavier than most people ever come to face.

We were family, sharing a deeply bonded friendship and love. For many years, we referred to each other as brother and sister. For decades, I understood him perfectly and accepted him unconditionally. In his life, Clem had withstood his share of disappointment and challenges, heartbreak and loss, but never had I known him to have to be so brave. Every morning, he woke up with the echo of a singular, unexpected doom resounding through his mind, reverberating off the walls of his house, disseminating into the periphery of a life he couldn't recognize as his own. None of it made sense, and he was smart enough to know it wasn't supposed to, it just was. It wasn't supposed to happen, but it did. "This is how things are," he said.

Clem had earned his place in the upper echelons of rock and roll through hard work, perseverance, magnetic charisma, and talent. He had experienced the best and worst that success brings, and I think, given enough time, he would have come to some sort of terms with this one thing he never planned for or thought about. We all live under the shadowy threat of no future and can only imagine the monumental task it is to reconcile the certainty of having no future—but to do so, while in the crushing wake of losing your identity and *raison d'etre*, took every ounce of his formidable energy and endurance.

We had vowed that no matter who else or what else came into our lives, we would be there for each other when needed. Both of us had called upon that promise in the past, showing up without hesitation. This was the ultimate showing-up. He faced death and I used every resource and intuitive act of compassion and understanding to soften and support a jagged and ragged transition away from life as he'd always known it. The exact right people also showed up, we circled close around and let love do the heavy lifting. When anything was taken away, we were all soothed by the love that surrounded him.

Clem's treatment stopped being effective late in March 2025, followed by his passing on April 6, 2025. His death was mourned around the world, not only for the loss to music, but for all who remembered his loyalty, kindness, impeccable manners, style, and unforgettable spirit. Clem's fans, friends, and loved ones should take comfort knowing that for six entire months after diagnosis—a significant part of his remaining time—Clem succeeded in his determination to keep being the man he wanted to be. Clem Burke will always be, forever and eternally, a strong, capable, vibrant force of life, and a powerhouse drumming rock and roll icon.

Kathy Valentine

ACKNOWLEDGMENTS

With gratitude and special thanks to Ajda, Daisy, and the entire HarperCollins team, along with Kathy, Tommy, Cheryl, Dawn, Bob, Merwin, and Ellen.

Additional thanks to:

<table>
<tr><td>Fred Armisen</td><td>Andy and Debbie Harris</td></tr>
<tr><td>Ismael Baiz</td><td>Nigel Harrison</td></tr>
<tr><td>Merwin Belin</td><td>Debbie Harry</td></tr>
<tr><td>Rodney Bingenheimer</td><td>Frank Infante</td></tr>
<tr><td>Andee Blacksugar</td><td>Matt Katz-Bohen</td></tr>
<tr><td>Gilby Clarke</td><td>Tommy Kessler</td></tr>
<tr><td>Jimmy Destri</td><td>Gary Lachman</td></tr>
<tr><td>Brendan Donahue</td><td>Peter Leeds</td></tr>
<tr><td>Dr. Steve Draper</td><td>Annie Lennox</td></tr>
<tr><td>John Ferriter</td><td>Craig Leon</td></tr>
<tr><td>Yfat Reiss Gendell</td><td>Jesse Malin</td></tr>
<tr><td>Mike Giblin</td><td>Toby Mamis</td></tr>
<tr><td>Amy Haben</td><td>Johnny Marr</td></tr>
</table>

Greta Musacchio

Glen Matlock

Christine Setzer

Nancy Sinatra

Dr. Marcus Smith

Robert Smith

Tina Spence

Ed Stasium

Chris Stein

Dave Stewart

Mike Sticca

Monika Tashman

Gary Twinn

Steven Van Zandt

Rick West

Mark Zelasko

PICTURE CREDITS

While every effort has been made to trace the owners of copyright material reproduced herein and secure permissions, the publishers would like to apologise for any omissions and will be pleased to incorporate missing acknowledgments in any future edition of this book.

All photographs are courtesy of the Clem Burke family archive, with the following exceptions.

Insert 1
Allen Tannenbaum page 6 (top right); Armando Gallo page 8 (middle); Bob Gruen page 2 (bottom); Bobby Grossman page 4 (bottom); Chris Stein page 2 (middle), page 4 (top), page 5 (bottom); Henry Diltz page 5 (top); Lynn Goldsmith page 3 (bottom), page 7 (bottom); Roberta Bayley page 6 (bottom), page 7 (top left), page 8 (bottom)

Insert 2

Alexander Thompson page 7 (bottom right); Brian Aris page 2 (middle), page 3 (top), page 3 (middle right), page 6 (bottom left); Chris Stein page 1 (top); Dave Stewart page 3 (middle left), page 4 (middle); Dawn Laureen page 6 (middle right); George DuBose page 5 (middle); Greg Allen page 4 (top left); Jay Blakesberg page 4 (bottom left); Lynn Goldsmith page 2 (top), page 2 (bottom); Marcus Smith page 7 (top right); Rob Roth page 8 (middle); Roberta Bayley page 1 (inset, middle); Thomas Manzi page 8 (top); Waring Abbott page 1 (bottom); Robert Matheu page 4 (top right), page 5 (top right, bottom left and right), page 6 (top)

ABOUT THE AUTHOR

Clem Burke was a founding member of Blondie, a band that has influenced and shaped the worlds of music, fashion, and art over the past fifty years. Blondie's chart-topping success, fearless spirit, and rare longevity led to an induction into the Rock & Roll Hall of Fame in 2006, an *NME* Godlike Genius Award in 2014, a *Q* Award for Outstanding Contribution to Music in 2016, the 2017 Silver Clef Outstanding Achievement Award, and more than fifty million albums sold worldwide to date.

Clem performed on every Blondie recording, including the *Billboard* number one chart-topping songs "Heart of Glass," "Call Me," "The Tide Is High," and "Rapture" (the first major hip hop hit to use original music rather than sampling other artists' beats). Clem was named one of the 100 Greatest Drummers of All Time by *Rolling Stone* magazine. He was also a Grammy Award winner for his recording of "Missionary Man" by Eurythmics. Some of Clem's many collaborators include Iggy Pop, Pete Townsend, Joan Jett, Bob Dylan, Wanda Jackson, Bob Geldof, and the Ramones.

Clement Burke
DRUMMER

Born:	November 24th, 1955
Hair:	Black
Eyes:	Brown
Weight:	160 lbs.
Height:	5' 11''
Favorite number:	Diane's
Favorite food:	seafood, steak
Favorite drink:	water
Favorite color:	black, pink, white
Favorite clothes:	black pegged pants, pink socks, black leather
Favorite movies:	"Don't Look Now," "Performance," "Beyond the Valley of the Dolls," "Rebel Without a Cause."
Favorite actor:	James Dean
Favorite actress:	Julie Christie
Favorite singer:	male — Mick Jagger, Iggy Pop, Steve Harley female — Debbie Harry, Marianne Faithful, Dionne Warwicke
Favorite record LPs:	"Who Sing My Generation," "Meet The Beatles," "12 x 5," The Rolling Stones; "Raw Power," "Too Much Too Soon," NY Dolls; "Indian Giver," 1910 Fruit Gum Co.; "Dedicated To The One I Love," Shirelles; "Saturday Nite," Bay City Rollers; "Runaway," Del Shannon
Current groups:	Rollers, Ramones, Runaways, Cockney Rebel
Favorite all time favorite groups:	Beatles, Stones, Kinks, Yardbirds
Favorite drummer:	Keith Moon
Biggest Influence:	Keith Moon
Personal ambition:	write, produce, make a movie
Professional ambition:	Blondie Greatest Hits album
Birthplace:	New Jersey
School:	No. 4
First instrument:	finger piano
Other instruments played:	bass, feedback guitar
Hobbies:	listening to records, photography, collecting 60's fan magazines
Ideal girl:	light brown hair, hazel eyes, slim build
Favorite books:	"Hell's Angels" by Hunter S. Thompson; "In Cold Blood" by Truman Capote
Favorite author:	Capote
Favorite poet:	Patti Smith
Favorite director:	Lindsey Anderson, Russ Meyer
Cities:	Hollywood, London
Teenage crush:	Marianne Faithful

In 2008, Clem received an honorary doctorate of music from the University of Gloucestershire in the United Kingdom for his groundbreaking work for the pioneering Clem Burke Drumming Project (in conjunction with the University of Chichester and Hartpury University). This science-based program studies the positive health benefits drumming has on mental health and brain function and the development of motor skills, language, creativity, and emotional well-being.

Drummers that inspired and influenced Clem's style include Earl Palmer, Hal Blaine, Ringo Starr, and Keith Moon. Clem, in turn, inspired a legion of drummers over the past five decades.